D1085018

Hoover Institution Publications 148

The Growth of American Government

THE GROWTH OF
AMERICAN GOVERNMENT

A Morphology of the Welfare State

Roger A. Freeman

1975
Hoover Institution Press
Stanford University
Stanford, California

The Hoover Institution on War, Revolution and Peace, founded at Stanford University in 1919 by the late President Herbert Hoover, is a center for advanced study and research on public and international affairs in the twentieth century. The views expressed in its publications are entirely those of the authors and do not necessarily reflect the views of the staff, officers, or Board of Overseers of the Hoover Institution.

"The Growth of American Government" has been supported principally by the William Volker Fund with supplemental support from the Smith Richardson Foundation.

Hoover Institution Publications 148
International Standard Book Number 0–8179–1481–1
Library of Congress Catalog Card Number 75–10553
© 1975 by the Board of Trustees of the
    Leland Stanford Junior University
Printed in the United States of America

Contents

Tables in Text

5. Issues and Prospects

Tables in Back

Preface

In the year 1975 the American people enjoy, more or less, a $1½ trillion economy and a $500 billion government. Most Americans — though certainly not all—regard rapid and steady economic growth as a highly desirable goal to be pursued vigorously by appropriate and effective public policies. But there is no consensus—in fact there is a broad controversy—on whether the concomitant absolute and relative growth of government is equally desirable, or whether it is desirable at all.

In recent years, the American public has become increasingly aware of the dramatic expansion in the range and intensity of governmental activities during the third quarter of the twentieth century. Many would trace this expansion back to the Great Depression of the 1930s and the New Deal. But the scope and magnitude of governmental programs have been growing for a much longer time, as Solomon Fabricant so effectively demonstrated in *The Trend of Government Activity in the United States Since 1900,* a comprehensive analysis of the vast expansion in the size and function of government during the first half of the twentieth century.[1] His study was based on data from 1900 to 1949. M. Slade Kendrick, in *A Century and a Half of Federal Expenditures,* carried federal expenditure data historically backward to 1789 and forward to 1952.[2] Both Fabricant and Kendrick showed that there was a consistent upward trend in public spending and concluded that it would continue as far as one could view ahead.

This book attempts to show the dramatic development in public expenditures and in government generally in the twenty years following 1952, a period that carries us from the later stages of the Korean War to the later stages of the Vietnam War.

During the first half of the twentieth century, governmental expenditures multiplied forty times, nearly three times faster than the nation's economy. Between 1952 and 1972—contrary to what is widely be-

---

[1] Solomon Fabricant, *The Trend of Government Activity in the United States Since 1900* (New York: National Bureau of Economic Research, 1952).

[2] M. Slade Kendrick, *A Century and a Half of Federal Expenditures* (New York: National Bureau of Economic Research, 1955).

lieved—governmental costs climbed only moderately faster than the Gross National Product (GNP), that is, 296 versus 234 percent. But this seeming slowdown and apparent stability hide two sharply conflicting trends: a cut to less than half of the share allotted to national security and a more than doubling in the slice given over to domestic programs. To put this in historical perspective: it required 163 years, from 1789 to 1952, for governmental expenditures for domestic programs to reach $34 billion; in the succeeding 20 years they virtually exploded from $34 to $257 billion. Such a dramatic expansion in a short span of time suggests that more took place than a mere change in magnitude. An over sevenfold growth in domestic programs signifies a decisive change in the role and nature of domestic government in the United States within the past twenty years.

If this rate of growth were to continue, domestic public expenditures would, within less than forty years, account for all of the GNP. That is obviously impossible. The expansion rate of domestic spending must slow down. But pressures for further expansion appear undiminished and are currently stronger than they have ever been. Therefore, sharp political and ideological conflicts over the magnitude and objectives of public spending are inevitable now and for many years ahead.

The basic philosophical and political issue is, of course, that of personal freedom. If we define personal freedom as the ability of the individual to make meaningful choices among known alternatives, then it follows that the extent of his freedom depends on the range of decisions he can make for himself and his family in comparison to those being made for him. One possible measurement of an individual's freedom is the share of his economic resources that he can allocate to his various wants according to his own wishes versus the share government allocates for him.

The individual's desire to control his own life, resources, and actions tends to conflict with government's claim to regulate, more or less deeply and extensively, the rules of the game and the conduct of affairs, through the distribution of resources. Hence the eternal struggle between man and his government.

It may be somewhat oversimplifying matters to say that social justice and civilized progress grow with the share of total resources channeled through government—or that the extent of individual liberty declines in the same proportion. Yet, there is a grain of truth in both assertions, big enough to make these propositions well worth debating.

Small wonder that in recent decades increasing attention has been focused on the division between the public and private sectors of the economy, on the slices of income and product that are under control of one or the other. As of 1972 total government expenditures were about 32 percent of the GNP and about 40 percent of national income.[3]

In this study, I aim to present the facts that can serve as the basis for a rational debate of the fundamental issues on the growth of domestic government in the United States. The idea for this project began with a paper entitled "The Service State at the Midcentury," which I presented at the annual conference of the American Society for Public Administration (ASPA) in 1965 and subsequently rewrote for *National Review* (September 21, 1965). Early in 1966, I restructured and expanded the ASPA paper into a speech, "Big Government - Friend or Foe?," which I delivered at the San Diego Open Forum. For that speech, which was reprinted many times, the Freedom Foundation at Valley Forge accorded me its George Washington Honor Medal Award as "an outstanding accomplishment in helping to achieve a better understanding of the American Way of Life."

I then received several suggestions to turn the paper into a comprehensive research project on the "Growth of American Government." Under that heading it was approved by the Hoover Institution on War, Revolution and Peace and occupied my time for several years. Urgent requests for special studies, reports, analyses, articles, and speeches of current topical interest interfered and delayed completion. I prepared a new version of the theme as the keynote address at the annual conference of the Governmental Research Association in 1970 under the title "The Wayward Welfare State." It appeared as an article in *Modern Age,* Fall 1971. For a summary in the *New York Times* (December 4, 1971), I was again given the Freedom Foundation's George Washington Honor Medal Award.

This volume contains an updated and substantially expanded version of the article "The Wayward Welfare State" (1–35) and a factual report and analysis of developments in governmental employment, revenues and expenditures between 1952 and 1972, with occasional glances at events prior to 1952, since 1972 and prospects during the balance of the century.

I am deeply grateful to W. Glenn Campbell, director of the Hoover Institution, and several of my colleagues who were helpful in offering

---

[3] According to national income accounts. Following definitions of the Bureau of the Census, governmental expenditures in fiscal year 1972 equaled 36.1 percent of the GNP and 44.3 percent of national income. Preliminary estimates suggest that data for 1974 will not differ significantly.

suggestions, giving me advice, and commenting on ideas and drafts. F. David Carr, research fellow at the Hoover Institution, worked with me; his assistance and contributions have been helpful. The typing and proofreading were ably performed by Penny McMullen, Anna Boberg and Dede Smith.

Responsibility for the facts I present and for the opinions I express remains, of course, exclusively my own.

Roger A. Freeman

Stanford, California

Technical Notes on Statistics

Statistics on governmental revenues and expenditures are prepared by several departments of the federal government that use different concepts and definitions. The statistics therefore differ from each other and reviewers have to exert great care not to compare data from different sources or sometimes even from the same sources published in earlier or later years. For several decades the most widely used source of federal financial data was the *administrative budget*. But as the use of trust funds and the volume of their transactions grew, the administrative budget (which excludes trust fund operations) reflected a shrinking share of total federal transactions. So a second measure came into broader use, *cash payments to the public*, more commonly called the *cash consolidated budget*. In fiscal year (FY) 1940 the difference between the administrative and the cash consolidated budget amounted to only $0.5 billion, but in FY1967 it totaled $29.4 billion: the administrative budget showed expenditures of $125.7 billion, the cash consolidated budget of $155.1 billion. United States Treasury accounts reported outlays of $158.4 billion, the United States Bureau of the Census of $166.8 billion. The federal sector of the National Income and Product Accounts (NIPA) showed in 1967 virtually the same total as the cash consolidated budget: $154.4 versus $155.1 billion. But that was a mere coincidence; in the preceding year the NIPA figure was $5.9 billion smaller, in the succeeding year $4.9 billion smaller than the cash consolidated budget.

In 1968 a new concept was introduced, the *unified budget,* which differs from all the other measures and has been used as the standard presentation of the United States budget ever since 1969. Preparation of the administrative budget and the cash consolidated budget were discontinued and data are not available for years after 1968. The unified budget, however, was computed back (by function) only to 1959. Therefore, it is impossible to make historical comparisons prior to 1959 or subsequent to 1969 using the major budgetary yardsticks.

The tendency to "debudget" transactions, which reduced the comprehensiveness and impaired the usefulness of the administrative budget from the 1940s on and led to its replacement by the unified budget in 1968, has since affected the unified budget. Several financing operations such as the Export-Import Bank, the Rural Electrification Administration, and the Rural Telephone Bank were excluded from the budget totals by statute. Other agencies were created, such as the Student Loan Marketing Association, the Environmental Financing Authority, and the Federal Financing Bank, whose transactions do not appear in the unified budget. Credit operations outside the budget totaled about $16 billion in FY 1974.[1] Great caution must therefore be exercised in using these statistics to make historical comparisons.

Unified budget data are released in the president's budget—submitted to Congress in late January or early February—with final figures for the immediately preceding fiscal year, estimates for the current fiscal year, and the president's recommendations and estimates for the succeeding fiscal year. Thus the United States budget submitted on February 5, 1974 had final data for FY 1973, estimates for FY 1974, and recommendations and estimates for FY 1975. But no comparison can be made with United States budget data for years prior to 1959, nor are state and local data available that tie in with the unified budget.

Bureau of the Census concepts have remained unchanged and statistics have been published annually since 1952; data are also available for selected years back to 1902. Not only are these statistics internally consistent, but also they are the most comprehensive data, and offer comparable information for state and local governments. The Bureau of the Census reports are the only source of comparable financial statistics for each state and major city and for other major units of local government. Although the Bureau of the Census reports offer very valuable data, they are long in preparation. Their annual report, *Governmental Finances in 1971/72,* became available only in January 1974, eighteen months after the close of the fiscal period.

The Social and Economics Statistics Administration (SESA) of the United States Department of Commerce publishes each year in its *Survey of Current Business* the NIPA, which contain revenue and functional expenditure data on a *calendar* year basis for the federal government and a combined total for all state and local governments. (No consistent state-by-state, city, county, and other local government financial statistics are available from any source except the annual reports of the Bureau of the Census.)

---

[1]*Special Analyses, Budget of the United States Government, Fiscal Year 1974,* p. 87.

SESA annual financial statistics are available back to 1952 and are published each year in July for the preceding calendar year. On the whole, they are the most useful source for historical comparisons, as far back as they go. The conceptual and magnitudinal differences between the SESA data and the unified budget are minute and a comparison between historical SESA data (to 1952) and current and future estimates contained in the United States budget are possible and practicable. For example, federal expenditures in the four fiscal years 1969–1972 totaled $824.4 billion according to the unified budget and $827.4 billion according to SESA statistics, a difference of only 0.4 percent.

Employment statistics of the SESA, the United States Bureau of Labor Statistics, and the Bureau of the Census are not directly comparable with each other; historical and other comparisons should be made only with data from the same source and within the same series. Equal caution must be exercised with numerous other statistics that emanate from different sources.

Many of the statistical tables and historical comparisons in this volume are based on the period 1952 to 1972. The year 1972 was chosen because it was the most recent year for which final financial data were available during the course of my research. In some respects it still is. The choice of 1952 as a starting year of the twenty-year period was governed partially by technical factors: it is the earliest year for which governmental financial data are available from the national income accounts. Also, it made a consistent decennial series possible because censuses of government were taken in each year ending with a 2 (except for 1913 instead of 1912). Such information is available from census sources for very few years, except those ending in 2, prior to the initiation of annual census surveys during the 1950s.

It is of concern that 1952 was in some respects not a "normal" year. Neither, of course, were 1932 nor 1942. For that matter it is difficult or impossible to define and identify a year that is "normal" in all respects and to prepare a time series with steady intervals. There may be concern over the fact that defense expenditures in 1952 were high when compared with the immediate postwar years 1947–1950. 1952 was in the later stages of the Korean war, just as 1972 was in the later stages—but prior to the end of—the Vietnam war. So, the years are comparable.

The fact that we selected 1952 as the starting year for many statistical tables does not imply that it should be regarded as a standard or norm—for defense or domestic expenditures. No year establishes a standard for the future because conditions and requirements differ from year to year and must be evaluated individually. Comparisons between 1952 and 1972 merely portray the changes that took place in the most recent twenty-year period for which sufficient statistical data are available. It does not mean to imply that 1952 was more "normal" than 1972. It may suggest that changes that took place between those years need to be viewed and possibly qualified in terms of other changes that occurred during that period.

The Wayward Welfare State: Preview and Summary

The birth and growth of the modern service state in the United States during the second third of the twentieth century may in historical perspective well have been the most significant governmental development of its time. To its architects the coming of age of the welfare state—as it is more commonly called—is a matter of supreme pride and immense satisfaction; it means to them that the American people have finally come to recognize their obligation toward the less fortunate in their midst, that they are willing and ready to make distributive social justice a reality. To its opponents it signifies the abandonment of the principle of personal responsibility, of a system of reward and punishment that made this country grow and prosper. It is to them the cause and mark of the decline and likely fall of a great nation that rejected its promise, forsook its destiny, and squandered its birthright.

The most visible manifestation of the growth of the welfare state, certainly the most amenable to measurement, is a vast expansion and intensification of public services in the broad field of social welfare, accompanied by a sharp increase in the size of public budgets and public payrolls. Dependence on government by a large number, and eventually a majority, of its citizens, whether as dispensers or as recipients of public benefits, is a distinctive mark of the welfare state.

Everybody knows that federal spending has been soaring over the past twenty years, far outpacing the growth rate of the nation's economy. Everybody also knows that the federal bureaucracy has dramatically expanded, at a much faster rate than the United States population or the civilian labor force. Everybody, that is, who has not looked at the record.

The fact is—and this may come as a surprise to many usually well-informed persons—that federal expenditures increased in the past twenty years at about the same rate as the GNP or personal income: they multiplied approximately three and a half times. To be sure, part of that increase

1

is only illusory and merely reflects a 40 percent shrinkage in the value of the dollar. But even so, it means that in *constant* (price-adjusted) dollars the national income and product as well as federal budget outlays doubled over the past two decades, a record of remarkably balanced growth and stability.

In overall terms, the federal budget and the economy grew at parallel rates between 1952 and 1972, during a period when many people thought that we were living through times of runaway, spendthrift budgets.

A study of the federal bureaucracy, which is widely believed to be proliferating at an exorbitant speed, yields a similar result: federal civilian employment increased only 8 percent between 1952 and 1972, whereas the civilian labor force and total civilian employment increased 39 percent; the population increased 33 percent.

We might then conclude that the United States experienced during those two decades a very modest expansion of governmental activity, well in keeping with the growth of the private economy, and a relative shrinkage of the central bureaucracy. Those are trends which many Americans would tend to applaud wholeheartedly.

But before we get carried away with such thoughts we might be well advised to study not only the magnitude of the change in governmental activity but also its nature and composition. Such an analysis would show that the seeming stability in the size of government was achieved only by financing a spectacular expansion of domestic services through a dramatic cutback in outlays for the military.

How Much is the Public Payroll Up?

Federal civilian employment increased only 8 percent between 1952 and 1972, while the United States population and labor force increased 33 and 39 percent respectively. But this covers a staff reduction of 19 percent in the Department of Defense, a combined increase of 26 percent in the Post Office and the Veterans Administration—less than the rate of population growth—and an expansion of 56 percent in the remaining agencies, which control all other federal programs.[1]

But the federal payroll is only the visible part of the iceberg, the part *above* the surface. Most domestic public services are partially or wholly

---

[1] Employment data taken from United States Civil Service Commission and United States Bureau of Labor Statistics sources.

financed by the federal treasury but carried out through state and local governments. It is the national government that offers, finances, encourages, and sometimes mandates the programs; most of the employees who implement them are statistically classified "state and local." Well over 500 categorical grant and loan authorizations are now in operation, and their cost jumped from $2.6 billion in 1952 to $36 billion in 1972—and an estimated $51.7 billion in the budget for FY 1975. If we want to get a proper picture of public employment, we need to add state and local employment statistics to federal payrolls.

State and local government employment increased 139 percent between 1952 and 1972, or three and one-half times faster than the civilian labor force and more than four times faster than the population. All civilian governmental employment in the United States (federal, state, and local)—including defense but excluding the armed forces—increased 92 percent, which is still almost three times the population growth rate. There was one civilian employee in government for every 7.6 in private employment in 1952. In 1972 there was one for every 5.0. If that rate of growth were to continue most of us would be working for the government soon after the turn of the century.

How Much is the Federal Budget Up?

A review of the federal budget shows similar developments. In the aggregate, revenues and expenditures have for many years been growing about as fast as the national economy. But when we analyze this seemingly moderate rate of expansion we find that the share of defense was cut in half while the share of domestic services tripled.

Defense costs went up 68 percent between 1952 and 1972, paralleling the simultaneous rise in prices. Expressed in *constant* dollars, military outlays in 1972 were no higher than they were in 1952; they were substantially lower than they were in 1967. In relative terms, defense spending fell during this period from 66 to 32 percent of the total budget, from 13.5 to 6.8 percent of the GNP. Spending for domestic public services meanwhile multiplied more than ten times (+962 percent) and its share of the budget jumped from 17 to 54 percent; the remaining 14 percent of the budget went for interest, veterans, international affairs, and space. Outlays for education, health, and welfare multiplied fifteen times—an increase of 1416 percent; outlays for all other domestic purposes combined multiplied more than six times (+543 percent).

Over two-thirds of the $174 billion increase in federal revenues and expenditures between 1952 and 1972 were allocated to domestic programs. Approximately one-half of the total budget growth went just to education, health, and welfare, approximately one-seventh to interest, veterans, international affairs, and space, and approximately one-fifth to national defense.

From the Warfare State to the Welfare State?

It is becoming apparent that the shift in national priorities, which some political and academic groups have been demanding for years, that is, "from the warfare state to the welfare state," has taken place. It probably would have been impossible to expand social welfare programs at the rapid rate we experienced since the mid-fifties without cutting into national defense. Congress could not have provided sufficient revenues by boosting taxes.

The welfare state has come of age in the United States, as it had earlier in some European countries. Interestingly enough it was not created by socialist or leftist governments. It was Otto von Bismarck who advanced welfare plans to forge an alliance between the *junkers* and the industrial workers against the rising forces of the liberals, the business and professional classes. This axis between statists on the right and statists on the left was renewed on several occasions, most clearly in Germany of the 1920s and 1930s when Nazis and Communists joined in attacks to bring down the liberal forces in the middle. But it was only in America, where the liberal tradition was stronger than in Europe, that the statists, in what was probably a shrewd move, assumed the label their opponents had held for so long: they became the new "liberals." The welfare state is the very antithesis of the original liberal idea, however.

In classical political theory, from Thomas Hobbes through John Locke to John Stuart Mills, the primary purpose and duty of the state is to protect the safety of its citizens, their lives and property, from hostile interests, both foreign and domestic. The secondary purpose of the state is to establish and enforce rules for the ordinary and peaceful conduct of civil affairs and to settle disputes among its citizens. Such was the tradition that guided the authors of federal and state constitutions. It still expresses the beliefs of a broad majority in this country.

Trends dating back to the nineteenth century and gaining strength during the first half of the twentieth century were toward a widening of the range of public functions, greater intensity in services, and perpetual growth in governmental finances and employment, as Solomon Fabricant demonstrated in *The Trend of Government Activity in the United States since 1900.*[2] In retrospect, however, viewing the record of the 1950s, 1960s, and early 1970s, these developments to midcentury were gradual and modest. The most dramatic expansion, particularly in the broad field of social welfare, took place in the third quarter of the twentieth century when government extended its responsibilities for its citizens and the range of decisions over their personal lives. Simultaneously, government became weaker in the discharge of responsibilities that had historically been regarded to be its foremost duties.

The Welfare State Comes of Age

The American welfare state has its roots in the Great Depression. In no year prior to 1930 did federal expenditures for domestic purposes come close to $1 billion. Even in the seven years of the New Deal they remained below $7 billion a year and did not reach $12 billion until 1952, twenty years after the birth of the New Deal.[3] In 1972 they totaled $131 billion.

Although its political, philosophical, and legal bases were laid in the 1930s, the American welfare state was launched barely twenty years ago, gathered speed in the late 1950s, and zoomed at a breathtaking rate through the 1960s into the 1970s. Its prophet is John Kenneth Galbraith, who propounded the theory that government and its services are being scandalously starved while the private consumer luxuriates. His solution: to tax the latter more heavily to support the former more generously.[4]

The counter argument notes that the consumer, who supposedly luxuriates, only consumes the goods he produced, or their equivalent value to which he has title. But the welfare state proponents recognize no such claim of the producer. They want to redistribute income and consumption more equally among high producers, low producers, and nonproducers, according to their own sense of social justice. They aim to overrule, through the political process, the rewards and punishments of the free market, disregarding the question of whether there can be a free society without a free market.

The case for the welfare state was presented well by George Katona of the Institute for Social Research, University of Michigan:

[2] Fabricant, *The Trend of Government Activity.*

[3] In constant dollars $12 billion were worth less in 1952 than $7 billion were in 1939.

[4] John Kenneth Galbraith, *The Affluent Society* (Boston: Houghton Mifflin, 1958).

This is the most serious argument against the mass consumption society: the consumer exercises his influence in a socially undesirable manner. It is Galbraith's accomplishment to have presented the argument to the American public in a most convincing way. We do not have enough schools and spend far too little on education; we do not have enough hospitals and spend far too little on the health of our people; there are too many slums which breed delinquency and crime; scarcity prevails in the entire domain of public expenditures, such as highways, parks, and recreation facilities.[5]

Whereas Galbraith blamed the consumer, Katona charged that "the largest part of government expenditures has been used for national defense, not for health, education, slum clearance and the like."[6]

If we are to test this claim we must consider not only federal expenditures but *all* governmental expenditures in the United States, that is, federal, state, and local. A review shows that outlays for national defense amounted to 50 percent of all governmental expenditures in 1952, 33 percent in 1962, and gradually declined to 21 percent in 1972.[7] The share of domestic services climbed from 37 percent in 1952 to 69 percent in 1972. The remaining 10 percent of governmental expenditures went for interest, international affairs, veterans, and space. Social welfare (education, income maintenance, health, etc.) currently receives 48 percent of all public expenditures, more than twice as much as the military.

Between 1952 and 1972 expenditures of all governments increased by $277 billion. Four-fifths of this huge amount were allocated to domestic services, less than one-eighth to national defense (see chart on p. 7).

But the absolute amounts may not be as significant as the trends. Between 1952 and 1972 outlays for defense increased 68 percent, for domestic service 645 percent, for education 705 percent, for income maintenance 1169 percent, for health, hospitals and sanitation 494 percent, for all other domestic services 429 percent. During the same period, personal consumption expenditures grew far more slowly, in total 235 percent: for food 131 percent, for clothing 175 percent, for housing and household operations 262 percent, for automobiles—so acidly criticized by Galbraith—326 percent, for recreation 295 percent.

Galbraith blamed inadequate spending for public services on exorbitant private consumption, Katona on excessive military outlays. The journal of one domestic special interest group editorialized recently:

---

[5] George Katona, *The Mass Consumption Society* (New York: McGraw-Hill, 1964), p. 62.

[6] Ibid., p. 64.

[7] See table 25.

"Congress has for years provided generous appropriations for certain programs almost without question while subjecting others—particularly domestic social programs—to the closest possible scrutiny."[8] But the record proves the contrary to be true. These have been the increases between 1952 and 1972: personal (private) consumption +235 percent, national defense +68 percent, and domestic government services +645 percent. The abovementioned journal continued: "What is needed desperately, therefore, is an even-handed approach to curb government spending. . . ." An "even-handed" approach among the various functions of government would mean restraint on domestic social programs, not faster expansion.

ALLOCATION OF INCREASE
IN GOVERNMENTAL EXPENDITURES, 1952–1972

	Dollars (in billions)	Percent	Dollars (in billions)	Percent
National defense			$32	12%
Domestic services:				
Education	$59	21		
Income maintenance	78	28		
Health, hospitals, and sanitation	17	6		
Other	69	25		
Total domestic services			223	80
Interest, international relations, veterans, and space			22	8
Total			$277	100

The Harvest of the Welfare State

Rates of increase of course do not necessarily prove that a function gets too much or does not get enough. That can be evaluated only by measuring what the expenditures actually accomplished, that is, how much progress was achieved, if any, in reaching or coming closer to program goals. The

---

[8] *AARP News Bulletin,* November 1973.

amounts now being spent—$257 billion for domestic services in 1972, of which $178 billion went for social welfare—and the length of time during which the programs have been growing rapidly are great enough to expect some tangible and measurable results. With outlays for education and for income maintenance each now exceeding $60 billion a year, we should at least have sharply reduced crime and other social ills and lifted education to new heights. But the evidence is to the contrary. Property crime, delinquency, and other types of social ills, new and old, have been increasing at a frightening rate.

The status and products of our educational system do not reflect the fact that eight times as much public money is now being allocated to it each year as two decades ago, while enrollment meanwhile only doubled. Too often, within the past decade, have educational institutions been the breeding places, and sometimes the cause, of civic strife and contempt of law. Schools and colleges no longer rank as high in the respect and affection of the American people as they did throughout most of our history.

Recurring conflagrations in our cities and on our campuses indicate that deep-seated unhappiness, frustration, and hatred characterize wide sections of our people. One of the ugliest pages in American history was being written just as the welfare state was put into practice. Our worst series of street riots began shortly after the passage of the Economic Opportunity Act of 1964. A succession of campus rebellions began soon after Congress passed several laws providing institutional and student aid and colleges began accepting and actively recruiting students who were below established standards. Our worst urban fights over the schools followed the expansion of compensatory education. Perhaps we can trace this widespread bitterness and upheaval to false hopes raised beyond any possibility of fulfillment and bound to be disappointed. We may now be seeing the results of acting as if all social ills could be cured by generous infusions of public money, of pretending that the effect of a law will be what its preamble says it should be.

Attempts to correlate tangible achievements with the resources applied to a program have cast great doubt on the idea that improvements are necessarily proportionate to the amounts spent or even tend to be favorably affected.[9] In case after case we must question whether there is a positive cost-quality relationship or whether expenditures have been counterproductive. Huge federal spending has not brought forth social miracles,

---

[9] See, e.g., Ira Sharkansky, "Government Expenditures and Public Services in the American States," *American Political Science Review*, December 1967.

but has instead created resentment among those who felt cheated when the promised results failed to materialize as the money was dissipated.

Why are the facts not brought out more clearly for the public? A major reason is that the specialists in the various areas of social welfare, and particularly the best known among them, are committed to expanded federal spending for the goals of their professional and special interest organizations. Those are the experts that are called in and relied on by government agencies, by some of the major foundations, and by the nation's leading press. Young graduates in the social sciences soon learn on which side the bread is buttered. They find out that good jobs, grants, and publicity go to the enthusiasts for enlarged federal spending, while the critics have a hard row to hoe. Small wonder that so many of our young people devise their strategies accordingly.

The American public seems to be far more conscious of the excessive growth of governmental activities in the past two decades and of the resulting potential dangers than are its representatives and most academicians. The Gallup Poll asked in October 1959 and again in August 1968 this question: "Which of the following do you think will be the biggest threat to the country in the future—big business, big labor or big government?" Among those who responded the percentage of those who feared labor most fell from 59 to 31 percent, of those who feared business from 21 to 14 percent. But the number of those viewing government as the greatest threat jumped from 20 to 55 percent.

The two biggest areas of governmental activity that have been growing most rapidly are welfare and education, which, in the aggregate, account for two-fifths of all public spending and, at present trends, may soon total one-half or more. The third major field is of course national defense, which has been proportionally shrinking in response to demands for increased welfare and education spending, which otherwise could not have been met.

In a carefully documented study of postwar budget formation Samuel P. Huntington, of the Institute of War and Peace Studies at Columbia University, found that in both the Truman administration before the Korean war and in the Eisenhower administration after the war there was a tendency to allocate to defense whatever money was left after expenditures for domestic programs and foreign aid had been estimated.[10]

---

[10] Samuel P. Huntington, *The Common Defense: Strategic Programs in National Politics* (New York: Columbia University Press, 1961). See also Warner R. Schilling, Paul Y. Hammond, and Glenn H. Snyder, *Strategy, Politics and the Defense Budgets* (New York: Columbia University Press, 1962); Maxwell Taylor, *The Uncertain Trumpet* (New York: Harper, 1960).

It has become regular practice in recent years to put pressure on the Pentagon for further cuts in the procurement of weapons systems or in the size of forces whenever demands from the domestic sector cannot be met easily by boosting taxes or enlarging the budget deficit.

Public Welfare in the Welfare State

Several European countries have a more comprehensive social security system than we have, and most have had it much longer. A few even have universal coverage for all their people, something which we have not fully achieved yet, and some pay small general child benefits. But no country in the world has anything like our program of Aid to Families with Dependent Children (AFDC)—nor would want to. That AFDC is a nightmare and a plague on the body politic is now more widely recognized than it was just a few years ago. Thus there have been efforts underway to abolish it and put something else in its place. But some of the plans most actively considered in recent years, such as a guaranteed annual income, a negative income tax, or the family assistance program, no matter how attractively packaged, labeled and merchandised, could get us from the frying pan into the fire, and saddle us with something worse than what we now have.

ADC—as it was initially known—came into being without public attention. It was not even mentioned in the extensive congressional debates that preceded the passage of the Social Security Act of 1935, because it was regarded as merely placing a federal financial underpinning under the widows' pensions, which all but two states were then paying. With the maturing of old age and survivors insurance, it was thought, ADC would gradually become unnecessary and peter out, as would other public assistance programs. Social Security has matured over the past thirty-nine years, now covers more than 90 percent of all workers, and pays monthly benefits to thirty million persons and their families. ADC was meanwhile perverted into something it was not intended to be: an escape from the necessity to work for a living by low-skilled people who refuse to accept jobs at a skill level they *can* handle, at a wage commensurate with the value of their output.

The child population (under 18) went up 41 percent between 1952 and 1972, but the number of AFDC recipients increased 456 percent and growth has only recently slowed down.

The orphans moved to Social Security long ago; currently fewer than 5 percent of the AFDC children's fathers are deceased. In 89 percent of the cases the father was "absent from home" in 1973: 43 percent of the fathers were not married to the children's mothers, 18 percent were divorced, and 28 percent had deserted, that is, separated without court decree. In nearly half the AFDC families there were illegitimate children.

Over the past twenty years AFDC has become the regular and accepted way of life for over three million women and men—for the latter usually indirectly or surreptitiously, and has widely replaced employment as the normal source of sustenance. It is now the preferred and respected mode of living, blessed with the government's seal of approval, in poverty or slum sections of major American cities. AFDC has become a major nutrient in the breeding grounds of crime, delinquency, illegitimacy, prostitution, and other forms of social ills, for a new generation to repeat and possibly excel in their parents' careers.

In his State of the Union Message in 1935 Franklin D. Roosevelt warned:

> The lessons of history . . . show conclusively . . . that continued dependence upon relief induces a spiritual and moral disintegration fundamentally destructive to the national fibre. To dole out relief is to administer a narcotic, a subtle destroyer of the human spirit. . . . The Federal Government must and shall quit this business of relief.

Truer words were never spoken: AFDC has turned into a cancer on society, planted and nursed by the federal government which has been getting deeper and deeper into "this business of relief" in the four decades since Roosevelt's warning. Not long ago a plan passed the House twice but was finally defeated in the Senate that would have tripled the number of recipients while changing the program's name to one that is not yet as discredited as AFDC.

The precept of the welfare state, as incorporated in various guaranteed annual income plans, is that there should be no connection between work and income. When the two congressional appropriations committees ordered a sample study of the welfare case load in the District of Columbia in 1962, to be directed and staffed by the comptroller general's office, they found out that 59 percent of the recipients were not eligible for the benefits they were getting. What was done about that? A national study was undertaken, staffed by state welfare departments, which, to nobody's surprise, reported that everything was all right and the incidence of ineligibility insignificant.

It is no mystery why AFDC recipients more than quintupled nationally since 1952—from two to eleven million—at a time of rising prosperity and employment: between 1952 and 1972 the average monthly benefit of AFDC families more than doubled, from $82 to $191, a 133 percent increase during a period when consumer prices rose 58 percent and grants in the Old Age Assistance Program were raised 64 percent. A study by the Citizens Budget Commission of New York in 1968 found that average monthly benefits in the ten states with the fastest rate of AFDC roll growth (median +161 percent) were twice as high as in the ten states with the lowest rate of AFDC roll growth (median +6 percent). Monthly AFDC payments averaged $177 in the former group of states, $88 in the latter. What incentives do persons of little skill and low productive capacity have to work for a wage that is not more than what they can get on welfare, and often less? Eligibility requirements have been gradually eased under federal direction (at least until 1972, when federal rules were tightened) and consist of little more than filing a claim that must be accepted at face value and not be investigated or verified. Residence rules have been abandoned under court orders as have virtually all other controls. Work requirements are nonexistent or nonenforced. Benefits per dependent were raised (and personal exemptions for income tax purposes boosted) by the same Congress that approved a $1 billion population control bill. Is this not like having a furnace and an air-conditioning plant going full force at the same time?

While New York City is not typical of the rest of the country, it epitomizes and foreshadows trends and developments elsewhere. A look at New York City welfare is enlightening.

The number of welfare recipients in New York City has more than doubled since 1966. In the world's financial capital more than one person out of every seven was on welfare in 1972. Eighty percent of the AFDC mothers were not born in the city, 70 percent were not reared there. They came from low-benefit, low-wage areas. Fifty-six percent of the welfare applications were approved in 1961, 79 percent in 1968. While per capita income in New York State is approximately 20 percent above the national average, AFDC money payments are 41 percent above the national average. From 1961 to 1971, the monthly allowance, including rent for a family of four in New York City rose from $188 to $326 per month, an increase of 73 percent. The total value of benefits to a man with a wife and two children, with no earnings, from public assistance, food stamps, school lunches, and Medicaid is approximately $5500.[11] That is more than he is likely to get on unemployment or earn in an unskilled job.

There are unskilled and low-skilled job openings around galore—but why should welfare recipients take them? Poor people may often be of low intelligence, but they are not stupid. The New York subway is filthy, household garbage is being collected at long and irregular intervals and left in alleys and streets in some sections of the city, parks are neglected and certain areas filled with refuse, rubble, and decay. But to expect welfare recipients to help clean up the city or at least their own neighborhoods, or work as domestics, would be deemed an indignity.

It is interesting to contemplate how clean the subways, streets, and parks are in Moscow and Leningrad—with whole swarms of men and women cleaning them all the time. But then, the Soviet Union offers no welfare or unemployment pay to able-bodied persons and its minimum wage was lifted from $54 to $81 a month in 1970. Ours was boosted by Congress from $277 to $399. The Soviet Union has a rule (Article 12, USSR Constitution) that "He who does not work, neither shall he eat." In the United States that principle of Saint Paul has long yielded to the welfare state precept that ties between the work and income should be weakened and eventually cut. We practice the first part of the socialist principle, "from each according to his ability, to each according to his work" (Article 12, USSR Constitution), but we would not think of practicing the second part. Soviet citizens are guaranteed the right to work (Article 118, USSR Constitution). Would the United States not be better off if it guaranteed everybody an *opportunity to earn* a living instead of accepting the principle that the government *owes everybody a living?* At this point, little effort is made to hold both parents responsible for the support of their children and to overcome the refusal of welfare recipients to take unskilled and semiskilled jobs.[12]

The War on Poverty has distributed huge sums among low-income persons, and placed militant radicals in well-paid key positions. It has financed and otherwise facilitated much of the violence that has plagued our cities in recent years. Some of the money was used to buy weapons and ammunition to train and organize sabotage and destruction.

[11] Blanche Bernstein et al., *Income Tested Social Benefits in New York: Adequacy, Incentives and Equity,* U.S. Congress, Joint Economic Committee, 1973, pp. 139, 141.

[12] This was well pointed out in an incisive analysis, *Welfare in New York City* (New York: Center for New York City Affairs, New School for Social Research, February 1970).

Parallel efforts in the poverty war, mandated by 1962 and 1967 Social Security Act amendments, to provide social services to welfare recipients to make them self-supporting have largely failed. A research study by the General Accounting Office in four major cities in 1973 produced almost no empirical evidence that social services to AFDC recipients had affected the likelihood that they will leave welfare or increase work while on welfare. The report's conclusions were decidedly negative.[13]

This confirmed the findings of an earlier study of the effectiveness of manpower training programs conducted for the Joint Economic Committee of Congress. The study suggested that in some cases cash benefits may prove to be more economical than occupational training.[14]

Some believe that pouring additional billions of dollars into the schools to raise the skills of children from low-income families offers them a way out of their predicament. "Education an Answer to Poverty" has been their watchword. Let us take a look at it.

Education: An Answer to Poverty?

Americans have always viewed and treated education with special affection. They know that much of the enormous progress that our civilization has achieved is the result of a tireless effort and huge investment in schools and colleges. Our most successful men and women, the leaders in most fields, are generally well educated, though often self-educated. Our least successful people, those with the smallest earnings, tend to rank low in educational achievements, are deficient in basic skills, and have attended school for fewer years than those higher up on the socioeconomic scale.

This has led many to seek the cause of the income differences among people in the number of years they attended school and in the amount of money that was spent on their respective schools. It has long been customary to measure educational quality in dollars spent per pupil, in the teacher-pupil ratio, and similar measures of *input*. Thus complaints about deficiencies in the *output*, the products of education, were answered with

[13] U.S. Comptroller General, *Social Services: Do They Help Welfare Recipients Achieve Self-Support or Reduce Dependency?* (Washington, D.C.: General Accounting Office, June 1973).

[14] U.S., Congress, Joint Economic Committee, *Effectiveness of Manpower Training Programs: A Review of Research on the Impact on the Poor,* paper no. 3 in *Studies in Public Welfare, A Staff Study Prepared for the Use of the Subcommittee on Fiscal Policy of the Joint Economic Committee,* 92d Cong., 2d sess., 1972.

the same plea: give us more money, hire more teachers and pay them more. The American people so did. Here is what has happened since the early 1950s:

PUBLIC SCHOOLS AND COLLEGES, 1952 AND 1972

	1952	1972	Percent Increase
Students in public education	27,862,000	52,152,000	87%
Employees in public education	1,884,000	5,646,000	200
Expenditure for public education	$8.4 billion	$67.5 billion	704
Number of students per employee	14.8	9.2	− 38
Expenditure per student	$301	$1,294	330

SOURCES: Enrollment: U.S. Office of Education, *Statistical Summary of Education, 1951-52,* 1955; idem, *Digest of Educational Statistics,* 1973.
Employment: Refer to Table 7a.
Expenditures: U.S. Department of Commerce, Bureau of Economic Analysis, *National Income and Product Accounts of the United States, 1929–1965,* Supplement to the *Survey of Current Business,* August 1966; idem, *Survey of Current Business National Income Issue,* July 1973.

But the evidence is overwhelming that there is little if any cost-quality relationship in the schools. James Coleman so found in the most extensive study of American public schools ever undertaken.[15] Christopher Jencks, in summarizing the ensuing national debate, concluded: "Variations in schools' fiscal and human resources have very little effect on student achievement—probably even less than the Coleman Report implied."[16] Hundreds of class-size studies show that students do not learn more in smaller classes.

---

[15] James S. Coleman et al., *Equality of Educational Opportunity,* Department of Health, Education and Welfare, 1966.

[16] Christopher Jencks et al., *Inequality: A Reassessment of the Effect of Family and Schooling in America* (New York: Basic Books, 1972).

While expenditures per pupil were increasing every year and the number of pupils per class was shrinking, learning achievements in the schools were falling: mean scores on college board tests (S.A.T.'s), have been declining dramatically for over a decade, from 478 (verbal) and 502 (mathematical)—out of a possible 800—in 1962-63 to 444 and 480 respectively in 1973-74.

In 1965 Congress was persuaded that a vast expansion of "compensatory education" programs would reduce the lag of one or several years in basic skills of children from low-income backgrounds. Now, nine years and more than twelve billion dollars later, the record of thousands of projects, from "Higher Horizons" and "More Effective Schools" in New York to "Bannecker" in St. Louis, from "Madison" in Syracuse to the Berkeley schools, all of them begun with great enthusiasm, tells a story of consistent failure to produce the educational improvement among so-called deprived children that their sponsors had hoped for and promised.

In his school reform message of March 3, 1970, President Richard M. Nixon reported that "the best available evidence indicates that most of the compensatory education programs have not measurably helped poor children catch up. . . . In our Headstart program, where so much hope is invested, we find that youngsters enrolled only for the summer achieve almost no gains, and the gains of those in the program for a full year are soon matched by their non-Headstart classmates from similar poor backgrounds." Subsequent reports have confirmed these findings.

These efforts at compensatory education resemble the quest of the alchemists who tried, for hundreds of years and at a huge cost, to do what we now know cannot be done.

Again, as in the case of public welfare, New York City offers an excellent proof of the futility of spending huge amounts of money without reforming our methods. "Our schools are the most lushly funded school system in the nation," boasted Mayor Lindsay, adding that "it has the best teacher-pupil ratio of any city—not just some but any city in the country" (*New York Times,* June 6, 1969). But his advisory panel had reminded him in November 1967: "The New York City school system, which once ranked at the summit of American public education, is caught in a spiral of decline."

New York City schools now have about the same enrollment as they had twenty-five years ago. The number of teachers has doubled. Expenditures have multiplied eight times and now average, on a per pupil basis, twice those of other large cities. But students in New York City schools lag substantially behind national norms (averages) and slip farther behind in reading scores year after year. Pupils in New York City schools with the highest expenditures and lowest class sizes lag the most; pupils in schools with the lowest expenditures and the largest classes are ahead in achievement scores.

Politicians have played a cruel hoax on the poor in urban communities by selling them "compensatory education" as a cure-all for their ills. Many schools in low-income neighborhoods, instead of teaching disadvantaged children marketable skills, offer courses that are irrelevant to their true needs. In the end the schools give them, in place of an education, a diploma which some of the recipients can't even read. When the failure becomes manifest, as sooner or later it must, the sponsors blame it on stingy government appropriations that should have been at least twice as high.

It is significant that publishers have found it necessary to have college textbooks rewritten to fit a lower reading ability level. The Association of American Publishers' student guidebook on how to read textbooks was originally written at the twelfth-grade reading level; it was recently rewritten at a ninth-grade reading level because too many college freshmen found the earlier editions too difficult to comprehend.

It is sad but not surprising that in the latest major survey of higher education, sponsored by the American Academy of Arts and Sciences, the deteriorating quality and the demise of general education constitute a central theme. The subject of an academic decline runs through the articles of many of the eighty-four authors.[17]

In their eagerness to make everybody fit for college, many institutions, even prestige institutions, have tried to make college fit everybody. Standards of admission and graduation were substantially lowered, at least for some groups, in a misguided quest for equality and a drive for quantity. The push for quantity has succeeded: the number of earned bachelors' and first professional degrees conferred by institutions of higher learning increased 200 percent between 1951/52 and 1972/73, the number of masters' and second professional degrees 293 percent, and the number of doctoral degrees 348 percent. This over a period when the United States population grew a mere 34 percent and the total labor force 39 percent. Small wonder that many of the graduates find it increasingly difficult or

---

[17] *American Higher Education: Toward an Uncertain Future, Daedalus,* Fall 1974 and Winter 1975.

impossible to obtain employment at a professional or technical level and are lucky if they can land the type of job for which a high school diploma would have been ample. Now that an oversupply of college graduates has been created, only those who by ability and drive are fully qualified are likely to find proper placement. Many of the others will be frustrated and embittered when they realize that they had been ill-advised, that they had been wasting their time and money—and the taxpayers' money—in a fruitless exercise.

One contributor to the Academy of Arts and Sciences' survey of higher education, Steven Muller, president of Johns Hopkins University, commented on it thus: "This is the first time that we've had a collection of pieces where there is substantial acknowledgement that quantity has affected quality and has affected it negatively."[18]

Private schools and colleges that offer students and their parents an alternative curriculum to state institutions and a freedom of choice have been pushed to the wall in recent years by unwise public policies. Many of the institutions face extinction within the next decade, at a huge additional cost to the taxpayers, unless remedial action is soon taken to reduce the severe penalty for attending a nonpublic school or college.

Well-Intended But Ill-Conceived

Most actions by governmental authorities concerning the schools are well-intended but too often they are ill-conceived and seem to aim at objectives other than improved learing. Some urban school systems appear to be engaged in a process to ruin not only public education but the cities they serve. They pursue policies which cause business enterprises and large numbers of the types of residents they need most to sustain their social and economic base, millions in the national aggregate, to move out as their only means of escape from the city's or the school district's jurisdiction.

To be sure, government has an essential role to play in many problems of our contemporary society. But in too many cases we must ask, Are you helping to solve the problem or are you part of the problem? Time and again, government has perpetuated a problem that otherwise would long have been solved. Sometimes it makes a mountain out of a molehill.

For more than three decades the United States government has been

---

[18] Steven Muller, "Anguish," *Chronicle of Higher Education,* December 2, 1974.

trying to boost the price of farm products and to reduce farm production, at a cost to the public treasury which has now run well over $100 billion. Our lawmakers worry periodically over the high cost of food and the inadequacy of our food base for an "exploding" population (though birthrates and population growth are at the lowest level ever and steadily dropping). When in 1973 food prices finally began to rise—in keeping with trends on the world's commodity markets—the government tried to restrain them by price controls, a method that has never proven effective and that led to supply shortages. In all the excitement over climbing food prices it is too easily forgotten that the share of food in the consumer's expenditure dollar shrank from thirty-two cents in 1952 to twenty-one cents in 1972, the lowest percentage in history and among the world's nations. It stood at twenty-two cents in 1973. Nor does it seem to be recalled that the farmer's slice of all personal income had fallen from 5.5 percent in 1952 to 2.2 percent in 1972. It jumped to 3.6 percent in 1973 but had fallen back to 2.3 percent by mid-1974. Is it a national calamity if these trends are halted or even temporarily reversed slightly? As time goes on we seem to be moving away from a free market instead of coming closer to it, although the country's largest farm organization has long advocated a free market as the most effective way of providing the consumer with his needs at reasonable prices.

We have poured more than $150 billion into aid to over 100 foreign countries. In some cases it has helped, but in many cases it has reaped a harvest of thistles and venom while supporting self-destructive policies of the recipient governments. Surely, it has earned us few genuine friends, if any, among other nations.

For over a century we have been trying to act as the Great White Father to the remnants of the Indian people, piling on new programs in recent decades—with meager and often tragic results.

While the United States Surgeon General issues warnings against smoking and the Department of Health, Education and Welfare calls smoking the leading cause for the 600,000 deaths a year from coronary heart disease, the 72,000 deaths from lung cancer, and the 25,000 deaths from chronic bronchitis and emphysema, the federal government continues to support the growing of tobacco, thereby, in the words of the American Medical Association, subsidizing "increased death and disability."

Many activities call for public regulation, but this sometimes turns into public strangulation, as it has particularly in the case of railroads and some other utilities. When the railroads could no longer sustain losses and began to go bankrupt, government had to nationalize passenger traffic. This means mainly that operational deficits, which were supposed to disappear, are now borne by the taxpayers. Our energy problem would not be half as serious if government had not intervened. Occasionally the use of governmental power is needed to prevent the formation of a monopoly, but in most cases only government can and does create a monopoly by encouraging, granting, or directly exercising it, often with huge losses (e.g., the Post Office). The most costly monopolies encouraged and aided by government are those exercised by the national labor unions.

Grants to state and local governments have long been a popular device to promote and finance favored public services. But the multiplication of authorizations to well over 500 programs in recent years has turned federal aid into an administrative nightmare, which, if continued much longer, will wind up in chaos. Plans to simplify intergovernmental aid by shifting some of the decisions to states and cities through grant consolidation, fiscal grants, or tax credits have so far been given the cold shoulder by members of Congress who feel that there is but little wisdom outside its own halls. Revenue sharing, instead of replacing categorical grant programs, was placed on top of the grant programs and thus added to the intricacy and confusion.

Officeholders in the executive and legislative branches of government continue to pay lip service to local autonomy and home rule by states and communities while further centralizing decision-making power in Washington through earmarked and conditional grants and tightened regulations. Virtually all functions of state and local governments are now so closely controlled by federal law and supervised by federal agencies that the reality of a federal system of government—of a wide dispersal of power among coequals—has become a fiction and has for practical purposes ceased to exist.

We have been complaining about rising prices, pointing fingers in several directions, and demanding that government discipline unions and management by guideposts, jawboning, fines, or controls. But only government itself can and does create inflation, largely through budget deficits, easy money, and lopsided labor policies, and only government itself can stop inflation—by exercising self-discipline, which so far it has shown no inclination to do. Huge budgetary deficits have become the rule and have led to double-digit inflation. Although the Federal Reserve Board has tried from time to time to use a restraining influence on the money supply and on reserve and margin requirements, it has been unable to apply such policies consistently and with sufficient severity. To conduct an anti-inflationary policy through monetary means alone, or almost alone, would result in a level of unemployment that appears politically intolerable.

Wage and price controls imposed in August 1971 brought only a minor and short-lived slowdown in the upward spiral. By 1973, prices were rising faster than they had prior to the imposition of controls. Moreover, for the first time in United States peacetime history, numerous shortages of essential goods developed throughout the economy, largely because the natural regulator and balancer between demand and supply, market pricing, had been deactivated by government edict.

Repeated experience has shown that controls can serve as a temporary *supplement* to proper fiscal and monetary policies but not as a *substitute*. In a rare display of agreement the national organizations of labor and business demanded repeal of wage and price controls. Congress obliged and let control authority expire but otherwise showed little inclination to diminish governmental powers over the private economy. Inflation and scarcities are therefore likely to continue until the American public and its leaders are willing to swallow the pill of consistent fiscal-monetary restraint.

The energy crisis, which became a major public calamity in 1973, is another example of well-intended government action that turned out to be counterproductive. "Our basic problem," said the president of the Edison Electric Institute, "is not a lack of government policy but rather a proliferation of government policies which are often uncoordinated and even contradictory." Hundreds of reports for many years had warned of an impending crisis in the supply of gas, oil, and electric energy, but lawmakers turned a deaf ear. When the predicted shortage materialized, those mainly responsible devised a conspiracy theory rather than admit the true causes. Regulation of the natural gas price at artificially low levels for the past twenty years stimulated expanded consumption of (and conversion to) gas while discouraging exploration and production. More recently, control of oil and gasoline prices, restriction of imports, withholding of off-shore leases, and reduction of tax incentives (such as the cut in the depletion allowance from 27.5 to 22 percent in 1969) had a similar impact on the availability and consumption of petroleum products. Discovery declined and known reserves could not keep up with demand, although there may be enough oil and gas in the ground to last for centuries. Many other government actions contributed to, and are mainly responsible for, the inadequacy in the supply of petroleum products and electrical energy: obstacles put in the way of companies which attempted to build new power plants or refineries, prevention for nearly five years of the construction of the Alaska pipeline, imposition of legal mandates which force sharply higher consumption of gasoline and discourage the wider use of coal (of which the United States has almost unlimited supplies). No government "crash program" can quickly end the difficulties resulting from unwise policies of the past and present. But a freeing of market forces could alleviate them in a shorter time than any alternative action.

A quarter of a century ago we started an urban renewal program, which, at a huge expense, has since destroyed three times as many dwellings as it has completed, and has built mostly apartments which the former residents of the area cannot afford. It has been called a "slum removal program" because it has mainly shifted slums from one section of the city to another, sometimes spawning "instant slums" to replace the old ones. The true welfare state enthusiasts blind themselves to the fact that slums are not decaying buildings but people whose attitudes and habits require more of a change than is provided by the replacement of decrepit dwellings with gleaming apartment towers.

In an effort to keep rents down, New York City has maintained, ever since World War II, rent control over 1.3 million apartments. When maintenance costs soared and losses mounted to unbearable levels, many landlords were forced to abandon their property. Over 130,000 apartments and houses, two-thirds of them structurally sound, were left to rot in New York City within four years; housing units are being retired twice as fast as new ones are opened.

Dozens of urban programs intended to improve housing conditions were enacted, extended or enlarged in recent years. What is their combined impact? What would one expect to happen in a market where private demand is high, costs and prices are rising at a faster rate than in the rest of the economy,[19] and government adds billions to the demand, offering generous subsidies and infusing large amounts of grants, loans, and guarantees? As a consequence, the price of houses and of construction generally, and inevitably also rents, increased at an even faster rate, driving additional millions of moderate-income families out of the housing market. Not surprisingly those families added their voice to the clamor for more housing subsidies—for middle-income families. We have here the classic case of a vicious cycle: government action intended to cope with a

---

[19] The Consumers Price Index climbed 58 percent between 1952 and 1972 but the residential construction index (Boekh) simultaneously jumped 109 percent, the building construction index 151 percent (*Engineering News Record*).

problem balloons it and creates the need for an expanded program. Most of the public housing authorities are in financial trouble, some near-bankrupt; though their buildings are supplied for free. Some of the public housing projects built within the past quarter century turned into slums, and a few became so dilapidated that they had to be torn down.

Not enough attention has been paid to Jay Forrester's *Urban Dynamics,*[20] which showed that to start solving the urban problem at the housing end is self-defeating. The city, he suggested, should aim to create an environment that will attract and generate jobs; if the people are gainfully employed, almost everything else will fall in line.

To be sure, there are fields in which enlarged governmental investment has proven eminently productive and yielded rich dividends. For example, the highway fatality rate fell from 7.4 (per 100 million motor vehicle miles) in 1952 to 4.5 in 1972. This means that in 1972 36,300 lives were saved which would have been lost had 1952 fatality rates continued, not to mention other costs of accidents that just did not happen. The major factor in the improved highway safety is undoubtedly the construction of modern automobile roads (freeways, turnpikes). Toll roads recorded a fatality rate of 2.05 (per 100 million vehicle miles) in 1971, compared with a 4.7 rate on *all* roads. In other words, turnpikes or freeways had only about one-third the death rate of other roads—despite the far higher speeds at which cars are driven on them. Had the toll road rate prevailed on all roads, only 25,600 persons would have been killed in 1972, instead of the 56,300 who actually perished in that year as a result of motor vehicle accidents.

But a loss of 56,300 lives a year, with most of the victims in their early or prime years—aside from hundreds of thousands injured or maimed—is still an intolerable loss. Accidents are one of the largest causes of death in the United States among young persons and middle-aged adults; about half of those accidental deaths are caused by motor vehicles.

The death toll remains high because most of the driving is still done on old-fashioned and inadequate roads. Not enough modern roads have been or are being built. Expenditures of all governments for highway purposes increased from $4.6 billion in 1952 to $18.4 billion in 1972, a 301 percent increase. This roughly equals the rate of increase in total governmental spending (296 percent) but looks puny compared with the expansion of outlays for social welfare (education, health, social security, public assistance, etc.) of 832 percent and a rise of 414 percent in all other domestic

---

[20] Cambridge, Mass.: MIT Press, 1969.

governmental costs. It does, however, far exceed the simultaneous growth (68 percent) in the cost of national defense.

Our highway system could be brought up to contemporary needs and standards—at the saving of tens of thousands of lives, much human suffering, and billions of dollars in property—without much if any rise in taxes. Highways can be self-financing, as the experience with toll roads has proven. People are willing to pay the price of better highways, voluntarily, without compulsion. But that runs contrary to the philosophy of those who believe that only mandatory action by government under sanction of law, rather than a free market, expresses a proper public policy. This is why the Interstate Highway Program provides federal funds—for 90 percent of the cost—only for tollfree roads. The construction of new toll roads virtually ended in 1956 and the building of modern roads was restricted largely to the amounts appropriated by government from taxes. The resulting cost in human lives, suffering, and property losses from motor vehicle accidents is huge and unconscionable.

Crime in the Welfare State

There is one job, one major duty in the domestic field, which government was always expected to do and which only government can do in a modern society: crime detection and prevention. It has turned this into the worst failure among its domestic activities.

No reliable statistics exist that would permit an accurate comparison of the incidence of crime in the United States and in other countries. But enough information is available to state that without doubt the United States has become the most crime-ridden country in the world. In no other megalopolis could its leading newspaper say, as the *New York Times* did on June 3, 1969: "This city's 8 million people live in daily fear of mugging, robbery and other violent crimes."

Nor is this simply a "crime wave," as it is often called. Waves crest and ebb, but the crime rate has been going almost steadily upward, with no sign of cresting or ebbing. According to FBI reports, the number of serious crimes leaped from 2 million in 1960[21] to 5.9 million in 1972.[22] That

---

[21] Data for years prior to 1960 are not strictly comparable with those for subsequent years.

averages out to a 9 percent increase each year—while population was growing approximately 1 percent per year.

Soaring crime is widely blamed on social conditions. There is an element of truth in this charge, but not in the sense in which it is usually meant to be understood: that society has neglected its poor. Spending under public income maintenance programs jumped from $7 billion in 1950 to $23 billion in 1960 and is now running at an annual clip of $150 billion. The number of families with a money income under $3,000 fell from 33.4 percent of *all* families in 1952 to 22.7 percent in 1959 and to 7.2 percent in 1972 (if counted in dollars of *1972 value,* from 18.3 to 14.3 and to 7.2 percent respectively); the number of families classified "below poverty level" fell from 18.5 percent in 1959 to 9.3 percent in 1972. But the number of female-headed families has gone up by more than two million since 1952. Several other indicators of social health also suggest that undesirable trends are developing while the welfare state increasingly permeates American society.

There really is no mystery about the cause of the soaring crime rate: would-be criminals did their homework, they checked the record, and came up with a simple fact: *crime pays.* A recent study concluded that the chances of going to prison are less than 1 in 200 for a man committing a felony in New York City. While the number of felonies committed in that city multiplied more than threefold during the 1960s, the prison population fell by about a third. The backlog of New York City's criminal court has been estimated at 700,000 cases; it would take two and one-half years to reduce the backlog at the present rate—if no new arrests were made.

In 1961 26 percent of the offenses known to the police were cleared by arrests, in the national average; this gradually declined to 19.6 percent in 1971 and improved to 20.9 percent in 1972. In other words, the criminal now has about four chances in five never to be arrested. A person arrested has five chances out of six *not* to serve time in prison or jail, although only 5 percent of those tried are acquitted. And the one in about thirty criminals who is unlucky enough to wind up behind bars serves on the average only 55 percent of the time to which he was sentenced. Is there any other moneymaking or ego-satisfying enterprise in which the chances are nearly as good?

---

[22] Reports by President Johnson's Commission on Law Enforcement and Administration of Justice suggested that twice as many major crimes are committed in the United States each year as appear in official police statistics. A Bureau of Census survey in the first six months of 1973 suggests that three times as many serious crimes may be committed as are recorded by law enforcement agencies.

Nor can this appalling record be blamed on the stinginess with which governments have been treating their law enforcement agencies:

POLICE EMPLOYMENT AND EXPENDITURES, 1952 AND 1972

	1952	1972	Percent Increase
Employment in state and local police departments	238,000	547,000	130%
U.S. population	157.5 million	208.8 million	33
Expenditures for police (federal, state, local)	$993 million	$6,654 million	570
National income	$291 billion	$ 942 billion	224

SOURCE: U.S. Department of Commerce,
Bureau of the Census, Bureau of Economic Analysis.

While the police employment-population ratio was nearly cut into half —from 1:662 to 1:382—the ratio of crime to population approximately tripled.

Data from New York City, Washington, D.C., and other major cities show the same picture: as the number of policemen and the size of police appropriations multiplied, so did crimes, often at surprisingly similar rates.

One of the country's most eminent experts on police science, James Q. Wilson, professor of government at Harvard University, concluded in a recent survey of police attempts to prevent crime: "And yet to close observers of police at work there is also some reason to believe that the number and deployment of the police have little or nothing to do with the crime rate."[23] He pointed out that the size of the New York City Police Department was increased by 54% between 1954 and 1974, when an experiment in Manhattan's 25th Precinct of doubling police strength in 1954 seemed to suggest positive results. But while New York City's population remained about constant between 1954 and 1974, crime increased even more rapidly than police manpower. A Kansas City experiment in the 1970s, sponsored by the Ford Foundation (through the Police Foundation), which sharply increased police patrols in one part of the city, left them unchanged in another, and abolished them in a third, found no

---

[23] James Q. Wilson, "Do the Police Prevent Crime?," *New York Times Magazine*, October 6, 1974. Subsequently Professor Wilson wrote: "Nearly ten years ago I wrote that the billions of dollars the federal government was then preparing to spend on crime control would be wasted and indeed might even make matters worse if they were merely pumped into the existing criminal justice system. They were and they have." James Q. Wilson, "Lock 'Em Up and other Thoughts on Crime", *New York Times Magazine*, March 9, 1975.

difference in the rate of reported crime or level of citizen fear among those city sections.

The former general counsel to President Lyndon B. Johnson's National Commission on the Causes and Prevention of Violence was reported as stating: "To the extent we tried dealing with the crime problem by increasing the number of police, we were doing something that everyone knew wasn't going to work. It was superficial relief from some symptoms. It is not a case of getting at the over-all causes."[24]

This does not suggest that police departments have been lying down on the job. Four hundred and eighty-eight policemen murdered in the line of duty between 1968 and 1972 testify to that. But it does suggest that there is something terribly wrong with our methods, with the procedures under which police are forced to operate, and with the rules imposed by courts whose concern seems to have shifted largely from the victims—and potential victims—of crime to the criminals who committed the offenses.

Nowhere is the basic philosophy of the welfare state—denial of personal responsibility—more clearly expressed than in our attitude toward crime and our treatment of criminals, in no other manner do we more manifestly reap the harvest of what we have sown.

Most of the many dozens of studies of rehabilitation programs show very little if any gain in reducing recidivism. Only the certainty of speedy and severe punishment consistently deters crime. Yet our courts have gone to ridiculous ends to protect the criminals but not the victims, as Judge Macklin Fleming of the California Court of Appeals showed in his recent book *The Price of Perfect Justice* (New York: Basic Books, 1975).

The American public is increasingly frightened by the jungle-like conditions in our cities and anxious to end this reign of terror. On June 30, 1972, *Life* published the results of a readers' survey on crime to which 45,000 responded. Eighty percent of the readers stated that they were afraid to walk their streets at night; nearly as many said they sometimes feel unsafe in their own homes. In a Gallup Poll asking whether the courts should deal more harshly with criminals the percentage of respondents who gave an opinion rose from 57 percent in the affirmative in 1965 to 82 percent in 1969. But neither the courts nor legislative bodies seem ready to take the drastic measures which at this stage may be necessary to restore law and order in the United States, at least to a level that is closer to

---

[24] Orde Coombs, "The Three Faces of Harlem," *New York Times Magazine,* November 3, 1974.

conditions which prevail in other civilized countries. Though much more money will undoubtedly be needed if crime is to be reduced, there is little hope that any amount will reverse current trends unless far more fundamental changes are made, until a semblance of safety is restored to our streets and homes.

Giant on Mudbrick Feet

Grave as the threat is from evergrowing crime, the most ominous danger to our long-range national survival lies in a gradual weakening of our national defense.

With an outlay of $81 billion and over two million men in uniform in 1974, our defense establishment offers a mighty and imposing sight. But the crucial point is that our potential enemies have for many years been building up their military strength while ours has been diminishing, measured by the only meaningful yardstick: the combined power we may have to face some day in a major confrontation at a future Armageddon.

Not that the Soviet Union or the People's Republic of China are planning to start a war with the United States. They both probably hope that a war may in the end not be necessary. They believe that they may achieve their immutable aim of eventual Communist world domination without a war if current trends continue long enough, because the United States will some day be in no position to oppose or resist any action affecting our vital interests or security our adversaries may choose to take anywhere in the world or to reject any demands they may raise in an ultimatum.

American military might reached its apex toward the end of World War II and has been on the downgrade ever since, falling dangerously behind in many crucial areas. The United States dismantled its defense establishment between 1945 and 1948, cutting outlays from $80 to $12 billion. That unilateral disarmament prompted aggressive action in Korea in which we barely escaped military disaster. At that point the defense budget was raised to $50 billion and is now running approximately one-fourth lower, if counted in dollars of *constant* value.[25] Governmental spending for domestic purposes meanwhile multiplied over four times in *constant* dollars. It is not widely enough known that the Vietnam operations were carried on to a

---

[25] U.S. Congress, *Congressional Record*, May 14, 1974, p. H3820.

large extent by depleting the rest of the defense establishment. This leaves us with "Swiss cheese" defenses, as several incidents in recent years suggest. Demands in Congress for further cutbacks in military outlays, ranging from $10 to $30 billion, for a "peace dividend" would, if met, weaken United States security seriously. As a matter of fact, the "peace dividend" has already been distributed, several times over, in the form of tremendous boosts in social welfare spending in recent years.

The most ominous development may be a significant change in the attitude toward national defense among the nation's lawmakers. For some years Congress tended to follow the advice of the Joint Chiefs of Staff and, as a rule, boosted presidential recommendations on defense appropriations—in the years 1960–1963 by an annual average of $1.5 billion. But in the years 1968–1973 Congress cut presidential proposals on the Pentagon budget by an annual average of $3.8 billion, with the size of the cut tending to increase. It totaled $5.2 billion in 1973, and the defense-budget cutters exuded great confidence that they would be able to do even better in the future. In the fall of 1974 Congress reduced the president's defense budget recommendations by $4.5 billion and substantially increased appropriations for domestic purposes.

Defense-budget reduction plans used to be advanced as required to balance the budget. But this seems no longer necessary. Representative Les Aspin, author of an amendment to impose a lower military expenditure ceiling, appealed to other members of Congress to go to work on their colleagues and "convince them that you've got to cut the defense budget if you want sufficient money for your own programs."[26] The implications of this approach—that domestic outlays are a congressman's "own" programs while national defense is someone else's concern—are portentous. The budget battle seems to turn into a contest between the Armed Services and the "Charmed Services" in which the former usually lose. Pressure groups for expanded domestic spending, ranging from the United States Conference of Mayors to the National Education Association, did "go to work" and the Aspin amendment cutting defense procurement by $1.5 billion passed the House.

A survey of the ninety-two members of the House of Representatives newly elected in November 1974 found that five out of six believe that the government is spending too much on defense and three out of four that more should be spent on social programs.[27] But the next two to three years

---

[26] *National Journal Reports,* October 6, 1973, p. 1481.

[27] *U.S. News and World Report,* December 16, 1974.

will be critical in the view of Pentagon strategists in setting the world balance of power for the 1980s.

We are now on the threshold of an entire new generation of weaponry for the automated battlefield of the future. That includes unmanned, remotely-piloted aircraft, automatic guns, cruise missiles, hover aircraft, laser-guided or TV-equipped bombs and missiles, battlefield sensors, surveillance and killer satellites and many others. They have three characteristics in common: they are highly sophisticated, they take many years to develop, produce, deploy and they are exorbitantly expensive. The question is whether Congress will have the vision and the courage to act or let our defensive strength fall behind.

The United States enjoyed a decisive military superiority over the Soviet Union at the time of the Cuban missile crisis in 1962, which is why the Russians yielded to President John F. Kennedy's ultimatum that their naval vessels steaming toward Cuba reverse their course. The Soviet Union has since been pushing one of the greatest armament programs ever ("talking peace but sharpening its sword"), has pulled abreast of us in many respects, and has gained a clearcut superiority in strategic offensive weapons, in megatonnage as well as in the number of delivery vehicles—land-based intercontinental missiles, missile-launching (and other) submarines, antiballistic missiles, and several other major weapons systems. There has been a decisive shift in the balance of military power. The USSR has a substantial lead in combat ground forces, which is widening with the cut of United States armed forces by over one-third, from 3.5 to 2.1 million. The Soviet navy was reported to be "now the world's most powerful navy" in the 1973 and 1974 editions of *Jane's Fighting Ships*. And the Soviet air force, with 10,000 front-line, combat-ready craft is ahead of the United States in numbers. The United States is now devoting less than 6 percent of its GNP to national defense—down from 13.5 percent in 1952—while the USSR is probably exerting at least twice that effort, and also reported to be allocating twice as much to defense research and development as we are.

Increases in our defense budget were more than consumed by higher prices and boosts in military pay, made particularly necessary by the conversion to a voluntary army. Cost per soldier jumped from $3,578 in 1952 to $10,398 in 1972 (and an estimated $12,448 in 1974).

Increasing complexity and sophistication of weapons systems shot prices up. The cost of tanks has been at least doubling every ten years, the cost of aircraft multiplying four to six times. This forced substantial cutbacks in numbers to stay within appropriations.

We obtained an antiballistic missile treaty at the Strategic Arms Limitations Talks (SALT) I because we were at the time ahead of the Soviets, which gave them a powerful incentive to make tangible concessions. That element was not present when a tentative SALT II agreement was concluded in Vladivostok. United States direct spending on strategic programs, in real terms, had dropped to nearly one-third between 1961 and 1974, while the Soviets had been building up.

The new ten-year pact sets rather high ceilings and puts virtually no limits on what the air force and navy can add. There is every indication that the Soviet Union will continue its build-up. Whether the United States will allocate sufficient resources to preserve its relative strength from slipping further appears doubtful at this time.

Under current trends, the Soviets are headed for a decisive military superiority.[28] We are simply running out of time. It takes five to ten years to develop, test, produce, and deploy a major weapons system. Whether our defenses will be strong in the second half of the 1970s, the 1980s, and beyond, or whether the United States will have to yield to nuclear or other forms of blackmail, is now being decided—by what we do about our missiles and missile defenses, about the navy's F-14 and the air force's F-15 fighters, the advanced manned strategic aircraft (AMSA) (now to be implemented as the B-1 new strategic bomber), the nuclear carriers and the 4000-mile range Trident missile submarine programs, the C-5A cargo plane, a possible reactivation of the MBT-70 main battle bank, and the army's SAM-D missile. The Joint Chiefs of Staff appear to be fighting a losing battle. And the warnings of our military experts are not sufficiently heeded.

What is needed above all is the will to preserve America's strength and its position as the leading force of the free world. In his inaugural address to the Congress on August 12, 1974, President Gerald Ford said: "A strong defense is the surest way to peace." The supply of greater military resources can come only from tighter control of nondefense expenditures or from taxes.

Many Unhappy Returns

That taxes are too heavy is a perennial complaint that in itself proves little if anything. If the majority of the people felt that taxes are oppressive

---

[28] "American Military Power Sliding Into Second Place?," *U.S. News and World Report*, November 4, 1974.

they could do something about it in a system of free government—by electing representatives who run on a platform of lower taxes rather than expanded government programs. Though the outright advocates of higher taxes, such as John Kenneth Galbraith and his followers, are distinctly in the minority, the spokesmen for enlarged public services seem to swing enough weight to have been successful in their drive. All governmental revenues (federal, state, and local) went up 310 percent between 1952 and 1972 while the GNP and the national income increased only 234 and 224 percent respectively. As a result, governmental receipts inched up from 26 percent of the GNP and 30.8 percent of the national income in 1952 to 31.9 percent of the GNP and 39.1 percent of the national income, respectively, in 1972.[29]

In the press and in political statements the weight and growth in taxes is often attributed to the demands of national defense. But this is contradicted by the fact that national defense outlays, as a share of the GNP, declined from 13.5 percent in 1952 to 6.8 percent in 1972 and are currently running below 6 percent. Some may contend that 1952 is not a fair base year for comparison purposes because the Korean war was then still going on. But the fact is that, except for the period prior to World War II (in an entirely different world situation) and the short period of American unilateral disarmament between 1946 and 1950, which led to aggression and near-disaster—we are now spending a smaller share of our income on the military than ever before. Eighty-eight percent of the 1952–1972 increase in all governmental spending and four-fifths of the increase in federal spending went for nondefense purposes. In other words, the growing weight of taxes in recent decades is clearly attributable to domestic programs, not to national defense.

Moreover, federal revenues increased between 1952 and 1972 only slightly faster (240 percent) than national income or product (224 and 234 percent respectively). State and local revenues—all of which are allocated to domestic services, mostly education and welfare—meanwhile jumped 518 percent. Steady rounds of state and local tax boosts mainly accounted for the growth in the tax load over the past twenty years, although the people themselves have more direct say about their state and local taxes than about federal taxes. Receipts from property taxes multiplied five times, from general sales taxes eight times, from personal income taxes

---

[29] Data based on national income accounts. Using the broader concepts and definitions of the Bureau of the Census, governmental revenues equaled 34.7% of the GNP and 42.6% of the national income in 1971–1972.

seventeen times (though complaints about rising property taxes appeared to be the loudest and most persistent).

Even so, the taxes of the American people are not extraordinarily high in comparison with the burden borne by the citizens of other major industrial nations—Sweden, Great Britain, France, Germany, Austria, Holland—who pay a higher share of their income to their governments in the form of taxes. This does not seem to have adversely affected their economic progress. In fact, there is little evidence to support or prove the common assumption that high taxes as such deter or impede economic growth. Some countries with very high levels of taxation and liberal programs of social insurance have achieved remarkable rates of economic expansion and high per capita incomes.

It could well be that the *form* of taxation has a far greater impact on economic development than its overall *magnitude*.

It is well known that the American tax structure is unique. No other industrial country has a tax system that is so heavily biased in favor of consumption and against capital formation in a determined attempt to redistribute income. Most major countries use a consumption tax as the mainstay of their revenue system; the United States is the only country that does not use such a tax at all at the national level. Nor does any other country rely for its revenue as heavily on income taxes as does the United States.

The individual income tax, now graduated from 14 to 70 percent, is by far the biggest single tax, yielding well over $100 billion a year. It is the pride and joy of those who see in it a major and effective tool for making progress toward their egalitarian goals. They do attack the income tax because it contains many "loopholes" which, it is asserted, enable many wealthy persons to escape bearing their fair share—or any share—of the tax burden. Closer examination shows that the individual income tax is indeed full of loopholes, however that term may be defined.[30] Only about half of personal income, as defined in national income accounts, is subject to the rate scale of the federal income tax. But most of the untaxed income—over $500 billion annually at the present time—accrues to persons in the lower-middle and low-income brackets, only a small fraction to those in the high brackets. The cry about loopholes for the rich, as it is widely heard, reminds us of the man who decried the mote in somebody else's eye but could not see the beam in his own.

---

[30] Someone once defined a loophole as a provision in the tax code from which the particular speaker—or the group he represents—derives either no benefits or not enough benefits.

To be sure, there are some "shelters" protecting or favoring certain economic activities, usually for a good reason. For example, to tax long-term capital gains as if they were regular income would be the most effective way to freeze investments and to bring the country's economic expansion to a screeching halt. To repeal mineral percentage depletion allowances, without an adequate replacement, would diminish exploration and discovery of oil and natural gas wells, which already have been cut to half in recent years. To do this while the country is critically short of energy sources, increasingly dependent on uncertain foreign supplies, and subjected to blackmail from abroad would be detrimental and could be disastrous to the country's prosperity and very existence. What is needed is added incentives for discovery and production of domestic energy sources, not discouragement.

The United States levies a higher corporate profits tax than any other country, although that tax is probably the most economically damaging tax in our system. Not because it taxes the stockholder, as is widely believed, but because it punishes the efficient producer, restricts industrial expansion, penalizes capital formation, and adversely affects our competitiveness in international trade. Its immense political appeal has prevented even a partial replacement of the corporate profits tax with a value-added tax that has become the main revenue source for most major European countries.

No tax has been on the receiving end of as many vituperative attacks for as long a time as the property tax; to some extent, for good reasons. But great progress has been made in recent decades in improving the assessment process and administration in general. Exemptions may be too generous in some states, but they average only about one-third of the base, compared with one-half the base on the federal individual income tax. Whatever its shortcomings may be, the property tax is the mainstay of local government, which could hardly maintain some semblance of autonomy without an independent source of revenue. There is no substitute for the property tax, without which the remnants of home rule of local communities would largely disappear from the American scene.

It is unfortunate that much of the talk about tax reform focuses on how to make it a more effective tool for taking money from some and giving it to others instead of shaping taxes as a positive means of promoting economic growth and stability in a neutral way. The primary goal of tax *reform* should, above all, be tax *reduction,* which can in the long run be achieved only through tighter control of public expenditures than chief executives and legislative bodies have so far seen fit to apply.

In Conclusion

The spectacular expansion of governmental activities from 1952 to 1972—as expressed in the increase in public employment, public spending, and taxes—has not produced the promised and hoped-for results. In many respects it has been counterproductive and has left the American people in a worse position than they were in before. The steady weakening of the nation's global and military power, and of its domestic tranquility, cohesion, and progress must to a large extent be attributed to the growth of the welfare state. If it continues its growth at the rate of these years, the future of the American commonwealth may indeed be in jeopardy.

A straight projection of governmental trends of the 1952—1972 period would produce results by the year 2000 that seem absurd. There would then be one person working for government for every 1.75 persons in private employment—compared with a ratio of 1:4 at the present time—and governmental spending would equal 70 percent of the GNP—compared with 36 percent in 1972. It is hardly conceivable that this could happen. Expansion of domestic public programs is therefore unlikely to continue at the 1952–1972 rate for much longer. To be sure, demand for ever bigger benefits and services is as vocal as ever and its appeal to the large numbers of current and potential recipients, as well as the voting power of those who receive from government but do not contribute, grows. But the harvest of the wave of social legislation of the 1960s, of the new or enlarged programs, has been so disappointing that resistance to unlimited expansion of governmental activities and intervention is likely to become stronger as time goes on.

The trend toward bigger government—in terms of heavier taxes, bigger spending, greater employment, tighter regulations of business and personal activities—therefore has a good chance of flattening out in the last quarter of the twentieth century. While some visualize the *millennium*—and the millennial year of 2000—as a time when government will play a much greater role in the daily life of the American people than it does now, the eventual outcome could well be quite different.

—1—

Overview

A dramatic expansion of governmental activities, of their scope and magnitude, not only in absolute terms but also in proportion to the population and the economy, is one of the most pervasive facts and trends of our times, virtually universal among the countries of the globe, industrial as well as "less developed." Such growth seldom occurs at an even pace. Usually it proceeds in spurts with occasional slowdowns or stops, but it seems to go on indefinitely. The perennial nature of that upward movement caused Solomon Fabricant[1] to conclude that it expressed a secular trend that would continue long into the future. So it has. Most Americans, if asked, would express their belief that the increase in governmental activities, in taxes, and in the size of the public bureaucracy has been particularly steep—or exorbitant—in recent years, in the two decades that have passed since the publication of the Fabricant study. But strange as it seems, the record shows that the past two decades have been a period during which the upward trend in taxes, public spending, and the public work force and employment has flattened out. It suggests that in *aggregate terms* the significant growth of government finances and employment took place *prior to and not since 1952.*[2]

Aggregate revenues of all governments (federal, state, and local) grew parallel to the nation's economy or GNP during the first decade of the twentieth century. But in the succeeding sixty years public receipts as a

---

[1] Fabricant, *The Trend of Government Activity*, pp. 153-55.

[2] U.S. Treasury reports on fiscal operations have been kept since 1789, but consistent and comprehensive statistics on the finances of all governments—federal, state, and local—are available only as far back as FY 1902 and for all subsequent years ending in 2. Government financial data consistent with national income accounts are available from the Bureau of Economic Analysis (formerly the Bureau of Business Economics) of the Department of Commerce on a calendar year basis back to 1952. For further details see Technical Notes, pp. xv-xviii. Only in the 1950s did the Bureau of the Census and the Bureau of Business Economics begin to prepare and publish annual governmental financial statistics, the former on a fiscal year basis, the latter on a calendar year basis.

percentage of the GNP jumped from 8.2 to 34.7 percent (table 1). That growth did not proceed at a consistent rate: the percentage which governmental revenues are of the GNP increased by 89 percent between 1913 and 1932, by 94 percent between 1932 and 1952, and by a mere 17 percent between 1952 and 1972. In fact, if we consider only the federal government, revenues as a percentage of the GNP *declined* between 1952 and 1972—from 21.3 to 20.3 percent—after multiplying about seven times (from 3.2 to 21.3 percent) between 1902 and 1952. In specific terms, the GNP multiplied 16 times between 1902 and 1952, federal revenues 110 times. Between fiscal years 1952 and 1972, the GNP grew 226 percent, federal revenues only 211 percent.

Though taxes obviously have increased in the past two decades, which in turn explains widespread and persistent complaints about a growing burden, they have done so at a rate that is moderate compared with earlier periods. Moreover, tax boosts have taken place mostly at state and local levels where they often depend on direct approval or veto by the taxpayers at the ballot box. The overall federal tax burden has not increased in the past twenty years because federal taxes were cut in the 1954, 1964, and 1969 revenue acts. A review of the aggregate expenditure and employment of all governments yields a similar picture: the increase in finances and employment, which had been spectacular during the first half of the twentieth century and earlier, dwindled to a crawl in the past twenty years.

In earlier times, the governmental payroll showed a long-range, consistent, sharp, upward trend, as Fabricant demonstrated in his study on government activity. From a total of 265,000 in 1870 it multiplied forty times to 10.7 million in 1952, while the United States population meanwhile multiplied only four times, from 39.8 million to 157.6 million (table 2). In other words, public employment grew ten times faster than population. The number of persons in the population per government worker meanwhile fell from 150:1 to 14.7:1. Between 1952 and 1972 it slid only to 13.0:1; population increased 33 percent, public employment 50 percent (table 2).

Public employment may be divided into two parts: *(a)* national defense (military and civilian), and *(b)* all other, mostly domestic public services. Table 3 shows sharply divergent trends between 1952 and 1972: the defense payroll dropped 28 percent, while the nondefense payroll jumped 117 percent. This means that a dramatic expansion in government workers for domestic services was largely—though not wholly—offset by a simultaneous drop in defense workers. There is now one government employee in domestic services for every 5.5 workers in private employment, compared with a ratio of 1:9.3 twenty years ago.

To put this in perspective: more persons were added to the governmental nondefense payrolls in the past 20 years than in the preceding 163 years since the founding of the republic. A population one-third larger in 1972 than it was in 1952 is now governed by a bureaucratic work force more than twice its former size.

Back in 1958 Professor C. Northcote Parkinson, the author of Parkinson's law, calculated in a somewhat jocular vein that if the uptrend in British public employment were to continue at the prevailing rate, everyone in Britain would be working for the government by the year 2195. In 1971 New York's Morgan Guaranty Trust Company applied the same idea to the United States and found that if things were to go on as they had been, every American would be on the public payroll by 2049—a century and a half sooner than in Britain.[3] This calculation was based on total civilian employment. If the Department of Defense were excluded, the event would occur far sooner.

The disproportionate increase in the public payroll for domestic services was brought about and made necessary by the vast expansion of existing programs and the addition of hundreds of new programs mostly in social welfare fields during the 1950s and 1960s. Program growth in the past two decades is demonstrated even more spectacularly in simultaneous expenditure trends.

Expenditures of all governments in the United States multiplied 239 times between 1902 and 1972 (table 4a), the GNP only 53 times. Such figures are of course misleading, because the dollar has lost much of its value and was worth only 17.7 cents in 1902 dollars in 1972. Conversely, one 1902 dollar was worth $5.65 in 1972 dollars. Expressed in constant dollars—converted by the use of the implicit price deflator for the GNP —the GNP multiplied 9.4 times between 1902 and 1972, governmental expenditures 42.5 times—or four times faster. Meanwhile governmental expenditures as a percentage of the GNP jumped from 8.0 to 36.1 percent (table 4b). That growth did not proceed at an even pace through the twentieth century. In the first decade the rise was slow: 0.8 percent of the GNP. In the succeeding two decades (1913–1932) it soared to 9.8 percent of the GNP, in the next two decades (1932–1952) it jumped to 11.0 percent of the GNP, and in the last two decades (1952–1972) it fell to 6.5 percent of the GNP.

---

[3] *The Morgan Guaranty Survey,* April 1971.

If we consider the federal government only, the growth rates fluctuated even more widely. There was no increase between 1902 and 1913, a 3.8 percent increase of the GNP between 1913 and 1932, and a 14.8 percent increase between 1932 and 1952, followed by a mere 0.8 percent increase between 1952–1972 (table 5b).

This leads to two conclusions: *(a)* most of the federal growth occurred during the 1932–1952 period and then slowed down to a trickle; *(b)* most of the government growth since 1952 is accounted for by state and local governments.

That federal expenditures grew so slowly in the past twenty years will come as a great surprise to many who have been under the impression that the period from 1952 to 1972 was one of extraordinary expansion of federal activities. The answer to this seeming contradiction is apparent from table 5a: aggregate federal spending grew slowly because much of the increase in outlays for domestic services was offset by a relative cutback in national defense. National defense dropped from 54 percent of total federal expenditures in 1952 to under 30 percent in 1972, while domestic services boosted their share of the budget from 19 to 55 percent. As a percentage of the GNP, defense dropped from 14.3 to 7.2 percent, while domestic services soared from 3.9 to 12.1 percent.

To put this in clear perspective: it took 163 years, from 1789 to 1952, for federal expenditures for domestic purposes to reach a level of $13 billion. In the succeeding twenty years they multiplied *tenfold,* jumping from $13 billion to $134 billion. In other words, in the past two decades we increased federal spending for domestic services *every two years* by as much as the total growth in the preceding 163 years. Even with a correction for the lower value of the dollar, this still is probably the most spectacular and most significant change in governmental finances and in the nature and concept of American government in the twentieth century. It would have been politically impossible to finance an increase of such magnitude by additional taxation. Federal tax boosts of small size have very rarely been enacted during peacetime, major tax boosts never. This dramatic expansion of federal domestic expenditures could be financed in only three ways: *(a)* by increasing tax receipts from economic growth and severity of tax rate scales due to inflation; *(b)* by sharply cutting the share of national defense in the federal tax dollar (as shown in table 5a); and *(c)* by continuous and sizeable deficits in the federal budget. Of the twenty fiscal years from 1953 to 1972, four were balanced (1956, 1957, 1960, 1969) for an aggregate surplus of $10.8 billion, while the other sixteen budgets produced a combined deficit of $134.8 billion. In those twenty years the public debt went up by $182 billion—aside from a boost of $145 billion in the state and local debt and several hundred billions in contingent liabilities of the social security and other retirement systems and various guarantee and loan funds.

The federal public debt had remained well below $2 billion prior to 1917 (except in the years following the Civil War), was lifted to $24 billion by World War I, to $43 billion by the depression and the New Deal, and to about $260 billion by World War II. It stood at $437 billion in 1972 and is estimated to reach $508 billion in FY 1975.[4]

This does not include other and far larger obligations resulting from various loan guarantee and pension programs, nor the unfunded liability of the social security system whose current value the treasury calculated at $2.4 trillion as of June 30, 1974. The Social Security Administration prefers an estimate under more favorable assumptions of a mere $1.3 trillion liability—still an awesome sum to consider.

---

[4] As a percentage of the GNP the federal debt declined from 76.8 percent in 1952 to 39.8 percent in 1972. It is estimated at 34.9 percent of the GNP for the end of FY 1975. *Special Analyses, Budget of the United States Government. Fiscal Year 1975,* table C-3. Of the $437 billion federal debt outstanding at the end of FY 1972, $114 billion was held by various federal trust funds and agencies, $71 billion by the Federal Reserve System, and $252 billion by the public.

—2—

The Public Payroll

From 1952 to 1972 the public payroll multiplied more than fourfold, from $35 to $150 billion. The 330 percent rate of increase exceeds somewhat if not spectacularly the simultaneous growth of 247 percent of employee compensation in private industries (from $161 to $557 billion). This more rapid expansion in government consists of two factors:*(a)*the number of public employees grew 52 percent, those of private jobholders only 35 percent; *(b)* average annual earnings per full-time employee advanced 183 percent in government, 146 percent in private industry. In 1952 the average worker in private employment was wage-wise 5 percent ahead of the public employee ($3,430 vs. $3,279); by 1972 he had fallen 10 percent behind the government worker ($8,440 vs. $9,264)(tables 6 and 9).[1]

The Expanding Bureaucracy

There is now *one* person working for government for every *four* employees in private industry producing the multitude of goods and services needed, consumed, and used by 210 million Americans or exported.

The sixteen million persons drawing their wages from public sources possess, with their families, a significant voting power, which they use to exercise influence on pay decisions by the legislative and executive branches of the governments they serve. It is becoming increasingly difficult for officials in either branch of government to vote against higher pay for public workers. This was clearly shown by the ease with which Congress in September 1974 overrode President Ford's decision to postpone federal pay hikes for three months. Considering that now about one

---

[1] Source: U.S., Department of Commerce, Bureau of Economic Analysis, *The National Income and Product Accounts of the United States, 1929–65 (1966)* and *Survey of Current Business,* July 1973. These data are similar to but not identical with those published by the Bureau of the Census from which tables 2, 3, 6 and 8 are derived. Therefore there are slight (statistically insignificant) differences between those figures (numbers and percentages) and those appearing in the other tables and discussed in the text.

person in every four in the United States obtains his livelihood through *workless* pay from the various social welfare programs, this constitutes an organized and powerful voting bloc of those who have a direct and strong stake and interest in pushing governmental programs to ever higher levels.

Most Americans, if asked where the greatest increase in governmental employment occurred, would immediately reply, "in the federal government." But analysis of public employment by level of government does not bear this out (table 7a). The number of persons on the federal payroll *declined* by nearly one million between 1952 and 1972 (from 6.2 to 5.2 million), while those on state and local payrolls increased more than six million (from 4.5 million to 10.8 million). Percentage-wise this means a 15 percent cut in federal employment, a 139 percent jump in state and local government. To be sure, the federal reduction of nearly one million consists of a cut in the armed forces of 1.1 million (=32 percent) and an *increase* in civilian employment of 200,000. But this still means an increase of only 8 percent in federal civilian employment during a period when the population of the United States expanded by 33 percent. The number of federal civilian employees per 1000 population fell from 16.4 in 1952 to 13.4 in 1972 (table 7b). This stands in stark contrast to developments in the first half of the twentieth century when federal employment multiplied tenfold while the United States population merely doubled. The *relative* decline in federal civilian employment in the past twenty years was the result of consistent and determined effort by chief executives and the Congress. It was the subject of much pride of achievement by several presidents.

The size of the government bureaucracy has always been politically a most sensitive issue in the United States. It goes back to grievances in the Declaration of Independence that King George III had "erected a multitude of new offices, and sent . . . swarms of officers to harass our people and eat out their substance."

Similar charges are still frequently being levied—most commonly by conservatives or by the party out of power—because they seem to feel that there is a direct relationship between the size of the federal bureaucracy and the power it exercises. Eugene C. Pulliam, publisher of several major newspapers, began his oft-copied speech, "Will the Federal Bureaucracy Destroy Individual Freedom in America?," as follows: "The most serious threat to freedom in America today—including freedom of the press —comes from a Federal bureaucracy which seems determined to gain control over every facet of American life."[2] The Republican Coordinating Committee preambled its *Declaration on Economy and Efficiency in Government* in January 1967 (when the Republican party was out of office) thus: "The Federal Government has become a bureaucratic jungle, rampant with overlapping, duplication and waste. A major carefully planned effort to review Executive branch programs and their administration is urgently needed. Such a study must be followed up by an active program to press for meaningful reorganization and reform."

Politically conscious presidents have always been very much aware of the traditional American dislike for a large bureaucracy. In his first budget message in January 1964, President Johnson wrote:

> Although both our population and our economy are growing and placing greater demands upon the Government for services of every kind, I believe the time has come to get our work done by improving the efficiency and productivity of our Federal work force, rather than by adding to its numbers.
>
> This budget proposes a reduction in Federal employment in 1965—from 2,512,400 to 2,511,200 civilian employees—and I have directed the heads of all departments and agencies to work toward reducing employment still further. This reversal in the trend of Federal employment results from a rigorous appraisal of personnel needs, determined measures to increase employee productivity and efficiency, and the curtailment of lower priority work. It will be accomplished despite large and unavoidable increases in workloads.

One year later President Johnson's budget message declared:

> The result of such efforts has been and will continue to be a reduction in the size of the Federal work force relative to the work being accomplished. The effectiveness of these controls may be seen in the fact that had Federal employment kept its 1955 relationship to total population, Federal employees would have totalled 2,747,000 on June 30, 1964, more than 275,000 above the actual number as of that date.

President Johnson's statements were correct. The number of federal civilian employees per 1000 population had declined from 14.3 in 1955 to 13.2 in 1964 and stood at 13.3 in 1965. But at that point the trend was reversed. In 1966 there were 14.6 federal civilian employees per 1000 population, in 1967 15.0, in 1968 14.9. Not surprisingly, there was no further reference to federal work force reductions in President Johnson's

---

[2] *Congressional Record,* October 27, 1971, pp. E11330, E11345 et seq.

budget messages after 1965. To be sure, much of the increase in federal civilian employment in the years after 1965 was caused by added numbers in the Department of Defense, due to the tremendous step-up of action in Vietnam, something that the president did not foresee in 1964 or in January 1965 when he submitted his budget for FY 1966.

Employment in the Department of Defense does not move in a parallel trend with civilian agencies and often moves in opposite directions. Therefore, to be meaningful, employment statistics must be divided functionally between the Department of Defense and domestic services. This shows that the 8 percent increase in federal civilian employment between 1952 and 1972 consisted of a 19 percent decline in the Department of Defense and a 37 percent increase in the "other" agencies.

A 37 percent increase in public employment for nondefense activities—mostly domestic services—does not seem to be out of line with a simultaneous population increase of 33 percent or with a growth in private employment of 28 percent. The big increase in the public payroll took place not in the federal government but at the state and local levels. As table 7a shows, state and local governments boosted their employment by 139 percent, which is more than four times the rate of population growth of 33 percent.

Why, we may ask, does the public have the impression that it was the federal bureaucracy that has grown excessively when the record shows that most of the increase took place at state and local levels? Because during that period much of the power of state and local governments was shifted to the federal level and most decisions seemed to depend on and come from Washington.[3] The range, nature, and magnitude of state and local programs and employment have become quite dependent on programs enacted by the Congress and on programs subject to federal rules and approvals to be obtained from Washington or regional offices of federal agencies. Thus, not surprisingly, the public views state and local employees as part of the federal bureaucracy. After all, this is where the orders and the money come from. Federal aid to state and local governments soared from $2.6 billion in FY 1952 to $36.0 billion FY 1972 (estimated at $51.7 billion in FY 1975); it turned from a minor item to a major factor in the federal as well as state and local budgets. The number of aid programs has grown from a few

---

[3] "Growth in public payrolls keeps mushrooming—growing fastest at state and local levels. It is the federal bureaucracy, however, that has emerged as the nation's elite work force in pay, privileges—and power" ("Washington Bureaucrats: 'Real Rulers of America,'" *U.S. News and World Report,* November 4, 1974).

dozen to well over 500, affecting—and more or less determining and controlling—most of the public services of state and local governments.

For the purpose of studying the growth of public employment, it is more expedient to divide governmental employment along functional lines rather than by level of government. A functional breakdown in table 8a shows that governmental employment in national defense and international relations declined by 28 percent between 1952 and 1972, while domestic services registered the following rates of increase: education 200 percent; police protection 129 percent; health and hospitals 120 percent; and all other functions 64 percent.

In absolute numbers defense employment dropped by 1.4 million persons, while domestic services jumped by 6.7 million, composed as follows:

INCREASE IN GOVERNMENTAL EMPLOYMENT IN
DOMESTIC FUNCTIONS, 1952–1972

	Numerical Increase (in thousands)	Percent Increase
Total	*6,728*	*100.0%*
Education	3,762	55.9
Health and hospitals	706	10.5
Police protection	327	4.9
Highways	150	2.2
Postal service	141	2.1
Natural resources	129	1.9
All other	1,513	22.5

SOURCE: Table 8a

Well over one-half of the increase in governmental employment between 1952 and 1972 was accounted for by education, about three-fourths of the total by the three services that were most widely claimed to suffer from personnel shortages during that period: education, health and hospitals, and police protection. These are also the functions which, as we saw earlier, recorded by far the highest *rates* of increase. In each of these fields, the growth rate in the size of the staff greatly exceeded the increase in the size of the clientele (students, patients, etc.). And they were certainly not the fields on which official efforts to restrain the public payroll focused.

Those efforts aimed at what is generally viewed as the "federal bureaucracy" and they were, at least partially, successful. Federal civilian employment fell by nearly 200,000 between 1952 and 1959 but regained this drop by 1965. President Johnson, then new in office, pointed out in his budget message of January 1964 that his proposals called for "a substantial reduction in total civilian employment in the Executive Branch." He directed federal department and agency heads to make strenuous efforts to reduce employment and set agency ceilings. Federal civilian employment climbed to nearly three million in 1967 and 1968, however, because of the new social programs which President Johnson pushed through Congress and because of the Vietnam war.

Disturbed by this 400,000 increase in three years—600,000 since 1959—Congress, in 1968, in its bill imposing a 10 percent income tax surcharge, directed government agencies to fill no more than three of every four vacancies in permanent jobs until employment was reduced to the level of June 30, 1966. These and similar attempts were continued with renewed vigor by the Nixon administration in 1969, and the federal civilian payroll dropped by 200,000 between 1968 and 1972 (see table 7a). But all of this expressed a cut in the Department of Defense. The remainder of the federal agencies, in the aggregate, did not increase the size of their payroll and maintained it approximately at an even level from 1968 to 1972—in the presence of inevitable complaints that the restraint hampered the administration of existing programs, and lowered employee morale. There was one federal nondefense employee for every 127 persons in the general population in 1952, one for every 124 in 1972, with only minor fluctuations in-between—a record of remarkable stability over a twenty-year period when hundreds of new programs were enacted, many existing ones were expanded, and federal expenditure for domestic purposes had multiplied tenfold.

The most significant employment developments between 1952 and 1972 can be shown in capsule form as follows:

	Percent Increase
Employment in private industry increased	35%
Employment in governmental nondefense increased	117 (table 9)
Employment in public education increased	200 (table 8a)
Employment in national defense declined	28 (table 8a)

That total governmental nondefense employment grew profusely between 1952 and 1972—from thirty-seven public workers per 1000 United States population in 1952 to sixty in 1972 (table 8b)—was not due to the addition of an extraordinary number of federal bureaucrats in Washington but to the growing number of "street-level bureaucrats" in state and local government employment in social and other domestic services, particularly education, health and hospitals, and police. This is why determined and repeated efforts to cut the public payroll through administrative reorganization—thereby saving taxes—have not been very successful. Structural reshuffling or consolidation of agencies may at times be advisable. But it is not likely to make a major impact on the size of the public payroll, which is set largely by the nature and scope of domestic public programs.

This was pointed out well by Rowland Egger a quarter of a century ago:

> The attempt to sell administrative reorganization legislation on the basis of tax reduction, however honorable the motives and however laudable the hopes of those who support administrative reorganization for this reason, is a snare and a delusion. . . . Administrative reorganization per se has never saved large sums of money. . . . The plain fact is that the only way to save significant sums of money in the federal establishment is to eliminate activities and reduce the scale of operations. . . . There is no royal road, no painless way, to governmental economy.[4]

Presidential and congressional declarations of intent to keep the public payroll down have always been restricted to *federal* employment. State and local government employment were deliberately boosted by up to 300,000 persons by the Public Employment Program (PEP) of 1971 in an effort to provide jobs mostly for low-skilled men and women who could not find employment in an open market at wages they would have to be paid under minimum wage laws or union contracts. In the fall of 1974 Congress enacted a sizeable expansion of PEP to provide additional jobs, primarily in the state and local services in which employment has risen most substantially within the past decade or two.

Productivity in Government

How the efficiency of the administrative structure and the worker's productivity in government compare with their counterparts in private

---

[4] Rowland Egger, "Painless Economy and the Mythology of Administrative Reorganization," *Proceedings of the Forty-second Annual Conference on Taxation,* National Tax Association, 1949.

industry is a most difficult and possibly unanswerable question. Overall, the number of employees in the public sector has risen faster than in the private sector: 52 versus 35 percent between 1952 and 1972 (table 9). Meanwhile, according to the national income accounts, the private product doubled in *constant* dollars, while the government product grew only by 50 percent.[5] At first glance this appears to show that private industry increased its output by 100 percent with 35 percent more employees, while government output grew only in proportion to the size of the staff. What it really expresses, however, is our present statistical inability to measure output and productivity changes in the public sector of the economy.

Productivity can be defined as the relationship between output and all associated inputs. Most commonly it is understood as labor productivity and expressed as an index number of output per man-hour. Bureau of Labor Statistics quarterly and annual series show output per man-hour in the private economy to have risen 85 percent between 1952 and 1972[6]—an annual average of 3.1 percent—which is in line with a secular trend of doubled manpower productivity every twenty-five years. But no measurement is available for output or productivity in government. Under present practices in the national economic accounts, general government services (as distinguished from government enterprises) are valued at the cost of wages and salaries paid to government workers.[7] In other words, input equals output with no change in productivity, overtime, up or down. nor is there a possibility of comparing productivity in the public and private sectors.

This also means that we now have no means of measuring the productivity of the entire American economy—at the most only the productivity of the 80 percent of the working force employed in private industry. Even there, measurements may be reliable in goods-producing industries but are tentative or uncertain in many personal services. Private goods and services are sold in the market and their value can therefore be calculated. However, no gauge has been found yet by which we can measure the value of public services that are not sold to consumers but "given away."

---

[5] Data from *Economic Report of the President,* February 1974, tables C-5–C-10.

[6] Ibid., table C-32. Productivity growth is the result of many factors, primarily capital investment, improved technology, and more effective management techniques. It does not necessarily—nor is it likely to—reflect greater efforts on the part of the workers, but more efficient use of their time, and to some extent probably more education and training.

[7] Jerome A. Mark, "Progress in Measuring Productivity in Government," *Monthly Labor Review,* December 1972.

There have been sporadic efforts over the years to develop yardsticks of productivity in government. Most of them were undertaken for the purpose of developing impartial aids to executive and legislative decision making on governmental spending proposals, the setting of authorizations and appropriations for specific programs. Some of these efforts were motivated by a wish either to justify or criticize existing or desired levels of appropriations for public services.

At a Symposium on Productivity in Government at Wingspread, Wisconsin, May 15–16, 1972, cosponsored by The Johnson Foundation and the University of Wisconsin Graduate School of Business, diverse views were aired: "There is a widespread feeling that government—from the little neighborhood school to the most sprawling federal agency—is doing too many things too poorly at too high a price."[8] Charges were levied at waste, mismanagement, bureaucratic empire building, and archaic civil service rules that cripple efficiency.[9] Other participants, however, "warned that over-zealous pursuit of economy and efficiency could endanger some of the nobler purposes of government—such as enhancing justice and equity." It was said that "when efficiency increases, social goals may suffer."

Early in the 1960s the Bureau of the Budget tried to explore the potential for constructing overall productivity indexes in five major governmental agencies, but the undertaking gradually fizzled out. Nor has PPBS, the Planning, Programming, Budgeting System, which for many years was hailed as the bright hope of bringing greater rationality, efficiency and more sophisticated decision making on public spending, produced the promised and expected results. Many of its former spokesmen and supporters have become thoroughly disillusioned.

Ratios of workload to staff are available or can be prepared in many fields of activity and often may give at least a rough indication of productivity trends over time. But the quality of the service is far harder to measure and such evaluations are frequently influenced by the commentator's friendly or critical attitude toward the goals or means of the program under review. Therefore, many evaluations in terms of approaching or reaching program goals are based on general observations, are subjective, and often highly controversial.

---

[8] "Symposium on Productivity in Government," *Public Administration Review*, November–December 1972.
[9] Ibid.
[10] Ibid.

In 1970 Senator William Proxmire, as chairman of the Joint Economic Committee of Congress, asked the comptroller general to have prepared a comprehensive evaluation of the possibilities for measuring productivity in the federal sector of the economy. The report, dated August 4, 1972, stated that while many agencies were making use of work measurement data there was little use of overall productivity measures.[11] A survey of seventeen federal agencies found related activities in 114 organizational units covering about half the work force. It concluded that techniques have been developed by which productivity trends could be measured covering between 55 and 60 percent of the federal civilian employees. The study group found that in the participating public services—numerically dominated by the postal service—productivity had increased 3.4 percent in the four-year period 1967–1971. As usual in reports of this type the group suggested that further efforts and studies be undertaken.

In a follow-up report submitted December 17-18, 1973, the comptroller general, as chairman of the study group, told the congressional committee that the survey now covered 187 organizational elements in forty-five agencies with 1.7 million man-years of employment. A six-year sample (1967–1972) "showed annual rates of productivity improvement which varied from 1.1 percent to 2.8 percent with an average annual gain of 1.7 percent."[12] They found that mechanization was the dominant factor behind productivity gains in industrial and manufacturing operations and that computerization of clerical operations had a major impact.

A subsequent survey covering about 1.7 million man-years or 61 percent of the employment in the federal civilian government in 200 units spanned the fiscal years 1967–1973. It reported an average annual productivity gain of 1.6 percent, which within sixteen functional groups ranged from −2.4 percent (for standard printing) to + 5.8 percent (for power and general support activities).[13] The postal service averaged an annual gain of 1.3 percent, agriculture and natural resources 2.0 percent, while medical services showed a decline of 0.7 percent. This compares with a produc-

---

[11] U.S. Congress, Joint Economic Committee, *Measuring and Enhancing Productivity in the Federal Sector,* A Study Prepared for the Use of the Joint Economic Committee, Congress of the United States, by Representatives of the Civil Service Commission, General Accounting Office and the Office of Management and Budget, JEC Committee Print, 1972.

[12] U.S. Congress, Joint Economic Committee, *Federal Productivity: Hearings before the Subcommittee on Priorities and Economy in Government of the Joint Economic Committee,* 93rd Cong., 1st sess., 1974, p. 21.

[13] Charles Ardolini and Jeffrey Hohenstein, "Measuring Productivity in the Federal Government," *Monthly Labor Review,* November 1974.

tivity gain of 3.1 percent in the entire private economy—5.8 percent in farming, 2.6 percent in nonfarming.

Promising as these efforts may be they are only an initial step toward a comprehensive measurement of productivity in government.

Work-load data and their relationship to manpower and expenditures have been used for many years in the budgetary process, by administrative departments to justify their appropriation requests and by the Budget Office and congressional committees to evaluate these requests. Most of those measures are crude and permit only very general and tentative conclusions. A few examples follow.

Postal employment grew 37 percent between 1952 and 1972 (from 508,000 to 697,000) while the volume of mail increased 77 percent (from 49 to 87 billion). This means that the number of mail pieces per employee grew from 97,000 to 125,000. Considering the intensive mechanization of the postal service in recent years we would normally expect an improvement. But we don't know whether it is commensurate with the investment in automation, or better or worse. Nor do we have an easy measurement of the quality of the postal service, of speed and reliability. Opinions are widely divided on whether postal delivery has accelerated or slowed down.

The Veterans Administration staff expanded only 5.6 percent between 1952 and 1972 (175,000 to 184,000) while the number of veterans grew by 49 percent (19.3 to 28.8 million). But the number of veterans pensions declined from 3.1 to 2.3 million.

Employment in the Department of Agriculture went up 47 percent between 1952 and 1972 (78,000 to 115,000) though the number of farms in the United States dropped by 45 percent (5.2 to 2.9 million) and the farm population shrank 56 percent (from 21.7 to 9.6 million). Superficially this may suggest the type of relationship in agriculture that C. Northcote Parkinson reported for the number of ships in the Royal Navy and the admiralty staff. But the more significant fact may be that the cost of stabilization of farm prices and incomes multiplied seven times between 1952 and 1972 (from $689 to $4,243 million).

The Internal Revenue Service staff grew 28 percent between 1952 and 1972 (56,336 to 72,085), almost parallel to the number of tax returns filed, which went up 26 percent (from 89 to 112 million). So the number of tax returns per employee dropped from 1580 to 1554—during a period of the most intensive mechanization and computerization. Audits meanwhile declined from 4.4 to 1.7 million and delinquent notices from 19.8 to 8.8

million. But this could well be due to greater sophistication in the selection of returns to be audited and the increased effectiveness of the IRS in educating the tax-paying public. Without substantial details on the thoroughness of the review and auditing process, we do not know whether enforcement was less strict in 1972 than in 1952 despite the smaller numbers. That the grade average in IRS went from GS 6.1 to GS 8.3 may suggest that a staff of higher competency was active in 1972 compared to twenty years earlier. But it may merely express a "grade creep," a relaxation of promotional standards in the service as a means of raising salaries beyond normal step advancement.

The four departments mentioned above are among the most amenable to productivity measurements and account for nearly two-thirds of all federal nondefense employment. But *all* federal departments account for only 1.7 of the 12.5 million total governmental nondefense payroll: 86 percent of the governmental nondefense payroll is in state and local government. Answers to the question on trends in governmental productivity should therefore more appropriately be sought in the fields that account for most of the governmental employment. Education alone employs nearly half of all public nondefense workers and the aggregate of education, health and hospitals, police, and highways accounts for about two-thirds (table 8a).

Enrollment in public education almost doubled between 1952 and 1972, but the number of teachers and other school employees tripled. There was one employee for every 14.8 students in 1952, one for every 9.2 in 1972.

ENROLLMENT AND EMPLOYMENT IN PUBLIC EDUCATION, 1952 and 1972

	1952	1972	Percent Increase
Students	27,862,000	52,152,000	87%
Employees	1,884,000	5,646,000	200
Employee-student ratio	1:14.8	1:9.2	

SOURCE: Enrollment: U.S., Office of Education, *Statistical Summary of Education, 1951–52,* 1955; idem, *Digest of Educational Statistics,* 1973.
Employment: See table 8a.

If we view only the public elementary and secondary schools, which account for about 90 percent of all public education, we find that there was one teacher for every 35.6 pupils in 1900, one for every 26.2 in 1952, and one for every 19.8 in 1972.[14]

In other words, trends in public education and in the American economy generally have been running in opposite directions. While throughout most of industry and agriculture, employee productivity, that is, the ratio between manpower input and product output, has increased consistently and substantially, it has just as consistently and sharply declined in public education. That trend was particularly distinct during the past twenty years but has been apparent far longer, at least back to the turn of the twentieth century. Many members of the educational establishment regard this as a most desirable process of upgrading the educational quality of the schools. But research has failed to show a positive correlation between class size or teacher-pupil ratio and the student's learning on measurable skills and knowledge. The *Encyclopedia of Educational Research* in 1950 summarized over 200 research studies of class size and pupil achievement: "On the whole, the statistical findings definitely favor large classes at every level of instruction except the kindergarten." Nor could the massive survey of American schools by James Coleman in 1966 find a correlation between class size and the pupils' learning.[15] Restudies of the Coleman report strongly confirmed those findings.[16] A survey of New York City's public schools in 1957/58 showed a negative correlation between small classes and achievements in reading and arithmetic.[17]

There is no conclusive evidence on whether the quality of school education has improved over the years, as many firmly believe, or deteriorated, as steadily falling S.A.T. test scores and other indicators, as well as widespread complaints and the failure of compensatory programs, suggest. Unfortunately, there is no fact-based national assessment of the educational level of students that would enable us to know on a year-to-year basis what progress has been made, if any, as the input of manpower and other resources on *a per student basis* multiplies. Technical means are available for measuring the cognitive achievement levels of students, and, in fact, millions of standard tests are being administered in schools

---

[14] Data on instructional staff and enrollment from: U.S. Office of Education, *Statistics of State School Systems, 1953-54,* 1957; U.S. Office of Education, *Digest of Educational Statistics,* 1973; U.S. Office of Education, *Projections of Educational Statistics to 1981-82,* 1973. The 1900 figure was derived using an estimate for total instructional staff.

[15] Coleman et al., *Equality of Educational Opportunity.*

[16] Frederick Mosteller and Daniel P. Moynihan, eds., *On Equality of Educational Opportunity* (New York: Vintage Books, 1972); Jencks et al., *Inequality.*

[17] Marilyn Gittel, ed., *New York City School Fact Book,* Institute for Community Studies, Queens College of the City University of New York, 1968.

throughout the country. In a few states uniform tests are used in the public elementary and secondary schools. But broad-scale testing and public reporting of the results are not favorably viewed by many in the educational establishment. It is opposed by several organizations for ideological or political reasons. There is then no tangible evidence that, nationally, educational quality has improved over the past twenty years. But manpower input has increased more than half again as fast as the "student output," which suggests that productivity has substantially declined in public education.

Efforts were initiated in 1969 for a National Assessment of Educational Progress, a federally funded project of the Education Commission of the States, an organization of governors, legislators, and educators. About one million students were tested and a report issued in 1974 for the first time pulls together all of the findings and examines them in the aggregate. As released at the commission's annual meeting in Miami on June 22, 1974, the results show a decline in about every knowledge and skill area in the sciences tested over the preceding three years (1969–70 to 1972–73), a period during which school expenditures increased substantially.[18]

Next to education, health and hospitals recorded the greatest employment increase, absolutely and relatively (see p. 45). In hospitals the average daily census of patients declined 9.5 percent between 1952 and 1972 while full-time personnel increased 138.7 percent. There was on the average less than one employee—0.84 to be exact—for every patient in 1952, while in 1972 there were 2.21 employees per patient.

AVERAGE DAILY CENSUS AND PERSONNEL IN HOSPITALS, 1952 and 1972

	Average Daily Patient Census*	Full-time Personnel†	Employees Per Patient
1952	1,336,000	1,119,000	0.84
1972	1,209,000	2,671,000	2.21

SOURCES: American Hospital Association, *Statistical Guides 1952*, 1953; idem, *Hospital Statistics 1972*, 1973.

* The average number of inpatients receiving care each day during a twelve-month period. Excludes newborns.

† Includes full-time personnel and full-time equivalents for part-time personnel. Source for 1952 figures unclear as to whether full-time equivalent for part-time personnel included.

[18] "A Report Finds Scientific Knowledge Has Declined Among Pupils in U.S.," *New York Times,* June 22, 1974; see also "Student Scores Drop in Tests," *Congressional Record*, June 25, 1974, pp. E4198-99.

Part of this near tripling of the manpower input per patient is due to the shortening of personnel hours and more ample staffing of hospitals. Much of it is the result of greater specialization, and the extended use of technicians to relieve physicians of duties that can be performed by less highly qualified professionals. Has this improved the quality of health care? The death rate of the United States population has remained virtually steady. It stood at 9.6 (per 1000) in 1952, and has been fluctuating between 9.3 and 9.7 ever since, with no apparent trend. The average length of patient stay has declined, which could be due as much to the tremendous rise in hospital costs as to better health care. The incidence of many major illnesses has been sharply cut—particularly of polio, brucellosis, diphtheria, measles, whooping cough, typhoid, tuberculosis. But it has increased in hepatitis, venereal disease, strep throat and meningitis. On the whole, it seems that health care has improved and that the decline in manpower productivity in hospitals was probably not as great as patient-staff ratios would indicate.

The third largest growth in public employment was in police protection: an increase of 129 percent in the number of employees during a 33 percent expansion of the United States population. There were 1.6 police employees per 1000 population in 1952, 2.8 in 1972 (tables 7a and b). Despite this sharply increased protection ratio, crime did not diminish—it soared. Between 1957 and 1972, the United States population grew 22 percent, the number of police employees increased 84 percent—nearly four times faster—while the estimated incidence of crime jumped 309 percent, from 1.4 to 5.9 million.[19] It is of course conceivable that the number of crimes instead of quadrupling over the past fifteen years might have quintupled or sextupled had police manpower been kept stable instead of nearly doubling. But the record provides no prima facie evidence of the effectiveness of adding numbers to the police protection staff when crimes quadruple while the staff doubles. The fault may more likely lie in the methods applied by the police, possibly because of restrictions imposed upon them. The record does not suggest that merely adding numbers of police is an effective or promising way of stemming the growth of crime.

The government activity with the fourth largest increase in employment during the years 1952–1972 was highways (see p. 45). The growth rate in that field during that period almost exactly paralleled population expansion. By all appearances there has been tangible progress

---

[19] Estimated crime data from Federal Bureau of Investigation, *Uniform Crime Reports*, (annual) 1958 to 1972. Data for years prior to 1960 are not strictly comparable with later data.

on highways: the average vehicle speed increased by 22 percent (from 49.5 to 60.3 miles per hour) and the fatality rate dropped from 7.4 to 4.5 per 100 million miles and from 7.2 to 4.7 per 10,000 vehicles.[20] The increased speed means a saving in travel time of nearly one-fifth, which amounts to a significant economic gain. What is even more important is that had the 1952 traffic fatality rate remained steady at 7.4 per 100 million miles, 36,300 more people would have been killed by motor vehicles in 1972 than actually were.

These gains of course cannot all be credited to increased effectiveness in highway manpower. Aside from progress in vehicle safety, and leaving aside the question of education leading to better driving habits, there was a sharp upswing in road construction, which nearly quadrupled highway expenditures from less than $5 billion annually in the early 1950s to between $14 and $18 billion in the past five years. But on an overall basis it appears that greater investment of manpower and other resources in highways has paid off.

These data on manpower productivity trends in the four largest categories of public nondefense employment—education, hospitals, police protection, and highways—are, as mentioned earlier, very crude measures that permit at best only generalized and tentative judgments. With more determined efforts practitioners could have developed far more refined and reliable methods for the evaluation of productivity trends in those four and other domestic services. Even in the area of defense some progress could be made on ascertaining trends in input-output relationships although there are definite limits to it. Only "the battle is the payoff," and though it can be simulated in maneuvers it cannot quite be equaled.

But productivity measurements, an indispensable tool in private industry, often are a two-edged sword in governmental activities. They may at times serve to support the demands of administrators and interest groups for increased appropriations and manpower. But often they may offer little encouragement for program and staff expansion and even discredit them or throw doubt on their advisability. Practitioners in the various functional areas therefore tend to use only selected data—those that support their requests—and they neglect or omit others that would provide a more balanced picture. If progress is to be made in evaluating productivity in government it will have to be achieved by researchers with no organi-

---

[20] U.S. Department of Commerce, Bureau of Public Roads, *Traffic Speed Trends, 1952*, March 1954; U.S. Department of Transportation, Federal Highway Administration, *Highway Statistics, 1972*, 1973; National Safety Council, *Accident Facts, 1954*, 1955.

zational, political, or ideological ties, or commitments to the programs and goals under review. They must be generalists who are not awed by the expertise of the specialists nor swayed by their claims.

We must recognize that, in contrast to private industry, where competition and the profit goal impose pressure for greater efficiency and a natural and generally reliable gauge of productivity, governmental programs have built-in counterproductive trends. It is a natural tendency for a public employee to want to handle fewer cases—pupils, tax returns, welfare families, crimes—in the belief that he could do a better job if he had a smaller workload, and most certainly have an easier life. For the supervisor there is a definite gain in stature, position—and even grade—by having a larger number of subordinates. This and the ideological commitments to the program goals and methods of their professional fraternities provide a powerful and well-nigh irresistible incentive for empire building.

Only elected chief executives are aware of the political attractiveness and profitability of a reduction in public bureaucracy and they will try to achieve it, whether in fact or, more often, through somewhat slanted presentations or claims.

Earlier I cited some statements of President Johnson. But many presidents and governors have pointed with pride at a reduction in size of their bureaucracy. The federal budget for FY 1975 stated that "the decline in total federal civilian employment since January 1969 has been substantial. The overall reduction in the executive branch from January 1969 through June 30, 1973 was 226,264 or 7.7%."[21] The statement is correct. According to the federal budget for FY 1970 (Special Analysis I) and FY 1975 (Special Analysis G) full-time permanent employment dropped 229,011 between 1969 and 1973. This is composed of a drop of 278,338 in the Department of Defense and an increase of 49,327 in the aggregate of all other federal departments.

That is not much of an increase over a four-year period, considering long-range trends in the public payroll. But over the same four-year span, state and local government employment jumped 1,587,000 (16.8 percent) while population grew 3.8 percent; federal aid to state and local governments doubled from $22.6 to $44.1 billion between FY 1970 and 1974. That is a remarkable record for an administration that prior to, upon, and after assuming office declared fiscal decentralization and the return of authority and responsibility to state and local governments to be one of its

---

[21] *Special Analyses, Budget of the United States Government, Fiscal Year 1975*, p. 101.

primary goals. It is evident from this record that reduction in the size of the bureaucracy was more apparent than real, more facade than substance. The size of the federal payroll was increased inconspicuously by shifting most of the increase to a category that was statistically not classified "federal." But the power of the central bureaucracy over the state and local apparatus in each functional area grew apace in keeping with the expansion of federally financed programs and the imposition of detailed controls. Horizontal or "layer-cake" government of three levels of government was converted to a chain of command from Washington to Podunk, to a vertical functional autocracy.

Efficiency of the public bureaucracy and productivity in governmental programs have long been viewed with suspicion by the general public, which in turn led to sporadic studies of administrative effectiveness by presidents or the Congress and attempts to limit the size and growth of the public payroll. This general attitude toward public service goes far to explain the instant and wide popularity of Parkinson's law when it was first published in 1955 and of the ready acceptance of criticism of the governmental bureaucracy, even among students of public administration.

In a review of recent academic studies of governmental bureaucracy in the *Public Administration Review* (March-April 1974), Kenneth F. Warren concludes: "The authors' consensus, with Mainzer dissenting, is that American bureaucracy is guilty of the gross mismanagement of the public interest. The real accountability crisis is that even if our bureaucrats act inefficiently and against our interests, as is too often the case, we cannot realistically hope for administrative abuses to be checked by the present 'watchdog' system."

In an earlier volume, *Democracy and the Public Service,* Frederick C. Mosher found that professionalism in governmental bureaucracy and the power of the civil service pose a distinct threat to democratic control, that is, they are self-serving rather than serving the public interest.[22] The sharpest recent criticism came from Richard S. Rosenbloom in the *Harvard Business Review* (September-October 1973): "The largest employer group in the United States has shown the least concern for worker productivity. This seems absurd in a society that prides itself on management and efficiency, but the fact appears to be indisputable. . . . Not only is productivity in these groups lagging, but little is being done about it." Rosenbloom adds, "One is less surprised at the absence of evident productivity

---

[22] Frederick C. Mosher, *Democracy and the Public Service* (New York: Oxford University Press, 1968).

growth in government when it is recognized that none of the major forces operating in the private sector applies in government."

In its self-image the governmental bureaucracy constitutes a group of dedicated public servants who labor diligently, efficiently, and untiringly at low pay to provide better service to the people of the United States. They continue to do so despite the criticism and open hostility often shown to them by some officials in the executive and legislative branches, by political appointees or opponents, by the media and, frequently, by an ill-informed and ungrateful public. On the other hand it is apparently true that "complaints keep cropping up that a caste of career public servants —enjoying locked-in job tenure under civil service—is trying to run the country, without much regard for policies laid down by elected officials."[23]

The establishment many years ago and the gradual strengthening of both the merit principle in the civil service, and the impartial competitive examination and evaluations for hiring and promotions have helped greatly to attract and keep qualified persons in governmental employment and to reduce the role of patronage and political pressure. Unfortunately, the procedural growth has also helped to protect the inefficient, by making it more difficult if not impossible to remove them. Worse still, inroads on the merit principle in recent years, which under the euphemism of "affirmative action" reintroduced political pressure and racial discrimination, have adversely affected the effectiveness of some public agencies at a heavy cost to the taxpayers.

The outright hostility that the educational establishment showed in the spring of 1970 toward a presidential proposal suggesting the concept of accountability in education was rather typical of an attitude that pervades much of the public service. But in view of the tremendous absolute and relative growth in governmental nondefense employment in recent decades the time may well have come to undertake a comprehensive study of productivity in the governmental service. At this time there appears to be at least good reason for doubt that manpower productivity in the public sector has risen comparable to the progress in private industry—if it has risen at all and not possibly declined.

Governmental Pay

In February 1962 President Kennedy recommended to Congress that federal pay rates be made comparable with prevailing private enterprise

---

[23] "Is Bureaucracy Out of Control?," *U.S. News and World Report,* May 17, 1971.

salaries for the same levels of work as determined from painstaking statistical surveys and careful job comparisons. Congress adopted this rule eight months later in the Federal Salary Reform Act of 1962 and subsequently reaffirmed the principle in the Federal Pay Comparability Act of 1970. Each year now the Bureau of Labor Statistics makes an extensive survey of professional, administrative, technical, and clerical salaries in private enterprise and the president is required to adjust federal rates accordingly to comparable levels.

In 1962 an employee in private industry earned on the average $116 more than a federal employee (earnings were $5,081 and $4,965 respectively). Relative positions had barely changed in the preceding ten years; the difference in 1952 had been $85 (earnings were $3,430 and $3,345 respectively). Between 1962 and 1964, however, positions were reversed, due to the Federal Salary Reform Act of 1962 and subsequent action: in 1964 a federal employee was on the average $101 *ahead* of his counterpart in private industry (earnings were $5,605 and $5,504 respectively). It was in the succeeding eight years, when federal pay was supposed to move parallel to private wages, that federal employees made the most substantial absolute and relative progress. In 1972 they were on the average $1,783 ahead of workers in private industry (earnings were $10,223 and $8,440 respectively). Between 1964 and 1972 average earnings of federal workers rose $4,618, in private industry only $2,936.

Over the entire twenty-year period 1952 to 1972, average federal earnings per full-time employee had risen 206 percent, private earnings 146 percent (see table 6 for source of data). State and local government earnings meanwhile increased 175 percent, more slowly than federal, but still faster than private wages. School salaries at state and local levels went up almost as fast as federal earnings (191 percent), but other state and local workers did not do as well.

Average annual earnings per full-time employee of all governments (federal, state, local) increased by $975 *more* than in private industry; adjusted to *constant* dollars, private earnings increased 56 percent between 1952 and 1972, governmental earnings 79 percent which is 41 percent faster (table 6). In relative terms, average annual earnings in government equaled 96 percent of earnings in private industry in 1952, 110 percent of earnings in private industry in 1972.

Official surveys comparing federal and private salaries are not as precise as they appear or as would be desirable. It is one thing to establish wage standards for stenographers and other routine clerical workers, for craftsmen and other blue collar workers, and for general technicians. It is something else to compare technical specialists with diverse skills in certain industries with those in governmental services. The higher the occupational level, the more difficult it is to compare knowledge, expertise, or responsibility, especially when dealing with positions that call for decision making or policy formulation. Although the annual surveys, which cover over 3,000 firms employing about one-fourth of the relevant labor market, are conducted by trained specialists of the Bureau of Labor Statistics and audited by the General Accounting Office, they leave considerable leeway for judgment; comparisons between jobs are sometimes tenuous.[24] Nor is there a provision for adjustment by location, though wage levels differ among the various locations and regions of the United States and between major metropolitan centers and rural areas.

Salaries are set at a level intended to attract able and competent persons in the federal service. Government, in establishing a "prevailing wage," wishes to compete with private firms for the most qualified employees. In drawing conclusions from "prevailing wage" reports we probably should keep in mind that the surveys are undertaken and supervised by federal employees whose own pay is not entirely uninfluenced by their findings regarding the relative job classifications and level of federal and private pay. As the country's biggest employer with a $53 billion payroll in 1972, the federal government exercises substantial market power and therefore makes an impact on what it is trying to survey. Also, as a monopoly, the federal government is not as dependent as most private businesses on cost factors and competitors, domestic or foreign, in setting wage rates.

State and local government jobs are not included in the annual surveys, yet the federal government often competes with—and sometimes outbids—state, city, or county governments or schools for specialists in the numerous social services provided by government. Nor do the surveys take into consideration the extent of fringe benefits—which now average more than one-fourth of the monetary compensation—the higher prestige and power vested in the federal service, and last but not least, the greater job security and tenure.

---

[24] In a highly critical review of the white collar comparability process in 1974, the U.S. Comptroller General concluded that "federal pay adjustments were not based on well-founded, logical premises that reflect the legislative pay principles" and the methods used "resulted in significant deviations from comparability for Federal employees and in inequitable pay distribution among employees" (Comptroller General to the Director of the Office of Management and Budget, and the Chairman of the Civil Service Commission, July 12, 1974).

One of the caveats in drawing firm conclusions from overall salary comparisons are the differences in "job mix" or skill level in the various governmental functions and departments as well as in some industries.

Federal pay is governed by several compensation systems. By far the largest is the General Schedule, which consists of 18 grades ("normal" grades G.S. 1–15, "super" grades G.S. 16–18) that are divided up into 10 steps each. General Schedule accounts for nearly two-thirds of all federal civilian employees, not counting the postal service, which has its own pay scales, as do the foreign service and certain medical services. Thirty percent of the civilian employees, mostly blue collar workers, are under various wage systems, largely in the Department of Defense, General Services Administration, Veterans Administration, and the Tennessee Valley Authority. The armed services have their own pay scale. Top policy positions in the federal government are classified by five executive levels with salaries set by law between $36,000 and $60,000.

The best possibilities for analysis are in the positions covered by the General Schedule. Between 1952 and 1961 G.S. salaries were raised three times—in 1955, 1958 and 1960—for a combined increase of 27 percent. Between the passage of the Federal Salary Reform Act of 1962 and the year 1972 there were eleven boosts with an aggregate increase of 72 percent. In the aggregate the fourteen increases in G.S. scales between 1952 and 1972 totaled 120 percent. Table 10 shows maximum and minimum rates of the General Schedule in 1952 and 1972 with increases ranging from 83 percent in the lowest grade, G.S. 1 (now little used), to a maximum of 182 percent in the highest normal grade, that is, G.S. 15. The top of the "super" grades, G.S. 16–18, is frozen at $36,000 by a provision in the law limiting compensation under the General Schedule to the established salary for Executive Level V. Efforts to raise salaries for top federal officials, including members of Congress, have failed.[25]

---

[25] On March 6, 1974 the Senate adopted by a vote of 71 to 26 a resolution disapproving salary boosts for federal executives, judges, and members of Congress. Senators obviously were afraid of the public reaction toward Congress raising its own salaries at this time. That continued the lid on the supergrades at $36,000 where it has been since 1969. Had it not been for that limitation the salary for G.S. 18 would have been $39,693 in 1972 and $41,734 in 1973.

In a release dated July 31, 1974, the Civil Service Commission reported that, according to a comparability study, the salary in G.S. 18, to be comparable with private industry, should be at $71,076, in G.S. 17 at $56,011, in G.S. 16 at $45,146. However, the General Accounting Office reported at about the same time to the Office of Management and Budget that the Bureau of Labor Statistics had made faulty calculations by giving disproportionate weight to high-paying jobs and that civil servants' pay generally had been illegitimately enlarged. *Wall Street Journal*, August 5, 1974.

Salaries of selected high federal officials were as follows:

	1952	1972	Percent Increase
President	$100,000	$200,000	100%
Member of Congress	12,500	42,500	240
Member of Cabinet	22,500	60,000	167
Associate Justice of the Supreme Court	25,000	60,000	140

While actual salaries in the various grades of G.S. increased between 80 and 179 percent, for an average of 125 percent, the overall average of all G.S. salaries increased 203 percent between 1952 and 1972 (table 11). This means of course that there has been a general upward shift in grades, usually referred to as the "grade creep." It is illustrated in table 12. The number of employees in G.S. 1–3 declined by 62 percent but the number of G.S. 11–12 positions expanded by 235 percent, G.S. 13–15 by 405 percent, and the "super grades" G.S. 16–18 by 649 percent; the number of *all* positions increased only 27 percent. The median G.S. grade, that is, the point at which there are as many employees above as below, moved from 3.9 in 1952 to 6.9 in 1972. The mean or average rose from 6.4 in 1952 to 9.0 in 1972.

The average G.S. grade increased among the agencies shown as follows:

AVERAGE G. S. GRADE

	1952	1972	Increase
Internal Revenue Service	6.1	8.3	2.2
Forest Service	6.2	8.5	2.3
Food and Drug Administration	7.1	9.3	2.2
Federal Highway Administration	7.9	9.9	2.0
Civil Service Commission	5.6	7.5	1.9
Office of Education	8.6	10.0	1.4

SOURCE: *The Budget of the United States Government,* FY 1954; *The Budget of the United States Government,* FY 1974, Appendix.

Some explain the grade creep as a process of upgrading the quality of the federal service: persons of greater competence are being hired and more employees are being promoted on individual merit. To induce technical specialists and outstanding administrators and executives to leave their present jobs and accept federal appointments they must be offered higher salaries, which, in the civil service, means higher grades.

This is probably true—to some extent. But the nature of much or most of the grade creep is a disguised salary increase in excess of the raises authorized by the Congress. It is also due to the expansion of federal domestic programs from $13 billion in 1952 to $134 billion in 1972 and a 37 percent growth in civilian employment.

Overall it appears that employee compensation has been increased more substantially in the federal service than in private industry. This is also true, to a lesser degree, in state and city governments and in the largest local government service, the public schools. It is well known that except in the case of rare and unusual specialties the number of applicants for civil service jobs usually exceeds the number of openings particularly at lower and medium occupational levels and that there is intense competition for vacancies among applicants who commonly use all the political and other pull they can muster. By all appearances, governmental openings are usually regarded as highly desirable by numerous jobseekers.[26]

Government Pensions

Employees who devote their working life to governmental service are entitled to receive adequate pensions after they have retired. The certainty of those annuities in addition to job tenure during good behavior gives them a proper feeling of stability and security during their active career.

In supplemental compensation, particularly in pensions, public employees appear to be ahead of the average worker in private industry and the comparability surveys and comparable setting of wage rates do not apply to such fringe benefits.

Much of the financial gains of government workers in recent years is not revealed in official wage and salary figures but hidden in pension rights that are payable years or decades later. While the cost of current salary raises soon shows up in higher budgets and may at state and local levels force tax boosts or, at the federal level, increase deficits, the cost of "improvements in pension provisions" is hidden in intricate formulas

---

[26] The City of San Francisco was swamped with applications in the summer of 1974 when the Board of Supervisors approved a $17,000 annual wage for street sweepers. New York City's $18,000 pay for firemen also set a goal for workers in private industry to aim for.

whose meaning and impact are not known for a long time. Elected top officials at federal, state, and local levels, when confronted with insistent demands for major salary raises, sometimes face the agonizing alternative of a tax boost or a paralyzing strike. One way out of this politically dangerous squeeze is to offer a generous pension hike, payable in a distant future. They are thereby not just postponing the day of reckoning but usually avoiding it forever. No one will figure out ten or twenty or thirty years later that the cause of a jump in the budget was that old pension boost. By that time the official or officials who had made the decision will no longer be in office, the pension claims will be a firm legal and inescapable obligation, and the resulting tax boost will be an "uncontrollable item" or "just one of those things." Public employees and their organizations often find liberal pension offerings to be an attractive compromise solution by which they can obtain more in future benefits than they could by alternative immediate salary raises. Resulting tax savings to the recipient employees also weigh heavily in favor of such deferred compensation.[27]

The public is almost always unaware of the huge pension commitments that are being piled up—and when it learns of them it is far too late to do anything about them. Because pension boosts create a sizeable long-range obligation for the community, former Mayor Frank P. Zeidler of Milwaukee suggested that they ought to be subjected to a referendum.[28] This might offer at least some safeguard for the taxpaying public. Sam Zagoria of the United States Conference of Mayors proposed that controversial new employee contracts be placed on the ballot, which could act as a restraining influence and might take decisionmaking officials at least partially off the hook.[29]

Public employee retirement payments multiplied more than ten times between 1952 and 1972—from $831 to $8,562 million—while salaries

---

[27] State legislators do not forget themselves when it comes to generous pensions. Due to a change in the law, approved in 1972, a California legislator who was defeated at the polls stood to receive an additional $213,678 in extra benefits between his current age of thirty-nine and age sixty. The California Assembly's speaker, who lost in the gubernatorial primary in 1974 after serving for ten years, would have received from his present age of thirty-eight for the rest of his life $8,292 a year, or $182,524 before his sixtieth birthday. When the newspapers revealed the details of this pension bill, however, a public outcry arose and the legislators repealed most of the added benefits at a special session in September 1974.

[28] Frank P. Zeidler, *New Roles for Public Officials in Labor Relations,* Public Relations Library No. 23 (Chicago: Public Personnel Association), p. 20.

[29] Sam Zagoria, "Resolving Impasses by Public Referendums," *Monthly Labor Review.* March 1973.

meanwhile only quadrupled.[30] At present rates public employee pensions will more than triple in the current decade. In some cities certain agencies already pay out in pensions as much as in current salaries and their number is increasing as self-bankrupting pension schemes mature.

There are now about 2,200 public employee pension systems in operation, more than 90 percent of them at state and local levels, covering over 16 million employees and their families. One-third of the more than three million current beneficiaries are federal-civilian, one-third state-local, and slightly under one-third military. Federal employee retirement funds held a balance of $28 billion in 1972 with uncovered liabilities well over twice that high. State and local employee retirement funds owned $68 billion worth of assets in 1972, certainly only a fraction of their long-range obligations. The actuarial value of all public retirement commitments is in the hundreds of billions. In contrast to the strict accounting for direct federal, state, and local debts, no comprehensive records are kept of the "contingent" retirement obligations of governments.

Nor are precise and reliable studies available to compare benefits of the various public employee pension systems with the retirement pay of employees in private industry. The latter consists largely of the old age and survivors part of the Social Security System in addition to annuities which many companies and some unions in several industries provide. But it appears that on the average, public retirees are better off. In some public systems a worker can retire on half pay after twenty years, regardless of age, while few private systems distribute benefits before age sixty.[31] Private pensions and annuities are usually based strictly on actual contributions which in turn are related to the wages received during the earning career. Under federal civil service retirement rates pensions are based only on the highest years. It used to be the five highest years until this was changed to the three highest years in 1969. In some retirement systems the pension is based on the earnings at time of retirement, even including overtime. Retirees under the Social Security System, mostly former workers in private industry, have their benefits based on the average of actual

---

[30] U.S. Bureau of the Census, *Historical Statistics on Governmental Finances and Employment,* 1969; U.S. Bureau of the Census, *Governmental Finances in 1972-1972,* 1973.

[31] The *New York Times* reported on October 27, 1974 in an article "Fiscal Experts See the City In Severe Financial Crisis": "Pensions contributions alone now cost the city more than $1 billion a year and by 1980 they are expected to rise to more than $2 billion a year. These benefits, paid for almost entirely by the city, now permit some categories of city employees to retire at age 65 after a lifetime career with combined pensions, annuity and Social Security payments that are higher than their salaries."

contributions, going back to 1951 when the maximum applicable wage base was far smaller than it is now ($4,800 in 1951, $13,200 in 1974).

The benefits of social security recipients are now annually adjusted for inflation by the consumer price index. But retired federal employees get an extra 1% pension increase every time their checks are adjusted for changes in the cost of living. At the time of the passage of that provision in 1969, the General Accounting Office warned of its tremendous long-range spiral effect. But Congress paid no heed.

Unionization in the Public Service

According to official figures a smaller segment of employees is unionized in government than in private industry. In 1972 2.5 million public employees belonged to labor unions, approximately one-fifth of the thirteen million civilian government employees. Simultaneously about one-fourth of nongovernmental employees were listed as dues-paying union members.

But this does not give a true picture because it omits the four million members of well over 600 professional organizations, many of which, more or less, act like and play the role of unions though they are not so labeled. The largest professional organizations are the National Education Association (NEA), with 1.3 million members (compared with only 380,000 in the American Federation of Teachers) and the American Nurses Association, with over 200,000 members. Their policies and activities have in recent years become increasingly indistinguishable from those of unions which belong to the AFL-CIO.

The United States Civil Service Commission reported in February 1974 that in 1973 56 percent of nonpostal federal employees were represented by unions. With 91 percent of postal employees unionized, approximately two-thirds of all federal civilian employees are now covered by exclusive recognition. Most of the growth has taken place in slightly more than the past twelve years—which is truly remarkable, considering the fact that nearly forty years have gone by since the passage of the federal National Labor Relations Act (Wagner Act), which facilitated and encouraged organization in the private sector of the economy. Unionization in the private sector stands at about 25 percent of all employment—a figure that has barely changed in many years—and seems unable to move beyond that point. Well over one-third of all civilian public employees (federal, state, and local)—and according to some sources about one-half—are now members of unions or quasi-unions such as the NEA, compared with a one-fourth union membership in private industry.[32] Although unionization in the public service goes back to before World War I—with the Lloyd-La Follette Act of 1912 and the birth of postal unions—"union growth in the public sector was insignificant until the start of the 1960s" according to a report of the Bureau of Labor Statistics.[33] "For reasons not fully understood even now, things changed unexpectedly and rapidly during the 1960s," the same report continued.[34]

A study of the record suggests that the growth of unionization in the public service in the 1960s should not have been unexpected or difficult to understand: it proved the most effective weapon in the hands of public employees to advance their financial well-being relative to workers in private industry and to the general economy. In the late 1950s less than a million public employees belonged to unions; by 1962 there were 1.2 million and by 1972 2.5 million—not counting those who were members of quasi-unions. The American Federation of State, County and Municipal Employees has become "the fastest growing union in the nation and fifth largest in the American Federation of Labor and Congress of Industrial Organizations."[35] But mere numbers do not adequately explain or express the simultaneous growth in power and effectiveness of public employee unions, let alone their increasing militancy.[36]

Historically, unions played almost no role in public employment up to the 1950s. There was virtually no collective bargaining, strikes were extremely rare, affected few workers, and usually produced very little for those who participated in them.

Public school teaching offers a good illustration. The dominant organization was the NEA, which regarded itself as a professional organization and not a union, though it lobbied with Congress and state legislatures for

---

[32] This is low compared with many other industrialized countries. In some countries such as Denmark, Belgium, Norway, Austria, Israel, unionization is between 60 and 80 percent of the labor force.

[33] Harry P. Cohany and Lucretia M. Dewey, "Union Membership Among Government Employees," *Monthly Labor Review*, June 1970.

[34] Ibid.

[35] Reginald Stuart, "Labor's New Managers," *New York Times*, October 27, 1974.

[36] The power of federal employee unions was clearly demonstrated when President Ford recommended that a 5.5 percent increase in federal salaries be postponed from October 1, 1974 to January 1, 1975. The Senate voted nearly two to one (sixty-four to thirty-five) on September 19, 1974 to approve a resolution overriding the presidential request. *Congressional Record*, September 19, 1974, p. S17126; see also "Federal Pay Rising Again—How Workers Will Fare," *U.S. News and World Report*, September 30, 1974.

state and federal aid and its local groups presented demands to school boards. The American Federation of Teachers, which belongs to the AFL-CIO, was small and unimportant except in very few locations such as New York City. In 1960 there was not a single collective bargaining contract in existence for teachers in public education; by 1970 there were 3,522 contracts in districts with 1,000 pupils or more and almost all personnel were covered by exclusive bargaining representatives in the country's large school systems. Not only had collective bargaining become the rule, it covered far more than salaries and other benefits and extended to the number of positions, class size, and numerous other policy subjects that used to be regarded as the exclusive prerogative of management, that is, boards of education and top administrators.

Between 1960 and 1961 and 1969 and 1970 the number of teacher strikes jumped from 3 to 180. There was an annual average of three teacher strikes in the school years 1960–1961 to 1962–1963, with 10,300 participants and 13,500 man-days lost. In the annual average of the school years 1967-1968 to 1969-1970, there were 142 teacher strikes, with 102,500 participants and 1,270,000 man-days lost.[37] Only one-fourth of the strikes were called by teacher unions, about two-thirds by "professional organizations."[38]

Developments in other governmental fields paralleled those in education: unionization, an insignificant factor prior to 1960, was a dominant fact of life by 1970. Increase in influence far exceeded numerical expansion of membership. Much of the change came about by the growth in political power exercised by the nationally organized labor movement. Though only one-fourth of the workers in private industry are unionized—a share that has not been growing for some years—their political impact on nearly half the members of both houses of Congress and on the executive branch, as well as on their counterparts at state and municipal levels, has become decisive.[39] In times of a labor crisis, when crucial decisions had to be made, few chief executives or legislative bodies dared

---

[37] *NEA Research Bulletin,* October 1970.

[38] The *New York Times* reported on September 22, 1974: "The nation's teachers organizations have vastly increased the amount of money they are giving to political candidates this year and have become one of the best financed interest groups in the nation."

[39] The activities of organized labor in influencing elections were well described and documented in Douglas Caddy, *The Hundred Million Dollar Payoff,* (New Rochelle, N.Y.: Arlington House, 1974). In an article entitled "Unions Jump Into Campaign," *U.S. News and World Report,* October 7, 1974, reported: "Now taking shape among American labor unions is the most strenuous campaign they have ever conducted in a congressional election. The goal of organized labor: Elect enough sympathetic lawmakers—mostly Democrats—to insure passage of favored legislation. The tactics: Raise a record amount of money and manpower to do the job."

to go against organized labor. Regardless of considerations of the economic or financial impact, the weight of government has almost always come down on the side of labor when the alternative meant open warfare. This was particularly evident when the operation of vital public functions was at stake.

A key turning point was President Kennedy's Executive Order 10988 of January 17, 1962, which sanctioned unionization for all federal employees. "As a catalyst to union organizing in the federal civil service, it was to prove comparable to the original National Labor Relations Act—the Wagner Act of 1935—in the private sector."[40] Its impact extended beyond the federal civil service and it set the pattern for public employment at all levels. "In less than a decade union membership at least tripled among employees of federal, state and local governments."[41] Bills pending in Congress subject to hearings in 1972 and 1974 would add the last touch: they would grant all public employees (federal, state, and local) the right to engage in collective bargaining and bring them under federal jurisdiction.[42] Although at this point only twelve states authorize broad collective bargaining rights for both state and local government employees, such negotiations in one form or another have become the prevailing practice through much of the country; some form of unionization of public employees is authorized in forty states. In some of the largest cities—New York, Philadelphia, Cincinnati, Detroit—almost all municipal employees are now unionized and in cities with a population of 10,000 or more about 60 percent of municipal employees are unionized.

To be sure, civil service strikes are just as illegal at federal, state, and local levels of government today as they were half a century ago when Calvin Coolidge was put on the road to the presidency for firing striking Boston policemen in 1919 with the famous statement that "there is no right to strike against the public safety by anybody, anywhere, any time."[43]

When he sponsored the Wagner Act as a charter of freedom for workers generally, Franklin D. Roosevelt said:

"A strike of public employees manifests nothing less than an intent on their part to prevent or obstruct the operations of government until their demands

---

[40] David Perlman, "The Surge of Public Employee Unionism," *American Federationist,* June 1971.

[41] Ibid.

[42] H. R. 9730 by Rep. Frank Thompson, H.R. 8677 by Representatives William Clay and Carl D. Perkins, 93d Cong.

[43] Only in Hawaii and Pennsylvania do state employees have the right to strike.

are satisfied. Such action, looking toward the paralysis of government by those who have sworn to support it, is unthinkable and intolerable."[44]

Yet there are now hundreds of public workers' strikes every year —their number having grown from 15 in 1958 to more than 400 in 1970 and 388 in 1973. Many of them have cut off vital public services without which people cannot live in today's cities. But no president, governor, or mayor nowadays has the courage to fire and replace striking public employees though the laws permit or even mandate it. Most of the mere handful of private employers who within the past ten to twenty years attempted to fire and replace striking employees failed, due largely to the force of government thrown decisively on the scales in favor of organized labor.

They merely proved that there is no policy but unconditional—or at best qualified—surrender to firm demands of organized labor in today's reality and that continued resistance for the purpose of upholding a principle has become quixotic besides being ruinously expensive. If unions and management were treated equally, that is, were subjected to the same prohibitions against collusion in restraint of trade, market forces could well provide the balance between the opposing interests. But efforts in that direction appear beyond hope at this time.[45] The presidents, governors, and mayors who refused to try to break a strike of public employees and gave in to their demands may have assessed the relative power and political facts of life more realistically than those who counseled or attempted resistance.

The courts also have come a long way since Judge T. Alan Goldsborough in December 1946 sentenced the United Mine Workers Union to a fine of $3.5 million and John L. Lewis to $10,000 for disobeying an order to postpone strike action. The conviction was upheld 7 to 2 by the United States Supreme Court because "the course taken by the union carried with it such a serious threat to orderly constitutional government, and to the economic and social welfare of the nation, that a fine of substantial size is required in order to emphasize the gravity of the offense of which the union

---

[44] Quoted in A. H. Raskin, "The Revolt of the Civil Servants," *Saturday Review,* December 7, 1968.

[45] Hearings scheduled for May 1974 on S2237-Ninety-third Congress by Senator Strom Thurmond and six cosponsors, which aimed to apply antitrust laws equally to management and labor, were called off when their sponsors abandoned the undertaking as hopeless.

was found guilty."[46] Although a court may occasionally still slap a mild fine on a union for disobeying an order, nothing like the United Mine Worker's case has happened since nor, in all likelihood, could happen in the political atmosphere that pervades all three branches of American government in the 1970s. A District of Columbia superior court imposed fines and jail sentences against leaders of the striking Washington teachers in September 1972—but vacated them on the following day. When a state superior court ordered a picketing ban in a San Francisco municipal strike in 1974, the mayor refused to enforce it because he "would not act as a strike breaker."[47]

New York City set the pattern for many other cities and for much of the country with a "nonstop crisis" since the mid-1960s, of slowdowns, strikes, strike threats, and sabotage by teachers, subway workers, nurses, doctors, policemen, firemen, garbage men, welfare workers, and others. To be sure, New York State had a strict law against strikes of public employees, the Condon-Wadlin Act. It was never enforced because officials deemed it to be too severe and punitive. So, after a twelve-day subway strike in 1967, the governor of New York sponsored a repeal of the Draconic law and its replacement by the more lenient Taylor Act. But a few months later, in February 1968, when the mayor of New York City tried to hold firm against striking garbage workers, the governor intervened. Instead of carrying out the mandate of the Taylor Act or calling out the National Guard as the mayor had requested, the governor within one day capitulated to the demands of the strike leaders. He had acted similarly a few years earlier in a New York City teachers' strike.

This gave public employees and their unions an object lesson which they learned well and which has been repeated many times since: strikes against government, though they are a felony under federal or state law, can be undertaken with impunity. Moreover, such unlawful strikes pay off in fat wage agreements because no public official has the courage—nor probably the political strength—to uphold the public interest against the self-interest and demands of the "street bureaucracy." Nothing succeeds like success.

Striking workers locked a dozen bridges in uncrossable positions in New York City, thereby stopping traffic, letting tons of waste pile up,

---

[46] The fine against the union was reduced to $700,000.

[47] When lower courts imposed jail sentences and fines on Philadelphia union chiefs for leading an illegal teachers' strike, the Pennsylvania Supreme Court canceled sentences and fines in October 1974.

turning the city into a pestilential garbage dump, letting huge amounts of raw sewage spew into metropolitan waterways, closing the schools, cutting off school lunches, and sabotaging New York City's citizens in dozens of other ways. They knew they could do it without punishment and they did it, time and again—at a handsome profit to themselves. When the city of Memphis tried to hold out against a strike of its garbage workers—and against demonstrations during which Dr. Martin Luther King was to lead a protest march but was assassinated—it was forced to back down by the federal government.

There is a difference between a strike against an individual business and a strike against government. If employees walk out on General Motors, the public can buy Fords or Chryslers, not to mention imported cars. But the public has no such choice in vital public service areas in which government exercises a monopoly. Citizens must rely on elected public officials who have sworn to uphold the law. But there is ample evidence in recent years that those officials are unwilling to enforce the laws, unable to stand up against pressure or blackmail.

A sizeable literature has developed in recent years on the unionization, militancy, and growing power of the public bureaucracy, much of it critical of apparent trends.[48] But there is no sign that those trends are in any way slowing down, being arrested or reversed. By all reports the power of the public bureaucracy over its own compensation and over public policies keeps on growing.

---

[48] The Brookings Institution engaged in a study of unionization of public employees with five volumes planned of which three have so far been published: Harry H. Wellington and Ralph K. Winter, Jr., *The Unions and the Cities,* 1971; David Stanley, with the assistance of Carole L. Cooper, *Managing Local Government Under Pressure,* 1972; and Jack Steiber, *Public Employee Unionism: Structure, Growth, Policy,* 1973. See also Sterling D. Spero and John M. Capozola, *The Urban Community and Its Unionized Bureaucracy* (New York: Dunellen Company, 1973); Robert J. Brown, *Teachers and Power* (New York: Simon & Schuster, 1972); *Report and Recommendations on Labor-Management Relations in the Federal Service,* Washington, D.C.: Bureau of National Affairs, 1970; "Government Employee Negotiations and the Public Interest," NAM Position Paper, *NAM Reports,* May 18, 1970; "Symposium on Collective Bargaining in the Public Service: A Reappraisal," *Public Administration Review,* March-April, 1972; and Sam Zagoria, ed., *Public Workers and Public Unions* (Englewood Cliffs, N.J.: Prentice-Hall, 1973).

—3—

Public Revenues: Government as a Siphon

In FY 1972 all governments in the United States—federal, state, and local —collected in taxes and other revenues an aggregate amount of $382 billion—out of a gross national product of $1,100 billion.[1] Governmental receipts set a new high and the amount of the increase over the preceding twenty years—up $282 billion over the $100 billion collected in 1952—also established a new record. Since the turn of the twentieth century public revenues have multiplied 225 times (from $1.7 billion in 1902) while the GNP multiplied only 53 times. This means that over the past seventy years government's intake has grown more than four times faster than the nation's income and product, from 8.2 percent of the GNP in 1902 to 34.7 percent of the GNP in 1972 (table 1).

Public revenues did not rise at a constant rate. In the first decade of the twentieth century they moved up parallel to the national economy. In each of the two succeeding twenty-year periods they nearly doubled *as a percentage of the GNP*. In the past twenty years, however, governmental receipts expanded only slightly faster than the GNP. That was, *in relative terms,* the slowest increase in governmental revenues in any twenty-year period on record.[2]

Growth between 1913 and 1932 was rapid because *(a)* income tax rates were boosted drastically during World War I and, though subsequently reduced, were never brought back to prewar levels; and *(b)* the GNP dropped sharply between 1929 and 1932 (the Great Depression). The jump between 1932 and 1952 was caused by record federal income tax rates imposed during World War II that were cut only slightly in the postwar

---

[1] As reported by the U.S. Bureau of the Census; see table 1. The Bureau of Economic Analysis which, like the Bureau of the Census, is a division of the Department of Commerce, uses somewhat different concepts and reports its annual totals on a calendar year basis. They therefore differ slightly from the Bureau of the Census data. There is, however, no difference in the apparent trends and in the conclusions to be drawn from them.

[2] Comprehensive statistics on governmental finances (federal, state, and local) are available back to 1902.

GROWTH OF GOVERNMENTAL REVENUES AS A PERCENTAGE OF GNP,
1913–1972

Fiscal Year	Governmental Revenues as a Percentage of GNP	Percentage Increase over Preceding Period	Percentage Increase
1913*	8.1		
1932	15.3	7.2%	89.0%
1952	29.7	14.4	94.0
1972	34.7	5.0	17.0

SOURCE: Table 1.* The decennial census of governments, usually taken in years ending with 2, was taken in 1913 instead of in 1912.

period, whereas state and local tax rates started soaring after the war and maintained their pace. Between 1952 and 1972 public revenues were pushed up only slightly faster than the GNP because much of the tremendous expansion in domestic expenditures of government during those years was offset by a relative cutback in national defense outlays to half their former share of the budget and the taxpayer's dollar.

In FY 1972 aggregate receipts of all governments equaled 34.7 percent of the GNP, 42.6 percent of national income, and 42.5 percent of personal income (table 13). If trends of the past twenty years were to continue, governmental revenues would equal about half of the national income as well as half of personal income, or about two-fifths of the GNP, soon after the turn of the century.

On a per capita basis, governmental revenues in FY 1972 equaled $1,828 for each person or $7,312 for a family of four. Is that burden too heavy to bear for the individual taxpayer with an average per capita income of $4,300? Is government levying too much in taxes to maintain adequate and stable growth in the nation's economy?

By some measurement government is not levying enough. Federal revenues fell short of meeting expenditures in sixteen of the past twenty years; receipts equaled only 95 percent of the outgo for the entire period; 5 percent of federal expenditures were deficit financed. The combined public debt doubled during those two decades, increasing by $313 billion—not counting numerous contingent obligations arising from social security, pensions, guarantees, and other commitments that total in the hundreds of billions.

GOVERNMENTAL DEBT, 1952 AND 1972

	Total (in billions)	Federal (in billions)	State-Local (in billions)
1952	$289	$259	$ 30
1972	602	427	175
Increase	313	168	145

SOURCE: Table 1.

Most of the state and local debt was incurred for capital projects and therefore is held by some to be offset by the addition of tangible values. But public works construction is a continuing and usually growing activity at state, city, and county levels and certainly at the federal level, and should therefore largely be financed on a current basis, particularly because there is no allowance for depreciation in governmental budgeting and accounting.

Some observers of the fiscal scene feel that government is not taxing enough and that, as a result, many vital public services are being starved while the consumer luxuriates. According to this view the consumer is allowed to keep more of his earnings than he ought to be permitted. Leading among those who hold that government is not getting enough is John Kenneth Galbraith who broke new ground in 1958 with his book *The Affluent Society*. The ensuing controversy is discussed in a later chapter.

Compared with other industrial countries, the American tax burden appears to be moderate. According to a report prepared by the staff of the Organization for Economic Cooperation and Development (OECD) early in 1974, the United States ranked sixteenth among twenty-three countries in regard to governmental receipts as a percentage of gross domestic product (table 14). At 31.5 percent[3] the United States was below the average of 34.6 percent, far behind Sweden with 50.1 percent, or Germany, Great Britain and France, which were shown between 38.0 and 39.0 percent. Of the major countries listed, only Japan with 22.3 percent, Spain with 23.4 percent, and Switzerland with 27.1 percent showed up lower than the United States.

Though much improved in recent years, international economic and fiscal comparisons are still somewhat tenuous and the figures cited above

---

[3] For calendar year 1972, from statistics of the Bureau of Economic Analysis, Department of Commerce, which are somewhat less comprehensive than Bureau of the Census data.

may be imprecise. But the fact that the tax load in many leading industrial countries is heavier than it is in the United States has long been known and appears to be well established.

Many of the countries with a heavier tax burden have long experienced respectable economic growth rates, often doing much better than the United States. Though it stands to reason that heavy taxes act as a depressant on economic growth, because they reduce the capital available for private industrial investment and expansion, the available data supply no proof that high taxes necessarily mean slower economic growth. One tentative conclusion we might draw is that the magnitude itself of taxes may not be as significant an adverse factor in economic expansion as is widely assumed. The composition of the tax structure—and possibly the use to which public funds are put—may have a greater impact on a nation's economy than the size of the aggregate. How much a country taxes its citizens may not be as important as how it taxes them.

Taxation in the Federal System

Federal and state governments exercise separate and independent taxing powers under the United States Constitution and state constitutions, whereas local governments, as subdivisions of the state, possess only such taxing powers as the state may delegate. For much of the time prior to World War II (except for the period of World War I), state and local governments collected about twice as much each year as the federal treasury. In 1941, federal receipts exceeded state-local receipts for the first time, and they have remained larger ever since.

Since 1946 the federal treasury has been taking in, on the average, about twice as much each year as all state and local governments combined. In other words, the relative position of federal and state-local treasuries was reversed between pre–World War II and post–World War II years. This seems to confirm the broadly held belief that the federal government has a much stronger taxing capacity than the states and that its relative strength is growing. Further proof appears to be adduced by the fact that between 1902 and 1972 state and local government revenues multiplied 152 times, federal revenues 342 times (table 1).

But some developments cast doubt on the belief in the federal government's growing fiscal power. For one, income fell short of outgo in sixteen of the past twenty years, as mentioned earlier. Moreover, between 1952 and 1972 federal revenues increased 211 percent, state-local revenues 457 percent. Consequently, the state-local share of all governmental receipts, which had been as low as 20.6 percent in 1944, increased from 28.4 percent in 1952 to 41.5 percent in 1972. As a percentage of the GNP federal revenues simultaneously *declined* from 21.3 to 20.3 percent, while state-local receipts increased from 8.4 to 14.4 percent of the GNP (table 16).

Historical analysis back to 1902 shows that state-local revenues always grew faster than federal revenues except during wartime (table 15). Between 1902 and 1916, as well as between 1945 and 1972, state-local revenues increased more than three times faster than federal revenues; between 1920 and 1940 federal receipts dropped while state-local receipts multiplied 2.7 times. In each of those periods federal revenues grew more slowly than the GNP, state-local revenues substantially faster.

It was only in wartime that state-local revenue growth came to a virtual standstill while federal receipts skyrocketed. In World War I (1916–1920) federal revenues jumped 640 percent, in World War II (1940–1945) 671 percent, while state-local receipts simultaneously advanced only 33 and 30 percent respectively. We find a similar picture, if less drastic, during the Korean War (1950–1953).

Between 1952 and 1972 federal revenues increased 211 percent, state-local revenues 457 percent (states +488 percent, local governments +425 percent). Federal receipts *dropped* from 21.3 percent of the GNP to 20.3 percent, while state-local receipts jumped from 8.4 percent of the GNP to 14.4 percent. Yet it was during that period that the view that federal taxes expand rapidly in response to economic growth, whereas state and local taxes are inflexible and lag, gained broad acceptance. This served to support the notion that enlarged federal aid to the states was necessary and imperative. Congress obliged, and the annual amounts of federal aid jumped from $2.6 billion in 1952 to $33.6 billion in 1972 (with an estimated $51.7 billion in the president's budget for FY 1975).

In the immediate postwar period, when the state-local share of governmental revenues had shrunk to nearly 20 percent of the total, some economic and political experts concluded that the fiscal powers of state-local governments had become insufficient to meet contemporary requirements and could hardly be enlarged. They predicted that the federal government would have to assume most of the revenue-raising responsibility and either render more aid to the other governments or assume the operation of major domestic programs. Now that state-local governments have increased their resources at a faster rate than the federal government and doubled their share of total governmental receipts—from 20.6 percent in 1944 to 41.5 percent in 1972—it sometimes is asserted that state-local governments have, by that extraordinary effort, exhausted their fiscal capacity and will in the future have to depend increasingly on the federal treasury. If state-local governments had not increased their receipts so spectacularly in the postwar period this would of course have been taken as proof that they were unable to do so and that recourse to the federal treasury was the only answer. This seems to be a "heads I win, tails you lose" proposition. The underlying issue appears to be not so much whether state-local governments *are able* to raise larger funds but whether it is *desirable* that they do so. The choice depends on whether we favor or oppose centralization of governmental power or certain types of taxes that are used more strongly at one level of government or the other.

Fluctuations of federal and state-local tax receipts—as shown in table 15—speak a clear and unequivocal language. The superior fiscal strength and powerful tax machinery of the federal government were able to outpace the supposedly weak, laggard, and antiquated state and local governments only during shooting wars—World Wars I and II and the Korean War —when the obvious and overriding needs of national defense forced a cutback (or at least restraint) in nonmilitary activities and a transfer of resources to the national government. Those were times of a major emergency, when the American people were willing to make otherwise unacceptable sacrifices. In nonwar periods states and local communities, with all their reported legal, economic, and political disabilities, managed to expand their receipts at a faster rate than the federal government or the growth of the national economy. They did so despite a very real handicap. Federal revenues, dominated by personal and corporate income taxes, tend to rise proportionately faster than the GNP, *at unchanged tax rates,* particularly during inflationary periods. State and local receipts are more likely to move in proportion to the general economic trend. They can be made to climb faster only by the politcially painful process of levying additional taxes or boosting tax rates. This is what state and local governments have been doing at an amazing pace, year after year.

This is surprising in view of the fact that the imposition of new state-local taxes, or the boosting of rates, usually requires an affirmative vote by the taxpayers themselves at the ballot box at the local level and often at the state level also. At the least it forces elected officials of local and state governments—mayors, governors, county commissioners, legislators, city councilmen—to advocate and stand up for tax boosts and to vote for them. That is exactly what they have been doing, except during war periods, time and again in every state of the Union. The record clearly refutes the oft-heard assertion that taxpayers will not vote to raise taxes on themselves, even for essential purposes, and that the large funds needed to sustain and improve vital public services can be raised only at the federal level. The fact is that Congress has hardly ever boosted federal taxes during peacetime or for domestic purposes, except for social security, though it has on several occasions voted to reduce them slightly. The tremendous expansion in federal funds for domestic public services (see tables 5a and b) was financed in three ways: *(a)* by sharp *relative* cutbacks in outlays for national defense (to half their share in the tax dollar between 1952 and 1972); *(b)* by reducing federal tax rates after each war *less* than the cut in military outlays would have made possible and keeping taxes considerably higher than the prewar level; and *(c)* by deficit financing, which lifted the federal debt from $259 billion in 1945 to $427 billion in 1972 (with a ceiling of $495 billion approved in mid-1974).

A combination of hefty tax boosts, an expanding economy, and a high rate of inflation enabled state and local revenues to increase at spectacular rates in recent years—by 40 percent between 1969 and 1972—while federal revenues increased by 12 percent. That abundance, in addition to federal aid, which jumped 77 percent between FY 1969 and 1972—with another 44 percent increase from 1972 to 1975 (budgeted)—produced sizeable surpluses in many state treasuries.[4] This set in motion for the first time ever a series of tax reductions in many states—cuts in income and sales tax rates, property tax relief, etc. That the state tax cuts of 1973 and 1974 will go very far or continue very long is unlikely. Spending pressures are so heavy and politically irresistible that happy surplus conditions and the time of tax cuts have probably passed.

State and local officials are of course very much aware of the political profit potential inherent in tax relief proposals. They also know the political risks of exercising tight expenditure control. One promising course between the Scylla of high taxes and the Charibdys of expenditure cuts is federal aid; thus the demand to increase further federal aid remains strong.

The drive for steep increases in federal aid to the states has been amazingly successful over the past quarter century. Much of the drive's strength is derived from the incessant pressure for expansion of domestic public services at a rate the public is unlikely to support if it means higher

---

[4] See "Good News for Taxpayers—Some States Rolling in Money," *U.S. News and World Report,* June 10, 1974.

taxes. Federal aid seems the way to get more generous public programs without having to pay higher taxes. Another argument in favor of federal aid is that the taxes from which the federal government derives most of its income are of a more desirable type than the major state-local taxes. Therefore the controversy over the tax structure, over federal versus state-local taxes and their respective economic, social, and political impact, plays a major role in a discussion of taxes and tax reform.

The American Tax System

In a society where demands for public services are low, the revenue needs of government can be met from just one or a few sources. But as governmental activities expand and fiscal requirements multiply, a variety of methods must be employed to exact the huge sums from a reluctant public. Attractive as the proposition of a single tax—the "ideal" tax—may be, it becomes utterly unrealistic when government claims 20 or 30 percent or more of the GNP. At that level even confiscatory rates of a tax would not suffice; they would become self-defeating and useless. Hence dozens of taxes have had to be conceived and imposed to conceal their total from the taxpayer and to make their bite less painful and less destructive. For reasons not immediately apparent to the untrained eye, the multitude of uncoordinated and overlapping taxes that Americans are called upon to pay to their federal, state, and local governments is called our *tax system*.

There is probably no more appealing idea in the field of intergovernmental tax relations than the concept of a clean separation of sources, with each government assigned certain taxes for its exclusive use. If that is not how the system now operates then it is not for the want of trying. But it never worked for very long, in the United States or anywhere else. Long ago, Germany, Switzerland, Canada, and several other countries allocated indirect taxes to the central government and direct taxes to states, cantons, or provinces. So incidentally did the United States for the first 120 years of its existence. But to public officials, as to human beings in general, the other fellow's grass always looks greener. So in the United States and in other federal countries central governments gradually ventured into direct taxes, while state and local governments adopted a widening range of excise and sales taxes. Eventually everybody was working both sides of almost every street. Three levels of government levy income taxes in the United States, three levels consumption taxes, two levels property and estate taxes.

Recommendations and attempts to reduce or eliminate tax overlapping have consistently failed. Governments are always on the prowl for more rather than fewer sources and are unwilling to give up what they have. The chance for tax separation or even a significant cutback in tax overlapping is slim indeed. Tax overlapping, however, is not as pervasive as a mere listing would make it appear. Analysis shows that there still is a distinct pattern of tax concentration at each level of government. The federal government collected 87 percent of all income taxes in 1972—slightly down from 96 percent in 1952—local governments collected 97 percent of all property taxes in 1972—virtually unchanged from 96 percent in 1952. The most significant change took place in consumption taxes, with the state share jumping from 37 percent in 1952 to 58 percent in 1972. Moreover, three-fourths of the 35 percent share of consumption taxes claimed by the federal government in 1972 consisted mostly of customs duties and excises on liquor, tobacco, and automotive items. All of these, except automotive items, have historically been prime federal tax sources. In fact they accounted for most federal revenues from 1789 to 1913, except during the Civil War. General retail sales taxes are levied only at state and local levels, with the states' share increasing from 78 percent in 1952 to 87 percent in 1972. A strengthened role of the states in income as well as sales taxation has been an important change in the past twenty years.

The dependence of each level of government on a particular type of taxation follows an identical pattern. Using the Bureau of the Census definition of taxes—which excludes social security contributions, as did the administrative budget that was in use until 1968—the federal government derived 82 percent of its *tax* revenues from income taxes in both 1952 and 1972, states obtained 58 percent of their taxes from consumption taxes in 1952 and 56 percent in 1972, local government obtained 87 percent of their tax revenues from property taxes in 1952 and 84 percent in 1972. It is evident that the picture has remained virtually unchanged over the past two decades. What really counts in the end, as far as the taxpayer is concerned, is the aggregate "mix" of all types of taxes imposed by all levels of government. That sets the nature of the country's tax system.

The American tax system is like no other in the world. In most other countries consumption taxes are the largest source of public revenue, with income taxes playing second fiddle. In the United States, consumption taxes are far outdistanced by income taxes. We are the only industrial country whose national government does not levy a broad-based major consumption tax.

The comparative picture for the United States and the other OECD countries is as follows:

INDIVIDUAL TAXES AS A PERCENTAGE OF TOTAL TAXATION
IN OECD MEMBER COUNTRIES IN THE AVERAGE OF 1968–1970

	Mean of All OECD Member Countries	United States
Taxes on goods and services	36.0%	19.0%
Taxes on incomes and profits	33.1	48.4
households	26.8	34.4
corporations	8.1	13.7*
Social security	21.7	18.6
Other taxes	10.1	14.1

INDIVIDUAL TAXES AS A PERCENTAGE OF GNP
IN OECD MEMBER COUNTRIES IN THE AVERAGE OF 1968–1970

	Mean of All OECD Countries	United States
Taxes on goods and services	10.9%	5.3%
Taxes on incomes and profits	10.7	13.5
households	8.6	9.7
corporations	2.4	3.8*
Social security	6.8	5.2
Other taxes	2.8	3.9

* Does not add to total because data for some countries are not available.

SOURCE: Organization for Economic Cooperation and Development, *Revenue Statistics of OECD Member Countries 1968–1970*, 1972.

Details for countries are given in tables 17 and 18, which are taken from the same source, *Revenue Statistics of OECD Member Countries 1968–1970*. The United States derives less of its public revenues from consumption taxes than any other OECD country and leans more heavily on income taxes than any country except Australia and Sweden.

Income Taxes

It is the extraordinary concentration on income taxation which causes some observers to praise the American federal tax system. "The federal taxing process has produced a magnificent tax system which compares favorably in its structure and administration with any in the world," declared Roy Blough, who had helped to shape the tax system while working in the United States Treasury and on the Council of Economic Advisers.[5] Others regard the strong emphasis on the income tax and the neglect of consumption taxes as detrimental to economic growth, questionable for social and political reasons, and unfair and oppressive.

One of the often cited advantages of the income tax is its elasticity: its yields increase with economic growth, but at a faster rate, and decrease —also at a faster rate—during an economic decline. Thereby the tax tends to counteract economic fluctuations and serves as an automatic stabilizer. Although the precise relationship between economic growth and tax receipts depends on the rate of inflation and various other factors, it has been estimated, most recently in a report of the Advisory Commission on Intergovernmental Relations (ACIR) (see below), that federal income tax yields grow 75 percent faster than the GNP, consumption tax yields at the same pace as the GNP, and property tax yields only at 75 percent of the GNP (i.e., 25 percent more slowly). This makes the income tax politically very attractive. In growth times, the income tax yields greatly enlarged amounts without the need to raise rates, whereas sales and property tax receipts increase only slowly and can be made more productive only by tax boosts—a politically distasteful and risky process.

It is therefore surprising that despite the built-in growth of the income tax, collections grew only 187 percent between 1952 and 1972, compared with a 378 percent growth in the aggregate of all other public revenues. The reason for the faster growth in nonincome tax receipts is simple: the federal income tax was cut in 1954, 1964, and 1969 while the rates of sales and property taxes were steadily boosted by state and local governments. To be sure, state income taxes were also raised but they play a minor role. Between 1959 and 1971 the fifty state legislatures enacted forty new major taxes and increased rates in 468 instances.[6] Why elected officials—at any level of government—prefer taxes whose yield grows substantially without the painful need to raise rates needs no explanation.

---

[5] Roy Blough, *The Federal Taxing Process* (New York: Prentice-Hall, 1952), p. 464.

[6] Advisory Commission on Intergovernmental Relations, *State-Local Finances: Significant Features and Suggested Legislation,* 1972.

GOVERNMENTAL REVENUES, 1952–1972

Fiscal Year	1952 (in millions)	1972 (in millions)	Percent Increase
All revenues	$100,245	$381,849	281%
Taxes	$79,067	$262,533	232
Income	50,983	146,556	187
Individual	28,919	109,974	280
Corporation	22,064	36,582	66
Consumption	15,689	57,589	267
Property	8,652	42,133	387
Other	3,743	16,255	334
Social security contributions	3,547	47,341	1,235
Other revenue	17,631	71,976	308
Exhibit: All revenues less income taxes	49,262	235,293	378

SOURCE: Table 16.

The tax that grew most rapidly between 1952 and 1972 was the social security tax. Expressing the tremendous expansion of the system, it increased 1235 percent, which is five times faster than the aggregate of all other governmental receipts. The property tax, presumably the most laggard tax, ranked second with a 387 percent increase. From 8.6 percent of all public revenues in 1952 it advanced to 11.0 percent in 1972. This was due largely to an enormous amount of construction and growth in property values, partially to rate boosts.

The 187 percent growth in income tax collections between 1952 and 1972 consisted of two components: *(a)* individual income taxes, which increased 280 percent (identical with the growth rate of the aggregate of all other public revenues); and *(b)* corporate profits taxes, which increased only 66 percent. Because the state income tax picture is more complicated—some states raised rates substantially, some did not; some states adopted new income taxes, some did not—it may be simpler to focus on development in federal income taxes.

Between fiscal years 1952 and 1972 collections of federal individual income taxes increased 256 percent, of corporate profits taxes only 52 percent. There were tax reductions in both fields, especially in 1954, 1964, and 1969: the corporate rate was cut from 52 to 48 percent, the excess profits tax was repealed, and depreciation rules were somewhat eased; individual income tax rates were lowered, and personal exemptions and standard deductions were raised. The main factor responsible for the differential rates in tax receipt increases—256 percent for individual taxes, 52 percent for corporate taxes—lies in the differential growth rate of personal income and corporate profits: between FY 1952 and FY 1972 personal income grew 240 percent, corporate profits (and inventory valuation adjustment) 104 percent.

This differential rate of growth expresses a long-range trend in income distribution in the United States that is not widely known but has significant implications for fiscal and economic policy. A decisive income shift from ownership to labor is evident. In *personal income* the share of labor and social benefits grew between calendar years 1952 and 1972 from 73.3 to 78.4 percent, the share of property and business meanwhile dropped from 26.7 to 21.6 percent. If we count only proprietors' income and dividends, we find that the business share dropped from 18.6 percent of the personal income to 10.7 percent, a cut in its relative share of 42 percent.

As a percentage of *national income* compensation of employees increased from 67.0 percent in 1952 to 74.7 in 1972, while proprietors' income and corporate profits and inventory valuation adjustment dropped from 28.1 to 17.8 percent.

As a percentage of *corporate income* compensation of employees rose from 76.8 percent in 1952 to 82.9 percent in 1972, while before-tax profits and inventory valuation adjustment fell from 23.3 to 17.1 percent.[7]

In 1974 statements were made with growing frequency that corporate profits had soared and that the trend of an income shift from corporate ownership to labor compensation had been reversed within the past two years. At first glance this appears to be correct: Between the third quarter of 1972 and the third quarter of 1974, corporate profits before taxes increased 61 percent, employee compensation only 22 percent. Those corporate profits figures, however, include huge "phantom profits" on inventory due to inflation. If allowance is made for the inventory valuation adjustment (which multiplied 7.5 times between the third quarter of 1972 and the third quarter of 1974, from $6.9 to $51.7 billion), corporate profits before taxes grew only 17 percent. This is less than the 22 percent increase in employee compensation. The national income share of cororate profits and inventory

---

[7] All data for national income, personal income, corporate income from *Economic Report of the President,* February 1974. By the third quarter of 1974 employee compensation had increased to 75.1 percent of national income, while proprietors income and corporate profits and inventory valuation adjustment had declined to 17.2 percent of national income (*Economic Indicators,* November 1974).

valuation adjustment shrank from 9.6 percent in the third quarter of 1972 to 9.2 percent in the third quarter of 1974 (down from 13.7 percent in 1952).[8] Moreover, if profits really had soared, as has been repeatedly claimed in statements intended to influence public sentiment and legislative policy, it would be hard to explain why the value of ownership in corporations—as expressed in stock market prices—fell 44 percent between January 1973 and October 1974. Considering the simultaneous decline in the value of the dollar—as shown in consumer and commodity price indices—corporate ownership lost more than half its value within less than two years. If corporate profitability and prospects had improved, investors would have been eager to expand rather than contract their holdings, to buy rather than sell in the market, and stock prices would have moved up rather than experienced a precipitous drop.[9]

Returning to our consideration of revenue developments between 1952 and 1972, we find in table 16 that, although some minor shifts occurred, the basic American tax structure remained unchanged. Federal income taxes still dominate the scene.

From time to time proposals have come up for the imposition of a broad-based consumption tax at the federal level. Because the retail sales tax is the fiscal mainstay of most states, federal plans focused more on a value added tax (VAT) which in recent years has become the prevailing tax in European countries, gradually pushing aside or replacing turnover or sales taxes. Though a VAT has many advantages, suggestions to use it in the United States, usually as a partial replacement for the corporate profits tax, have never gotten very far. The reason for the failure of the VAT to

---

[8] Data for national income accounts from *Economic Indicators*, August 1973 and November 1974. Between the third quarter of 1972 and the third quarter of 1974 corporate profits and inventory valuation adjustment dropped from 16.3 percent of corporate income to 15.6 percent, employee compensation increased from 82.9 percent of corporate income to 83.9 percent (*Survey of Current Business*, July 1973, November 1974). For further data on profit trends see "Why Today's Rise in Profits Is Not All It Seems," *U.S. News and World Report*, November 4, 1974; "Third-Quarter Profits: the End of an Illusion," *Monthly Economic Letter*, First National City Bank of New York, November 1974; Edwin L. Dale, "Inflation is Distorting Corporate Profits, Too," *New York Times*, December 1, 1974; and "Dividends: Slowing Down," *Newsweek*, November 25, 1974.

[9] Lord Keynes wrote in 1932: "Unemployment, I must repeat, exists because employers have been deprived of profit. The loss of profit may be due to all sorts of causes. But short of going over to Communism there is no possible means of curing unemployment except by restoring to employers a proper margin of profit" [John Maynard Keynes, *Essays in Persuasion* (New York; Harcourt, Brace, 1932), p. 275]. In the 40 years since this was written other factors have come into play that cause unemployment: wage rates mandated or supported by government which exceed the productive capacity of unskilled, young, or marginal persons with low drive. and the availability of workless pay from various public programs which compete effectively with gainful employment.

gain broader acceptance is the same reason that is responsible for the "underdevelopment" of consumption taxation in the United States: ideological and political preference for progressive over proportional taxation. Proportional taxation is basically neutral among taxpayers and leaves them in the same relative position after taxes as they were before taxes.

Increasingly, however, many conceive it to be a prime purpose of government to redistribute income and wealth, from those who earn and have more to those who earn but have less ("from those who earn it to those who yearn it"). This is done extensively by major domestic expenditure programs in the social welfare field. But taxes also play a significant role in the effort to more nearly equalize incomes. Just how effective a job they are doing remains controversial. By extensive manipulations—such as treating long-range capital gains as if they were current income—and farfetched assumptions some authors have concluded that the American tax system is approximately proportional.[10]

On the face of it, it is mainly the graduated rate scale, which has ranged from 14 to 70 percent since 1964, that provides the progression in the federal income tax. But much or most of its progressive impact derives from the fact that it leaves half of all personal income untaxed.

The Internal Revenue Code proclaims its intent to tax "all income from whatever source derived." But then it undercuts that sweeping statement by allowing a myriad of exclusions, exemptions, deductions, and credits. According to oft-repeated and widely believed assertions most of the untaxed income accrues to the rich. If true, this would counteract the intent

---

[10] See, for example; Joseph A. Pechman and Benjamin A. Okner, *Who Bears the Tax Burden?* (Washington, D.C.: Brookings Institution, 1974), p. 10; see also idem, "Who Paid Taxes in 1966?," *The American Economic Review*, May 1974: "In summary, the U.S. tax system is essentially proportional for the vast majority of families and therefore has little effect on the distribution of income."

Pechman and Okner were able to produce such results by extensively "adjusting" family income from concepts of personal income used in national income accounting. For example, they treated not only realized capital gains as current income but also unrealized capital gains such as those resulting from the impact of inflation on inventories, they attributed retained earnings of corporations to their stockholders' family income, and they excluded income which resulted from employer contributions—treating such benefits as income in the year in which the employer contributions were made rather than when the benefits were received.

The authors admitted that "high effective tax rates at the lower end of the income scale are probably due primarily to the use of a one-year accounting period for measuring income. When the accounting period is limited to a single year, there is a heavy concentration of retired-person families and of individuals with temporarily low income in these income classes. . . . Thus the annual tax burdens shown . . . for the lowest income classes are probably not representative of the tax burdens of families whose incomes are low when measured over longer periods" (Pechman and Okner, *Who Bears the Tax Burden?*, p.8).

of the planners to impose a heavier tax as individuals move up on the income ladder. Closer analysis, however, proves that most of the tax-free income is in the lower brackets.

Unfortunately no statistics are available that detail *personal* income by income brackets and could then be related to *taxable* income on income tax returns. The Department of Commerce discontinued such statistics in 1964. Annual sample surveys of the Bureau of the Census estimate money (cash) income by size groups but they cannot be related to tax returns. The aggregate money income according to the bureau survey for the calendar year 1972 totaled $687 billion, which is $252 billion short of the $939 billion personal income, according to national income accounts.[11]

Of the $939 billion in personal income, $445 billion showed up as taxable income on federal income tax returns. This means that $494 billion or 53 percent of all personal income remained untaxed.[12] Who received that huge amount of about half a trillion dollars *tax-free* in 1972? The only income breakdown by size brackets presently available that can be related to taxable income and to tax liability is *adjusted gross income* (AGI) on income tax returns.

The AGI on individual income tax returns in 1972 totaled $747 billion. Most of the "missing," that is, unreported, income of $192 billion consists of social benefits (social security, public assistance, unemployment compensation), untaxed labor income (employer contributions to pension and welfare funds, nontaxable income in kind, etc.), nonreported income (persons with income below taxable levels who do not file evasion), and imputed income (imputed rent on owner-occupied homes, etc.).

It is apparent from the nature of the personal income that is not included in AGI on tax returns that most of it—except possibly imputed income —accrues to persons in low-income brackets. Only an insignificant fraction goes to persons in high-income brackets. In other words, the overwhelming share of the $192 billion difference between personal income and AGI in 1972 went to persons at the lower end of the income scale.

The $302 billion difference between AGI and taxable income (TI) can be broken down by income brackets by an analysis of tax returns. Table 19 shows that, overall, 40 percent of AGI is untaxed. But this percentage is highest (78 percent) at AGI under $5,000; it then gradually declines to 33

---

[11] U.S., Bureau of the Census, *Money Income in 1972 of Families and Persons in the United States,* Current Population Reports, series P-60 no. 90, December 1973.

[12] Counting certain offsets (income that is taxable but not treated as personal income in national income accounting, such as capital gains or social insurance contributions) untaxed income probably totaled about $550 billion or more in 1972.

percent between $15,000 and $25,000, and to 23 percent between $100,000 and $200,000. It rises to 33 percent in the $1 million-and-over bracket.[13] The lowest percentage of "tax-free" income—23–28 percent—lies between $25,000 and $1 million.

The meaning of this is clear: most of the untaxed income accrues to persons in the lower-income brackets. This is not due to "loopholes" but to tax alleviation deliberately conferred by Congress. Nor, to be sure, is the far smaller share of income that remains untaxed in higher brackets attributable to "loopholes."

Most of the tax differentials—or "loopholes" according to their critics—were put in the law not by accident, oversight, or inadvertence, or to protect the rich from having to pay their fair share of taxation. They were inserted, almost always after extensive public hearings by the two tax-writing committees of Congress, to achieve one or both of the following objectives:

1. To provide greater equity, horizontal or vertical, among taxpayers and different types and magnitudes of income by taking into account differing circumstances and offering relief for hardships
2. To provide incentives to taxpayers to engage in or enlarge activities that are held to be desirable as a matter of public policy. This is done by offering rewards to some and imposing penalties on others.[14]

Intensive hearings on the tax structure and tax reform were held by congressional committees in 1954, 1959 and 1969 and with less comprehensive investigations in other years. Congressional action on tax reform resulted in far more exemptions of formerly taxable income than subjections to the tax of formerly untaxed income. Several million people were freed from any obligation to pay federal income taxes. Tax cuts enacted in March 1975 exempted additional million of persons from any income tax liability. Thus the incidence of "representation without taxation"—of citizens who have the right to vote but do not have to pay a share of the taxes—continues to grow apace. This bears an ominous portent for the preservation of responsible free government in our society.

---

[13] Due mostly to larger charitable contributions, which equal 3.0 percent in the average of all itemizing returns, 4.6 percent with AGI between $100,000 and $200,000, but jump to 18.3 percent in the $1 million-and-over bracket. Charitable contributions on $1 million-and-up returns (of which there were 1,011) averaged $385,809 per return.

[14] For details see my book *Tax Loopholes: The Legend and the Reality* (Washington, D.C.: American Enterprise Institute for Public Policy Research; Stanford, California: Hoover Institution on War, Revolution and Peace, 1973).

It may go a long way in explaining the growing fiscal irresponsibility in Congress and other legislative bodies as well as in executive departments.

It has often been asserted that loopholes inserted in the tax laws by Congress to protect the wealthy enable many of them and particularly millionaires to pay little or no income tax. Here are the facts on tax returns with $1 million or more AGI in 1972: 1,011 such returns were filed of which four reported no tax liability (whether some of these were found taxable in subsequent audits is not known). The remaining 1,007 returns reported an average AGI of $2,110,308 each and ATI of $1,443,284 (68 percent), on which a tax of $995,930 was paid, equal to a tax rate of 47 percent on AGI and 69 percent on TI, close to the 70 percent top rate of the income tax scale.

Most of the nontaxable income (difference between AGI and TI), which for four returns resulted in reported nontaxability, was accounted for by interest payments on money borrowed to invest elsewhere and earn a return, charitable contributions, state and local taxes, casualty losses, and foreign tax credits (for taxes paid to foreign governments on operations in their countries).[15]

The oft-repeated charge that middle-income groups bear a disproportionate share of the federal income tax has an undeniable political appeal. Everybody likes to feel sorry for himself and, after all, the tax takes a big slice out of the salary. But it has no basis in fact as the following statistics show:

SHARES OF THE FEDERAL INCOME TAX
BY MAJOR INCOME BRACKETS, 1972

AGI	*Share of AGI*	*Share of Tax Liability*
Under $7,000	15.8%	6.5%
$7,000 to 19,999	56.8	49.3
20,000 and over	27.4	44.2
	100.0	100.0

It is evident that the middle-income group, between $7,000 and $20,000, received 56.8 percent of all AGI, paid 49.3 percent of the tax, and was not overcharged. The $20,000-and-up group got 27.4 percent of all income but paid 44.2 percent of the tax, more than its proportionate share.

[15] The four nontaxable returns with an AGI of $1 million and over had an average AGI per return of $2,363,000 but itemized deductions of $2,877,000 each. Interest payment accounted for $1,258,000, charitable contributions for $166,000, state and local taxes for $47,000, and casualty losses and other deductions for $1,406,000.

The overall impact of the federal income tax is steeply progressive, as table 19 shows. In 1972 the tax rate on AGI grew from 5.2 percent in the under-$5000 bracket to 47 percent in the $1 million-and-over bracket, the tax rate on TI grew from 15 percent in the low bracket to 69 percent in the top bracket.[16]

The income tax is the "leakiest" tax in our system. Whereas between one-fourth and one-third of the base is exempt for sales and property tax purposes, about half of all personal income is beyond the reach of the Internal Revenue Service.

On the face of it, it appears that the situation had improved between 1952 and 1972. In 1952 39.8 percent of all personal income was taxable,[17] in 1972 47.3 percent. The share of personal income subject to the federal income tax gradually increased between 1952 and 1969 from 39.8 to 51.8 percent but not because changes in the tax law made formerly exempt income taxable. Rather, this trend was caused largely by inflation and rising income levels, which pushed more of the income above personal exemptions (then stable at $600 per person) and into taxable brackets. Under the impact of the Tax Reform Act of 1969, which was adopted by Congress and sold to the public on the proposition that it would narrow "loopholes," the taxable percentage of personal income receded from 51.7 percent in 1969 to 49.6 percent in 1970 and to 47.3 percent in 1972; 1972 was the year when the final forward provisions of the 1969 act became effective.

If the 1969 ratio of taxable to personal income had been in effect in 1972, $42 billion of income that was not taxable under the existing law would have been taxable. Considering the natural increase from inflation and rising incomes, it is likely that approximately $70 billion of income that was not actually taxed excaped to taxation in 1972 in direct consequence of the Tax Reform Act of 1969.

The political implications of the income tax are obvious. In 1972 slightly more than half (51 percent) of the federal individual income tax returns reported an AGI under $8000; 37 percent of the AGI was taxable on these returns and an income tax of 7.2 percent was paid on AGI and

---

[16] All data for 1972 federal income tax returns were derived from U.S. Department of the Treasury, Internal Revenue Service, *Preliminary Statistics of Income, 1972: Individual Income Tax Returns,* March 1974.

[17] Taken from Joseph A. Pechman,"Erosion of Individual Income Tax," *National Tax Journal,* March 1957.

16.1 percent on TI.[18] Less than 1 percent—0.8 percent to be precise—of all returns in 1972 reported an AGI of $50,000 or over; 76 percent of the AGI was taxable and an income tax of 31.4 percent was paid on AGI and 41.3 percent on TI.

When Congress is discussing and deciding tax policy issues, with whom is the legislator likely to place his bet? With the 51 percent (AGI under $8000) or with the 0.8 percent (AGI $50,000 and over)? This alternative explains the growing tendency, particularly apparent since the "close-the-loopholes" drive arose in the late 1950s, to free increasing amounts of personal income in the lower brackets from taxation and to increase the burden where the fewest votes are. It also explains the general bias that favors consumption and penalizes capital formation in the American tax system.

Expansion of individual income taxation was particularly strong at the state and local levels where collections multiplied fifteen times between 1952 and 1972 while all personal income multiplied only three and one-half times. The weight of the state income tax therefore became four times as heavy.

Most state income taxes were adopted in the 1930s, a few in earlier years; by 1937 there were thirty-one states levying a personal income tax. But when federal income tax rates soon after soared to unprecedented levels, states sought greener pastures and no state enacted a new income tax between 1938 and 1960. But then fiscal pressure became irresistible and by 1972 forty-four states were levying a personal income tax. Most states had meanwhile raised their former rates one or several times or tightened the tax in other ways. Some states had conferred on cities and other local governments the right to levy an income tax. All income taxes, individual and corporate, equalled 6.5 percent of all state and local revenues in 1952 and 12.4 percent in 1972, slightly over half the amount those governments gathered from consumption taxes.

Corporate Profits Taxes

Corporate profits taxes relatively eased between 1952 and 1972. The rate was reduced from 52 to 48 percent and the temporary excess profits

---

[18] This does not count the millions of persons who filed no income tax returns. Seventy-five percent of all returns reported an AGI under $13,000, 91 percent under $20,000 in 1972.

tax, imposed during the Korean war, was repealed in 1954. The role of the tax has shrunk also because corporate profits have relatively declined, that is, their share in the national economy has diminished (see pp. 85–87). Even so, profits are overstated in corporation reports. Depreciation tends to be understated substantially because, under existing tax accounting rules, it is computed on a historical basis rather than on current values and inventory gains at times of rapid price inflation are partially fictitious.

But there can be no question about the wide acceptance and appeal of the tax: "The corporate income tax is undoubtedly the most efficient system for collecting federal revenues yet devised by a frequently ingenious Congress. Indeed it may be the simplest mechanism ever developed by a modern state for exacting vast sums of money from an economy."[19] Certainly, the corporate tax is the least expensive tax to collect for the government. Much of it comes in big chunks, most of the work is done by the taxpayer, and audits are facilitated by strict accounting rules. But the broad popularity of the corporate tax is due to a general belief that it is borne by the corporation, that is, by the stockholders. It stands to reason that the more heavily the government taxes business, the more generously it can afford to treat consumers.

The important question—on which economists widely disagree—is Who pays the corporate profits tax: the stockholders, by lower dividends; the employees, by lower wages; or the consumers, by higher prices? There is no simple answer that holds true for all industries and all corporations at all times. The weight of evidence suggests, however, that in the long run a major part of the corporate profits tax is shifted forward in the price. The corporate tax rate varied from 11.0 to 13.5 percent in 1925–1929 and the net (after-tax) earnings of leading manufacturing corporations averaged 11.0 percent on net worth. In 1970–1972, when the rate stood at 48 percent, the net return still averaged 11.0 percent.[20] This suggests that all of the increase in the tax rate from 11.0–13.5 to 48.0 percent was shifted to the consumers.

If corporations are to attract the capital they need for modernization and expansion they must offer net (after-tax) returns that are competitive with alternative investment possibilities. Is it conceivable that, if there were no 48 percent corporate tax, profits would be twice as high as they now are? It appears likely that the long-run incidence of the corporate profits tax does

---

[19] Edward T. Thompson and Charles E. Silberman, "Can Anything be Done About Corporate Taxes?," *Fortune,* March 1959.

[20] First National City Bank of New York, *Monthly Economic Letter,* April 1973 and earlier issues.

not differ very significantly from a consumption tax. But the economic impact of the corporate profits tax is certainly different. It punishes the efficient producer, restricts industrial expansion, penalizes capital formation, and adversely affects the competitiveness of American industry in international trade. Still, the myth that it is largely borne by big business seems to assure the corporate profits tax a prominent place in the American tax system for as far as we can see ahead.

Consumption Taxes

Overall, consumption taxes approximately maintained their role in the American tax system between 1952 and 1972. They slightly increased as a percentage of the GNP, from 4.6 to 5.3 percent, and declined as a percentage of all governmental revenues, from 15.7 to 15.1 percent (see Table 16).

Objections to consumption taxes relate to their regressivity: they equal a higher percentage of the income of persons at the lowest income levels—who usually spend all receipts immediately on consumption goods—than of the income of the rich who save part of their income. In the absence of a national general consumption tax no conclusive and universally applicable finding on regressivity of consumption taxes can be made. Some state sales taxes, particularly thost that exempt food bought in grocery stores, are proportionate to income through much of the middle-income range and regressive only at both ends of the scale. Some sales taxes are more regressive. Opposition to consumption taxes is based not only on their regressivity but also on the fact they are not, as a rule, progressive, that is, they do not shift income from the higher to the lower brackets.

On the whole, sales taxes tend to offset, to a small extent, the sharp progressivity of the graduated income tax. This is held to be their fundamental fault. Those who view redistribution of income to be government's primary task regard a tax that does not add to progression and is proportional or even regressive as distinctly evil. Those who believe that all citizens who have the right to vote on public issues—directly or by voting for representative—ought to bear part of the burden, favor consumption taxes as a necessary part of the overall tax system. They do not deem it necesarily wrong when taxes are based not on a person's contribution to society (as expressed in earnings) but on his consumption of the products of other people's efforts.

Consumption taxes dominated the federal revenue system for the first century and a quarter of the Republic. They have been playing a sharply declining role in more recent years. In 1913 they still contributed 64 percent of all federal receipts but they dropped to 13 percent in 1952 and to a mere 9 percent in 1972. Collections of consumption taxes doubled between 1952 and 1972 (+115 percent) but other receipts tripled (+225 percent) (table 16).

Consumption taxes experienced internally divergent trends. Customs duties, which are economically and statistically treated as consumption taxes, multiplied more than sixfold while merchandise imports went up only fivefold. As a rule, import duties were increased not for revenue purpose but to raise tariff walls and, in some cases, for regulatory ends. Such protective action succeeded in boosting the average customs rate on all imported merchandise from 5.1 percent in 1952 to 6.1 percent in 1972. Imports equal only about 5 percent of the United States GNP, however, and do not play a major role in the American economy.

Gasoline tax receipts multiplied more than five times.[21] This resulted from the raising of the rate from two cents to four cents per gallon and the more than doubling (+127 percent) of gasoline consumption. The gasoline tax rate was doubled and a few other highway user or motor vehicle taxes were newly imposed or raised for the purpose of financing the Interstate Highway System and other highways. Only within the past few years have long-standing attempts to divert some highway user taxes to urban rapid transit purposes begun to succeed.

Most alcohol and tobacco taxes were maintained at existing rates as were telephone and firearms taxes and airway user levies. Much of the rest of the federal excise tax system was dismantled. All retail excise taxes (except on motor fuel) were repealed, as were stamp taxes, admissions taxes, and manufacturers and excise taxes (on appliances, matches, film and photographic equipment, sporting goods, musical instruments, light bulbs, and numerous other items). Collections from federal excise taxes, except gasoline, increased only 60 percent (from $8 to $13 billion) between 1952 and 1972 while all personal consumption expenditures went up 235 percent.

While most other countries strengthened their consumption taxes between 1952 and 1972, the United States cut its own substantially, thereby further widening the tax structural differences between itself and the rest of the world. The United States is the only industrial country whose national

---

[21] Data from *Annual Report of the Commissioner of Internal Revenue*, 1953, 1973.

government does not levy a major and general consumption tax. State and local governments increased their share of consumption tax collections from 41 percent in 1952 to 65 percent in 1972 through a series of new adoptions, steady rounds of rate boosts, and various tightening mechanisms. General retail sales and gross receipts taxes, which are by far the largest type of consumption taxes, were levied by thirty-one states in 1952, by forty-five states in 1972. There are presently thirty-nine states that impose taxes on income as well as on retail sales. Sales tax rates now vary from 2 to 7 percent with a typical rate of 4 percent, up from about 2 percent in 1952. Personal consumption expenditures multiplied three and one-half times but state sales tax collections multiplied eight times (from $2.2 to $17.6 billion), due partially to the addition of fourteen states, partially to higher rates.[22] Current sales tax rates, however, are still substantially lower than consumption tax rates in most European countries.

Social Security Taxes

Social security taxes grew at a faster rate than any other type of federal taxes and not much more slowly than state-local income taxes. Between 1952 and 1972 social security revenues jumped from $3.5 to $47.3 billion, a thirteenfold growth. Rates and tax base were repeatedly boosted in an attempt to keep up with steadily expanding benefits under the Old Age and Survivors Program and related social security programs. The Bureau of the Census classifies those receipts not as taxes but as "insurance trust revenue." As a compulsory exaction for public purposes, however, they qualify as earmarked taxes.

The main charge against the social security tax—and exclusive reliance of financing benefits from that tax—is regressivity. The tax is levied at a rate of 5.85 percent against the employer and the employee each, for a combined total of 11.7 percent of the wage up to $14,100 annually from January 1, 1975 on. Therefore all income above the cutoff of $14,100 is not taxed. It is a counterpart to the federal income tax in which there is a cutoff at the lower end, $2,050 for an individual and $2,800 for a couple. The combined social security tax rate multiplied 3.9 times between 1952 and 1972, from 3.0 to 11.7 percent, and the maximum wage subject to tax multiplied 3.9 times, from $3,600 to $14,100. In other words, the max-

---

[22] Retail sales taxes exempt food and other items in some states, but include transactions that are not retail consumption. To relate sales tax collections to personal consumption expenditures is rather crude but gives at least an approximate picture.

imum tax on the employee multiplied 15.3 times, from $54 to $825 for a person with a wage of $14,100. For a person with $3,600 earnings, the tax has multiplied only 3.9 times since 1952. The charge of regressivity against the social security tax would be justified if it were a tax like any other. But it is not. The cutoff wage base of $14,100 aplies not only to the tax but also to the benefits. In other words, while wages over $14,100 are not taxed, neither are benefits computed on a base in excess of that amount. Moreover, the benefits are skewed in favor of low-income earners throughout the scale so that persons in lower brackets are awarded monthly payments that are substantially larger in proportion to their contribution than payments awarded to persons in higher brackets.

If the contributions and benefits of social security are viewed together—as they must be if the evaluation is to be fair—they are clearly progressive, that is, individuals at the lower end of the income bracket get far more in relation to what they paid in than those at the higher end.

The Property Tax

No tax has been as bitterly assailed and maligned as the property tax, none is as widely and distinctly unpopular. Nor is there a tax whose decline and fall has been predicted more often or with greater assurance. Nearly a half century ago the standard textbook on the property tax said: "If any tax could have been eliminated by adverse criticism, the general property tax should have been eliminated long ago. . . ."[23] Twenty-five years later an eminent economist predicted: "Glancing ahead now, over the next two decades, I would expect to see the property tax all but wither away. Further relative decline is a forgone conclusion, but I would go beyond this and predict that in absolute terms property taxation is headed for oblivion."[24] As it happened, between 1954—the latest year for which statistical data were available at the time these words were spoken (at the 1956 National Tax Conference)—and calendar year 1973, property tax collections jumped from $10 to $47 billion. Withering away indeed!! Year

---

[23] Jens Peter Jensen, *Property Taxation in the United States,* (Chicago, University of Chicago Press, 1931), p. 478.

[24] George W. Mitchell (then economist for the Federal Reserve Bank of Chicago, now a member of the board of governors of the Federal Reserve System), "Is This Where We Came In?," *Proceedings of the Forty-ninth Annual Conference on Taxation* (National Tax Association, 1956), p. 492.

after year, however, articles are published under titles such as "The Trouble With Property Taxes"[25] or "What's Wrong With the Property Tax?."[26]

Despite its adversity the property tax has been growing at an amazing pace. Between 1952 and 1972 property tax collections multiplied five times (+387 percent) while all other governmental revenues went up only 270 percent, and income taxes merely 187 percent (see page 85 and table 16). As a share of all public revenues, property taxes grew from 8.6 percent in 1952 to 11.0 percent in 1972; they equaled 2.6 percent of the GNP in 1952, 3.8 percent in 1972. This is the more surprising because no tax is as restricted as the property tax by various intricate constitutional and statutory limitations in most states, none is as dependent for rate boosts on the taxpayers' approval at the ballot box. In hundreds of local elections, the voters, although grumbling, regularly approve property tax increases on their homes and the oft-predicted property taxpayers' revolt never develops. Most state governors called for property tax relief in their "state of the state" messages within the past few years and some was granted, mostly for elderly homeowners. But when the voters in four states—California, Michigan, Colorado, and Oregon—had an opportunity at the November 1972 elections to vote for proposals that would abolish or further restrict the use of property taxes, they defeated those proposals overwhelmingly. Maybe they realized—better than politicians were willing to admit—that the size of their total tax bill is set more by the magnitude of public expenditures than by the form in which taxes are levied. Perhaps they were also aware of the dependence of home rule and local autonomy—whatever vestige there is of it—and of decentralized decision making on an independent local source of taxation and that there is no adequate local substitute for property taxes.

To be sure, the role of the property tax changed decisively in the course of the twentieth century. Most of the change occurred between 1932 and 1944 when, under the impact of the depression and World War II, the share that property taxes are of public revenues dropped precipitously from 43.6 to 7.1 percent, due largely to the spectacular expansion of the income tax and the "freezing" of property taxes. Prior to the mid-1930s, property taxes had usually accounted for 40–45 percent of all governmental receipts. After World War II the property tax recovered but never regained its

---

[25] Robert Cassidy in *The New Republic*, May 15, 1971.
[26] *Changing Times*, May 1974.

former position. It has been contributing between 10 and 11 percent of public revenues since the mid-1950s. The burden of the property tax, at 3.8 percent of the GNP in 1972, is barely higher than it had been in 1902 when it stood at 3.4 percent. The aggregate of all other governmental revenues meanwhile soared from 4.8 percent of the GNP in 1902 to 30.9 percent in 1972.[27] It is the combined burden of the other taxes that makes the property tax so hard to bear.

As a percentage of total national wealth property taxes have increased by about one-third since the turn of the century.

PROPERTY TAXES AND NATIONAL TANGIBLE WEALTH, 1902 and 1968

	National Tangible Wealth (in billions)	Property Tax Collections (in millions)	Property Taxes as a Percentage of National Tangible Wealth
1902	$ 92	$ 706	0.76%
1968	3,079	30,673	1.00

SOURCES: National wealth for 1902: Raymond W. Goldsmith, Dorothy S. Brady, and Horst Menderhausen, *A Study of Savings in the United States,* Princeton, N.J.: Princeton University Press, 1956), vol. 3, table W-1 (pt. 2), p. 14.

National wealth for 1968: U.S. Department of Commerce, *Statistical Abstract of the United States, 1973,* p. 343.

Property taxes: See table 16.

The extraordinary increase between 1952 and 1972, when property tax collections multiplied fivefold (table 16), represented a catch-up process to make up at least in part for the lag during the preceding twenty years (1932–1952), when property taxes less than doubled while the GNP multiplied fivefold. As a percentage of the GNP, property taxes then fell from 6.7 to 2.6 percent. In the succeeding twenty years (1952–1972) they climbed to 3.8 percent of the GNP.

---

[27] Between 1952 and 1972 property taxes grew at a faster rate than other taxes. As a percentage of the GNP they increased from 2.6 to 3.8 percent, that is, by 1.2 percent of the GNP. All other governmental receipts grew by 3.8 percent of the GNP (from 27.1 to 30.9 percent). See table 16.

Most of the $33.5 billion increase in property taxes between 1952 and 1972 was levied on newly created or increased values. New construction totaled $1,935 billion (in *constant* 1972 dollars) of which $1,363 billion was private construction: $762 billion residential, $601 billion commercial, industrial, etc.[28] A 2 percent property tax on $1,363 billion of new private structures alone (not counting the land) would amount to $27 billion in taxes. This, of course, does not take into account either the value of structures destroyed or abandoned or depreciation. But destruction and depreciation were largely offset by a simultaneous rise in values. The composite construction cost index increased 101.4 percent between 1952 and 1972, while the Consumers Price Index went up only 57.6 percent.[29] That pushed up the value of existing buldings; older houses did not lose in value but often sold for more than they had cost ten or twenty years before. Land costs and acreage multiplied even faster than construction costs. Moreover, privately held real estate was helped through various public improvements such as roads, street lighting, bridges, sewers, schools, hospitals, etc. New public construction totaled $572 billion (in *constant* 1972 dollars) between 1952 and 1971. It was generally not taxable, but helped to raise values of adjoining private real estate.

No charge is levied more frequently against the property tax than that it singles out the homeowner and places a discriminatory and intolerably heavy burden on him. On closer analysis that charge makes no sense whatsoever. All United States residents, and all taxpayers, are either homeowners or renters. Would it be fairer to place a larger share of the load on the renters? They pay a proportionate share anyway: landlords recoup the net cost of property taxes and other costs, plus a profit, through rents. Currently 65 percent of all occupied dwellings are inhabited by their owners, 35 percent are rented.

Some economists have developed a theory in recent years according to which the residential property tax does not rest on the user but falls on

---

[28] Computed from U.S. Department of Commerce, *Construction Statistics 1915–1964, A Supplement to Construction Review,* 1966, and subsequent issues of *Construction Review* to 1973. The totals cited above do not include a huge number of additions, restorations, and remodeling.

[29] Construction costs have been rising faster than other price indexes, consumers or wholesale, for as long as those indexes have been in existence. Between 1915 (earliest year available) and 1972 the consumers price index (CPI) increased 312 percent, while the composite construction cost index went up 769 percent, or two and a half times as much. Source: see footnote 28. See also U.S., Bureau of the Census, *Historical Statistics of the United States Colonial Times to 1957,* 1960; *Economic Report of the President,* January 1974.

capital and is either less regressive than widely assumed or may even be progressive.[30] It is doubtful, however, that this theory will be widely accepted.

Property taxes now account for 11 percent of all governmental revenues. About 47 percent of all property taxes is derived from residential property and 65 percent of that from owner-occupied homes. This means that homeowners contribute about one-third of all property tax collections, which accounts for a mere 3.4 percent of all governmental revenues in the United States. Since homeowners as a group are economically somewhat better situated than renters, they account for at least 70 percent of all income received in the country, though they equal only about 65 percent of the population. In all likelihood they contribute directly or indirectly at least 70 percent of all public revenues. This means that the homeowner pays about 5 percent of his total tax burden through the property tax, 95 percent directly or indirectly through other forms.

Why then is the property tax so unpopular? Because it is the only tax of which the average homeowner and taxpayer is painfully aware because he has to pay it directly to a tax collection agency. Most of the income tax is deducted from his pay before he ever sees it, sales taxes are collected in small amounts on purchases, and business taxes are, when shifted forward, included in the price of goods and services and thereby hidden. Both the visibility of the property tax and the need to actually pay it over at a particular time in a sizeable amount are primarily responsible for the general aversion to this type of tax.

Another oft-repeated charge is that property taxes are not only full of exemptions which erode the tax base but also regressive because they place a heavier burden on residences and low-priced homes than on commercial property and high priced homes.

It is of course true that there are many exemptions in the property tax, especially for public, educational, and charitable properties. In the national average about one-fourth of all real estate is thus left free of tax. But we should remember that the federal income tax reaches only half of all personal income (see p. 89). By comparison with the federal income tax, therefore, the property tax looks pretty good with regard to its tax base and exemptions therefrom.

---

[30] Henry Aron, "The Property Tax: Progressive or Regressive? A New View of Property Tax Incidence," *The American Economic Review*, May 1974; Richard A. Musgrave, "Is a Property Tax on Housing Regressive?," *The American Economic Review*, May 1974.

Assertions that residences are assessed at higher ratios to their market value than commercial or industrial properties are conclusively refuted in the property value reports of the quinquennial surveys of the Bureau of the Census. Nor is there a shred of evidence in the annual statistical reports of the Department of Housing and Urban Development (Federal Housing Authority) that low-priced homes are taxed at higher ratios to value than high-priced homes.[31] Because the acquisition price of a family home tends to rise more slowly than family income, there is a regressive tendency apparent in the relation between real estate taxes and family income for both new and existing homes in the Federal Housing Authority statistics, mostly at the extreme ends of the income scale.

This is part of the broader problem of individuals or families who live in homes whose value is disproportionate to their resources, who occupy living space beyond their means, or who try to maintain general standards in excess of their income. In the case of earned income this simply means that people aim to consume more than they produce. That raises problems, particularly in the case of some elderly homeowners, which have been turned into a political issue with emotional connotations. It could be effectively resolved by deferring some of the taxes for the period of the aged person's occupancy. Many states have adopted "circuit breakers," which forgive rather than postpone the taxes. This helps the person's heirs to inherit a bigger estate and appears to be an overly generous remedy.

Residential real estate taxes average about 2 percent of market value, with variations from 1 percent or less in some southern states and Hawaii to nearly 3 percent or more in such cities as Boston, Milwaukee, Newark, Philadelphia, and Buffalo. At a time when governmental revenues and expenditures equal between 42 and 44 percent of national or personal income (see table 13) there seems to be nothing wrong with allocating about 5 percent of that total—or the equivalent of less than 2 percent of the GNP—according to the consumption of living space.

Homeowners are certainly not singled out for extra burdens. In fact, they obtain benefits under provisions of the Internal Revenue Code that are denied to renters. The deduction for income tax purposes of mortgage interest and real estate taxes and the nontaxability of imputed income from owner-occupied homes offset a substantial part of the home property tax bill. The renter, who pays for these items in his rental, is granted no such benefits and is at a serious disadvantage. On balance, the homeowner does

---

[31] U.S., Department of Housing and Urban Development, *Statistical Yearbook.*

taxwise much better than the renter. If there is tax discrimination, then it is *for* and *not against* the homeowner. This explains the remarkable growth of condominiums in recent years—with the main development yet to come.

It is, however, true that the federal income tax deduction of real estate taxes (and other state and local taxes) introduces an element of regressivity: a person in the top bracket offsets 70 percent of his deductible items in his tax liability, a person in the lowest bracket only 14 percent. What this amounts to is that state and local taxes are really not as regressive by their own characteristics—if at all—as by their treatment in the federal income tax. This could be corrected by shifting from deductions from AGI to tax credits against tax liability.

Many of the deficiencies or inequities in the property tax are the result of inadequate or faulty administration. Assessments are frequently made at a fraction of the value mandated by state constitutions and statutes, often at one-third or one-fifth of current market value. This leads to great unevenness—but strangely enough the courts, when called upon to provide redress, have shown a great reluctance to order administrators to set values as provided by law. At least some progress has been made in providing greater horizontal equity, as the narrowing *coefficient of dispersion* of assessed values in the quinquennial surveys of the Bureau of the Census proves.

A widespread and detrimental practice, however, is the undervaluation of land versus improvements. If anything, there ought to be greater emphasis on land values than on improvements. This could have a most wholesome impact on urban and suburban areas in curbing decay and encouraging sound development.

Though in ill repute, the property tax is an essential and important part of our tax system, indispensable if some semblance of meaningful local government is to be preserved.

— 4 —

Public Expenditures: Government as a Well

In FY 1972 an aggregate amount of $397 billion was spent by governments in the United States (see table 4a)—61 percent of it by the federal government, 20.4 percent by the fifty state governments, and the remaining 18.6 percent by 78,218 local governments.[1] Outlays exceeded revenues by $15 billion, all at the federal level.

Public spending has been setting a new record nearly every year since inception, multiplying 239 times since the turn of the twentieth century; the GNP multiplied only 53 times. This means that governmental outlays have grown 4.5 times faster than the nation's income and product—from 8.0 percent of the GNP in 1902 to 36.1 percent of the GNP in 1972 (see tables 4a and b). In other words, government's "living standards" expanded in the course of the twentieth century more than four times faster than those of the average American family.

Upward Trends

Public spending did not rise at a constant pace. Wars, economic and political fluctuations here and abroad, and other events speeded up or slowed down the *rate* of growth. But spending never went back to its prior level after an upswing. The secular trend points strongly and consistently up.

When we look at the dollar amounts it appears that most of the increase took place in recent years. In the first decade of the twentieth century the increase in public expenditures was minimal ($1.6 billion). Dividing the

---

[1] Local governments include 3,044 counties (virtually unchanged for many decades); 18,517 municipalities and 16,991 townships (both changed little); 23,885 special districts (whose number is increasing); and 15,781 school districts, whose number has been going down consistently, from 196,000 in 1918 to 59,000 in 1952. The spending shares shown above were computed by attributing expenditures to the governments that originated the funds, that is, raised the taxes. Without such an adjustment, intergovernmental grants would be shown twice—with the granting and the grantee government.

remaining sixty years into three twenty-year periods, the respective *increases* in public outlays were successively $9 billion, $87 billion, $298 billion (table 4a). But if we view developments in *relative* terms and express magnitudes in percent of national economic totals we obtain an entirely different picture.

In the first decade of the twentieth century government expenditures grew only slightly faster than the GNP. They jumped at an extraordinary rate in the next twenty-year period and have been slowing down *relatively* ever since.

GROWTH RATES OF GNP AND GOVERNMENTAL EXPENDITURES IN TWENTY-YEAR PERIODS, 1913–1972

Fiscal Year	GNP*	Governmental Expenditures*	Governmental Expenditure Growth Rate as a Percentage of GNP Growth
1913–1932	82%	287%	250%
1932–1952	404	703	74
1952–1972	226	298	32

SOURCE: Tables 4a and b
* GNP and governmental expenditures are for *fiscal* years.

GROWTH OF GOVERNMENTAL EXPENDITURES AS A PERCENTAGE OF GNP 1913–1972

Fiscal Year	Governmental Expenditures as a Percentage of GNP	Increase Over Preceding Period	Percent Increase
1913	8.8%		
1932	18.6	9.8%	111%
1952	29.6	11.0	59
1972	36.1	6.5	22

SOURCE: Tables 4a and b.

The most significant fact that emerges from the statistics presented above is that governmental expenditures, though they increased by nearly

$300 billion between 1952 and 1972, expanded at a moderate rate in those two decades when compared to the simultaneous growth in the nation's economy and viewed in the perspective of historical trends. It must of course not be forgotten that World Wars I and II occurred during the 1913–1932 and 1932–1952 periods respectively and affected expenditure totals. The role and impact of national defense on governmental spending trends is discussed later.

In FY 1972 governmental expenditures, by census definitions, equaled 36.1 percent of the GNP and 44.3 percent of both national income and personal income. If trends continue upward at recent rates, public spending will reach and exceed 50 percent of national income and personal income in the course of the 1980s.

Using definitions of national income accounts, governmental expenditures in *calendar* year 1972 equaled 32.1 percent of the GNP, 39.4 percent of national income, and 39.5 percent of personal income (see tables 21–25).

International comparisons of governmental expenditures are imprecise despite substantial progress made in accounting and statistical methods by the economics divisions of the United Nations and the OECD within the past ten to fifteen years. The most recent comparison by the OECD (table 20) ranks the United States twelfth among twenty-three countries. Current governmental expenditures in the United States are shown in table 20 at 30.9 percent of gross domestic product in 1971. Even at 32.1 percent, according to national income accounts, the United States would hold the same rank among the twenty-three countries: exactly in the middle. Several major European countries, with Sweden in the lead, allocate a larger share of their resources to government than the United States; Switzerland, Spain, and Japan allocate less. The arithmetic mean for the twenty-three countries equals 29.7 percent, slightly below the 30.9 percent shown for the United States.

In evaluating these data, however, it should be remembered that most countries, *except* those in a warlike situation, as well as the Soviet Union and other Communist countries, devote a smaller share of their resources to national defense than the United States. While military outlays equaled about 7 percent of the GNP in the United States in 1972, they varied between 2 percent and slightly over 4 percent in many European countries. This means that many of those countries, and particularly the leading industrial non-Communist nations, devote a larger share of their national product and of their public expenditures to the support of domestic services than the United States.

There is no adequate statistical basis at this time for a more specific comparison between the United States and other countries of nonwar-connected expenditures. Although the United Nations publishes in its annual *Statistical Yearbook* public revenue and expenditure reports from many countries, in most cases they do not include governments below the national level (state, province, municipalities, etc.) and their comparability with United States statistics is very doubtful because of differences in comprehensiveness and definitions.

A Declining Share for National Security

For a meaningful analysis of public expenditures—whether international or historical for the United States—a distinction must be made between outlays for national security and those for domestic purposes. Tables 4a and b show historical breakdowns for *(a)* national defense and international relations, *(b)* veterans benefits and services, *(c)* interest on general debt, and *(d)* all other functions, mainly for domestic public services.

It is apparent that national security outlays (national defense and international relations) were relatively insignificant prior to World War I, averaging less than 1 percent of the GNP. After a short-lived jump in World War I—to a maximum of $13.5 billion or 16.7 percent of the GNP in FY 1919—they dropped back to slightly over 1 percent of the GNP in the 1920s and 1930s. World War II lifted national security costs to unprecedented heights—to a maximum of $85.5 billion or 42.3 percent of the GNP in FY 1944—with a subsequent low of $16.1 billion or 6.6 percent of the GNP in FY 1948 (of which $10.6 billion, equal to 4.4 percent of the GNP, were for military functions).[2] The Korean conflict and the ensuing cold war lifted the cost of national security abruptly to 14.3 percent of the GNP in 1952, from which level it has been declining ever since, to 7.2 percent of the GNP in 1972. It was running below 6 percent of the GNP in 1974.

Explosion in Domestic Spending

It was in domestic spending that the most dramatic development took place between 1952 and 1972. From 6.0 percent of the GNP in 1902

---

[2] Data for FY 1919 from Kendrick, *A Century and a Half of Federal Expenditures.* Data for 1944 and 1948 from U.S., Bureau of the Census, *Historical Statistics on Governmental Finances and Employment,* 1967 Census of Governments. 1969.

domestic spending moved up gradually to 9.0 percent in 1922 and to 13.9 percent in 1932. There was then a slight decline to 12.1 percent and 12.2 percent in 1942 and 1952. This means that it took half a century, from 1902 to 1952, for public outlays for domestic functions to double their share of the GNP, from 6.0 to 12.2 percent. In the succeeding twenty years it more than doubled again, from 12.2 to 25.7 percent. The following table shows that while the sharpest rise in defense costs took place between 1932 and 1952 (World War II and the cold war) the steepest rise in domestic costs occurred between 1952 and 1972.

GOVERNMENTAL EXPENDITURES FOR NATIONAL SECURITY AND DOMESTIC SERVICES AS A PERCENTAGE OF GNP, 1913–1972

Fiscal Year	National Defense and International Relations	Domestic Services	Increase and Decrease in Percentage Points of GNP	
			National Defense and International Relations	Domestic Services
1913	0.7%	7.1%		
1932	1.1	13.9	+ 0.4%	+6.8%
1952	14.3	12.2	+13.2	− 1.7
1972	7.2	25.7	− 7.1	+13.5

SOURCE: Table 4b

Developments in domestic spending from 1952 to 1972 are put into focus even more clearly in an analysis of federal expenditures (tables 5a and b).

In 1952 federal expenditures for domestic services totaled $13.4 billion; since that time they have multiplied *ten* times.[3] This means that between 1952 and 1972 as much was added to federal outlays for domestic purposes *every 2 years* as had been in the preceding *163 years* (since 1789). In other words, federal involvement in public services and benefits prior to 1952, including the New Deal of the 1930s, had been relatively small. A real explosion occured in the twenty years subsequent to 1952. This is what happened in terms of the GNP: outlays for domestic purposes equaled 1.1

---

[3] Domestic services as defined in tables 5a and b: all expenditures except national defense and international relations, veterans benefits and services, and interest on the general debt.

percent of the GNP in 1902, 2.8 percent in 1932 (the depth of the depression), and 3.9 percent in 1952; between 1952 and 1972 they jumped from 3.9 to 12.1 percent of the GNP. Where did the funds, equal to 8.2 percent of the GNP, come from? Not from higher taxes, because federal taxes were repeatedly, if only slightly, cut so that federal revenues declined by one GNP percentage point, from 21.3 to 20.3 percent.

More than four-fifths of the funds that made it possible between 1952 and 1972 to blow up federal domestic spending to three times its former GNP share and ten times its dollar amount came from cutting national security's share into half: outlays for national defense and international relations dropped from 14.3 to 7.2 percent of the GNP. The remainder beyond the result of economic growth was "raised" by changing from a balanced budget in 1952—a surplus of $230 million—to a huge deficit of $18.8 billion (=1.7 percent of the GNP) in 1972.[4]

That the nature of the federal government underwent its most significant change ever between 1952 and 1972 is apparent from the allocation of its resources. In 1902 87 percent of the federal expenditures went for what may be called the "traditional"federal functions: national defense, international relations, post office, veterans services and benefits, interest on the general debt, financial administration, and general control. All other outlays accounted for a mere 13 percent of the budget. Half a century later, after two world wars, the Great Depression, and the New Deal, the share of those "other" outlays had grown very moderately to 19 percent. By 1972, however, those "other" outlays accounted for 53 percent, or a *majority* of federal spending. Most of those services, largely in the social welfare field, had previously been either insignificant or nonexistent. In other words, until about twenty years ago, the dominant functions of the national government were—as they had been for over 160 years—national defense and related programs, ministerial activities such as the post office, and general and financial administration. Those activities then accounted for more than four-fifths of federal financial resources.

Between 1952 and 1972 the national government came to play not only a larger role than it ever had before but also a far different role. Social services and income redistribution, previously of minor significance or unknown, have become the major and controlling elements in the budget

---

[4] According to Bureau of the Census definitions and reports. According to the Bureau of Management and Budget, the surplus amounted to $49 million in FY 1952 (consolidated cash budget) and the deficit to $23.2 billion in FY 1972 (unified budget). Source: *The Budget of the United States Government, Fiscal Year 1975*, p. 331.

DISTRIBUTION OF FEDERAL EXPENDITURES BETWEEN "TRADITIONAL"
AND OTHER FUNCTIONS, FISCAL YEARS 1902, 1952, AND 1972

	1902 (in millions)	Percent	1952 (in millions)	Percent	1972 (in millions)	Percent
Traditional functions						
National Defense and international relations	$165		$48,187		$ 79,258	
Veterans benefits and services	141		2,428		6,882	
Interest on general debt	29		4,262		17,114	
Post office	126		2,612		9,366	
General control and financial administration	34		608		2,245	
Total	495	87%	58,097	81%	114,865	47%
All other expenditures	77	13	13,471	19	127,321	53
Total expenditures	$572	100%	$71,568	100%	$242,186	100%

SOURCE: U.S., Bureau of the Census, *Historical Statistics on Governmental Finances and Employment,* 1967 Census of Governments, 1969; idem, *Governmental Finances in 1971–1972,* 1973.

and thereby the core function of the United States government. It is most remarkable that such a fundamental change, from the concepts that had prevailed from the inception of the Republic to the "service state" or "welfare state," could have been brought about without amending the Constitution. To be sure, some amendments, such as the Sixteenth (income tax) and the Seventeenth (direct election of senators) may have contributed toward that end. They were passed much earlier but their full impact took some years to be felt. In the final analysis, the change in the basic nature and purpose of the federal government was brought about by statutory and appropriative action of Congress, mostly on the initiative of incumbent presidents, aided by both a reinterpretation of several provisions of the Constitution by the Supreme Court, particularly with regard to the substantive meaning of the welfare clause (Art. 1, sec. 8) and the equal rights clause (Amend. 14, sec. 1), and the deactivation of the Tenth Amendment. Someone reading the leading newspapers and journals about public expenditure trends or reviewing hundreds of speeches on the subject in and out of Congress would normally reach the conclusion that the years 1952–1972 were characterized by an enormous increase in military spending, financed by cutting domestic services and starving social welfare programs. But the record shows that just the opposite was taking place. Interestingly enough this was particularly evident from 1969 on when an administration with a program of public frugality and fiscal restraint held office. When we compare expenditures between FY 1969 and FY 1975 we find these facts:

Federal Expenditures in Fiscal Years 1969 and 1975(A)

	1969 (in millions)	1975* (in millions)	Dollar Increase (in millions)	Percent Increase
Total	$184,548	$304,445	+ $119,897	+ 65
National security	89,264	95,104	+ 5,840	+ 7
National defense	81,232	87,729	+ 6,497	+ 8
International affairs	3,785	4,103	+ 318	+ 8
Space research and technology	4,247	3,272	− 975	− 23
Interest	15,791	29,122	+ 13,331	+ 84
Veterans benefits and services	7,640	13,612	+ 5,972	+ 78
All other (domestic purposes)	71,853	166,607	+ 94,754	+132

Source: *The Budget of the United States Government, Fiscal Year 1975,* table 17.

* As estimated in the president's budget.

The picture that emerges is truly astounding. It took 180 years, from 1789 to 1969, for federal expenditures for domestic purposes to reach a level of $72 billion. In the succeeding 6 years that total more than doubled, jumping from $72 to $167 billion, an increase of 132 percent. If this rate of growth were to continue for the next quarter century, federal expenditures for domestic purposes would amount to $5.7 trillion in FY 2000.

A growth in outlays for domestic purposes of that dimension over the next twenty-five years is hardly conceivable, save under conditions of a runaway inflation in which the dollar loses much or most of its remaining value. Such inflationary conditions could be created if the size of budget deficits of the early 1970s were to continue or increase further. But this is improbable. Nor does it appear likely that the military budget can be cut much further while maintaining a national defense that is worth having.

How the Domestic Spending Growth Was Financed

Tax boosts of the magnitude required to maintain the fantastic growth rate of domestic spending that has prevailed in recent years are extremely unlikely to be politically or economically acceptable in the years ahead. Congress hardly ever enacted major increases in federal taxes except under emergency conditions or for purposes of national defense and social insurance contributions.

It seems probable then that the rate of increase that domestic functions in the social welfare field enjoyed in the past six years will have to slow down sharply. But when we listen to the chorus that complains about the austerity of the early 1970s–the miserliness, cutbacks, threatened or actual vetoes, and fund impounding—and when we view bills under consideration in Congress, we may wonder when and how such a slowdown will occur.

The record is clear. Defense cutbacks were the main source from which resources for increased social programs were drawn in the past six years. As the table, Federal Expenditures in Fiscal Years 1969 and 1975 (B), on page 114 shows, social programs increased their share of the United States budget by 15 percentage points as defense lost 15.2 points; social programs increased their percentage of the GNP by 3.3 points, defense lost 3.0 points.

FEDERAL EXPENDITURES IN FISCAL YEARS 1969 AND 1975(B)

	Expenditures 1969 1975 (in millions)	Per-cent In-crease	Percentage of Total Expenditures 1969 1975	Percentage of GNP 1969 1975
Total expenditures	$184,548 $304,445	+ 65%	100% 100%	20.5% 20.9%
National defense	81,232 87,729	+ 8	44.0 28.8	9.0 6.0
Social welfare	55,881 137,890	+147	30.3 45.3	6.2 9.5
Income security	37,748 100,071	+165	20.5 32.9	4.2 6.9
Retirement and dis-ability	30,028 75,114	+150	16.3 24.7	3.3 5.2
Unemploy-ment	2,583 7,065	+174	1.4 2.3	0.3 0.5
Public assistance	4,273 14,505	+240	2.3 4.8	0.5 1.0
Social service	864 3,387	+292	0.5 1.1	0.1 .2
Health	11,604 26,282	+126	6.3 8.6	1.3 1.8
Education and man-power	6,529 11,537	+ 77	3.5 3.8	0.7 0.8
Other domes-tic functions	15,973 28,717	+ 80	8.6 9.4	1.8 2.0
All other expenditures	31,463 50,109	+ 59	17.1 16.5	3.5 3.4

SOURCE: *The Budget of the United States Government, Fiscal Year 1975,* table 17.

The biggest percentage increases in major functions took place in income maintenance (165 percent) and in health (126 percent). Education and other domestic functions advanced 77 and 80 percent respectively; "all other expenditures," mostly interest and veterans programs, advanced 59 percent.

The ironic part of this is that in the two fields that advanced most rapidly in the past six years, income maintenance and health, huge new federal programs were proposed but failed of adoption. In 1969 the administration recommended the Family Assistance Plan, a form of guaranteed annual income, which would have immediately more than doubled the number of public assistance recipients. The bill passed the House of Representatives twice but was rejected by the Senate in 1972. National health insurance plans were proposed by the administration and in a more generous form by members of the Senate majority. If passed they will add huge amounts to current outlays. Those bills are still pending at this writing—as are suggestions for guaranteed annual income plans that are far more expansive (and expensive) than the Family Assistance Plan would have been.

Several measures to boost education funds were proposed and adopted in recent years but the campaign for major federal aid to educational institutions—public schools and colleges—failed again, though it had been conducted for more years and by more sizeable organized forces, and probably with firmer determination and effort, than most similar movements in other fields.

Had the proposed major health, education and welfare bills been enacted, federal spending would certainly have climbed even faster than the exorbitant rate at which it did go up in the past six years.

National defense outlays are shown as having increased $6.5 billion or 8 percent between 1969 and 1975. But this tells only part of the story. Half the dollar increase went for increased benefits to retired military personnel. Pay boosts—including those caused by the conversion to a voluntary army—to a sharply reduced military force totaled more than the other half of the cost increase.

An increase of 8 percent in expenditures for defense during a period when the general price level went up 42 percent would suggest a reduction of 24 percent in *constant* dollars. But this far understates the actual reduction. The size of the armed forces was reduced from 3,506,000 to 2,152,000 (planned for 1975), a cut of 39 percent in manpower strength, while the military payroll went up 25 percent. Research and development fell behind in *constant* dollars but the sharpest cutback took place in procurement. A 32 percent reduction in the dollar amount at a time of price increases of 42 percent amounts to an effective decline of 52 percent.

SELECTED ITEMS OF MILITARY EXPENDITURES, FISCAL YEARS 1969 AND 1975

	1969 (in millions)	1975 (in millions)	Increase or Decrease (in millions)	(%)
Total national defense	$81,232	$87,729	+$6,497	+ 8
Less: retired military personnel	2,444	5,685	+ 3,241	+133
Remainder	78,788	82,044	+ 3,256	+ 4
Less: military personnel	21,374	26,611	+ 5,237	+ 25
Remainder	57,414	55,433	− 1,981	− 4
Operation and maintenance	22,227	24,917	+ 2,690	+ 12
Research and development	7,457	8,890	+ 1,433	+ 19
Procurement	23,988	16,359	− 7,629	− 32
All other	3,742	5,267	+ 1,525	+ 41

SOURCE: *The Budget of the United States Government, Fiscal Year 1975,* table 17.

Outlays for national defense, not including military retired pay—expressed in *constant* dollars—were reported by the Office of Management and Budget to be lower in FY 1974 and FY 1975 than in any year since the post–World War II disarmament period of 1947–1950; they were estimated 23 percent *below* FY 1952 in FY 1975.[5] Nondefense outlays in *constant* dollars were estimated 250 percent (=3.5 times) *above* FY 1952 in FY 1975.

Expansion of domestic programs is of course no reason per se for raising defense expenditures at a similar rate. The requirements of national security must be evaluated in the light of the strength and actions of our potential adversaries, who have been arming at a rapid pace, especially in the past twelve years. If the justification for reducing defense appropriations from 64 percent of the total budget in FY 1952 to 27 percent in FY 1975 (excluding retired military pay)[6] is that such a reduction seemed to be the most feasible way or the only way by which funds for the desired larger

---

[5] *Congressional Record,* May 14, 1974, p. H 3820

[6] Ibid.

social programs could be obtained, because neither tax boosts nor higher deficits were likely to be politically possible, then that is a different story. That was made particularly clear in the National Urban Coalition's *Counterbudget.*[7] The strategy to be used with members of Congress was explained by Representative Lee Aspin, author of an amendment cutting defense procurement appropriations adopted by the House on July 31, 1973. He said that it was necessary to convince congressmen "that you've got to cut the defense budget if you want sufficient money for your own programs."

Comparisons of the magnitude of defense outlays between the Soviet Union and the United States are extremely tenuous because there are no reliable data on classification methods or on pricing in the Soviet military budget. But it appears that the Soviet military expenditures have doubled over the past two decades,[8] and the relative military strength of the two countries, according to several reports, has shifted in favor of the Soviet Union in recent years.

According to CIA estimates the Soviet Union is now spending more for military purposes than the United States and has nearly twice as many men under arms.[9] With the Russian GNP less than half the size of the American GNP, the Soviet Union is devoting more than twice its GNP share to defense than is the United States. Congressional estimates of the cost of Vietnam operations and of potential savings ranged between $20 and $29 billion a year, and hopes were expressed that an equivalent "peace dividend" would be available after the war. These hopes, however, overlooked the fact that many of the military exercises, maneuvers, and other activities would have to go on in any case and that much of the Vietnam operations were carried on by depleting the rest of the defense establishment of its best forces and equipment. Military manpower was reduced by 1.3 million between 1969 and 1975, that is, by over twice the number of soldiers who had been in Vietnam.

To what extent development and procurement of advanced weapons systems can safely be reduced, at a time when our potential opponents in their pursuit of military superiority continue an intensive armament program with ever more sophisticated weapons, is a difficult question to

---

[7] Robert S. Benson and Harold Wolman, eds., *Counterbudget: A Blueprint for Changing National Priorities 1971–1976* (New York: Praeger, 1971).

[8] *Congressional Record,* December 12, 1972, p. S 22618.

[9] "Not All Is Going Well in Russia," *U. S. News and World Report,* September 9, 1974.

answer. The fact is that United States defense procurement has been cut to half its size over the past six years.

Of the total federal expenditure increase between 1969 and 1975 of $120 billion, 79 percent went for domestic purposes, 11 percent for interest, 5 percent for veterans services and benefits, and a mere 5 percent for national defense; the latter was not used for an increase in military strength, manpower, or weapons, but entirely for higher military pay and pensions.

A comparison of governmental expenditures in 1952 and 1972 on a calendar year basis by national income account concepts is shown in tables 21–23. While the specific figures differ from those on a fiscal year basis by Bureau of the Census or unified budget concepts, they reflect identical trends over the twenty-year period.

Table 21 discloses that while national defense outlays grew 68 percent, close to the rate of price increases, outlays for health, education and welfare multiplied fifteen times—from $5.9 to $89.7 billion. To be sure, the federal government participated in the financing of education and health only in an insignificant way in 1952, contributing 4 and 13 percent respectively. By 1972 its share of education costs had advanced to 10 percent, of health costs to 72 percent. While national defense accounted in 1952 for 66 percent of all federal outlays, domestic services absorbed more than half the total budget by 1972.

Expenditures of state and local governments (table 22) were entirely for domestic purposes and advanced from 7.3 percent of the GNP to 14.2 percent between 1952 and 1972.[10] Protagonists of domestic expenditures still claim, however, that those services are being starved. With population growing 33 percent and prices rising 58 percent, a constant level of state and local services would have required in 1972 slightly over twice the outlays of 1952. But aggregate spending multiplied 6.5 times, education and welfare 8 times.

When we view the combined expenditures of *all* governments in the United States, federal, state, and local (table 23), we find that the cost of domestic services increased at ten times the rate of defense (645 percent increase vs. 68 percent) and that domestic services had advanced from 37 percent of all outlays to 69 percent, from 10.0 percent of the GNP to 22.3 percent. A year-to-year comparison of federal expenditures between 1952

---

[10] Includes expenditures from federal grants. Therefore table 22 (state and local expenditures) and table 21 (federal expenditures) together total more than table 23 (governmental expenditures). Federal grants to state and local governments would have to be netted out to equal total governmental expenditures.

and 1972 (table 24) shows that defense outlays fluctuated within a narrow range between 1952 and 1965, jumped from $50 to $80 billion under the impact of expanded Vietnam action, and have remained at approximately that level ever since. Domestic expenditures followed an unrelenting upward trend throughout the period with no slowdown noticeable during the years of maximum Vietnam action. But when defense outlays stabilized at the $80 billion level, domestic outlays started to advance at an unprecedented rate.

It may be of interest to follow the growth of domestic expenditures by presidential terms:

GROWTH RATE OF FEDERAL DOMESTIC EXPENDITURES
BY PRESIDENTIAL TERMS, 1952–1972

1952–1956	48%
1956–1960	75
1952–1960	158
1960–1964	41
1964–1968	66
1960–1968	134
1968–1972	76
1968–1976	76
(projected at 1968–1972 rate)	

SOURCE: Computed from table 24.

It is apparent that domestic expenditures grew at a faster rate in the second terms of the Eisenhower and Kennedy-Johnson administrations than in the first, and that the growth rates were higher during the Eisenhower and Nixon administrations than they were during the Kennedy-Johnson administrations. This is contrary to what is widely believed and what might have been expected from the announced goals of those administrations. There was certainly no slowdown in domestic spending growth during the Vietnam War, though there was a speed-up when it ended.

The 76 percent rise in federal domestic expenditures during the first four years of the Nixon administration was more than 50 percent faster than in the first terms of Presidents Eisenhower, Kennedy, and Johnson. If the 1968–1972 rate is projected to 1976, domestic expenditures will have increased by 211 percent between 1968 and 1976—the steepest rise in any eight-year period under review.

Table 25 shows the year-to-year growth in the cost of domestic services in the aggregate of all governments from 1952 to 1972, with each year establishing a new record.

Domestic Spending Growth in Perspective

Domestic spending gained momentum and grew by increasingly greater amounts as time went on (see table 25). Five-year amounts of increase averaged $4,310 million between 1952 and 1957; $6,599 million between 1957 and 1962; $10,780 million between 1962 and 1967; $22,899 million between 1967 and 1972. To be sure, the *rate* of growth remained stable for much of the twenty-year period, but jumped in the last five years of that period as follows:

$$1952–1957 \quad + 62\%$$
$$1957–1962 \quad + 59\%$$
$$1962–1967 \quad + 60\%$$
$$1967–1972 \quad + 80\%$$

The true dimension of the trend in governmental domestic spending can probably be appreciated more fully if it is compared with simultaneous developments in personal consumption expenditures:

GOVERNMENTAL EXPENDITURES FOR DOMESTIC PURPOSES AND PERSONAL CONSUMPTION EXPENDITURES, 1952 AND 1972

	1952	1972	Percent
	(in billions)		Increase
Governmental expenditures for domestic purposes	$ 34.5	$257.5	645%
Personal consumption expenditures	216.7	726.5	235
Governmental domestic expenditures as a percentage of personal consumption expenditures	16%	35%	

SOURCE: Table 23.

The picture appears even clearer when we compare public and private spending in *constant* dollars and on a per capita basis:

PUBLIC DOMESTIC AND PRIVATE PERSONAL SPENDING
PER FAMILY OF FOUR, 1952 AND 1972, IN 1972 DOLLARS

	1952	*1972*	*Percent Increase*
Governmental expenditures for domestic purposes	$1,342	$ 4,931	267%
Personal consumption expenditures	8,418	13,916	65

SOURCE: Table 23 and *Economic Report of the President,* 1974, table C-18.

An average family of four expended (in 1972 dollars) for its personal consumption in 1952 $8,418 and in 1972 $13,916, an increase of 65 percent. Governmental spending for domestic purposes for a family of four meanwhile jumped from $1,342 to $4,931, an increase of 267 percent.

This suggests an increase in public versus private consumption of unprecedented dimensions, a spectacular shift from the area of free choice to the area of compulsion. In 1958 John Kenneth Galbraith complained in *The Affluent Society* that the consumer was luxuriating by being permitted to spend too large a share of his earnings according to his own vulgar whims while vital public services were being starved. The above cited data show how strong the trend is in reversing a situation which in Galbraith's opinion then existed.

This does not mean, however, that the slice of government was being increased by reducing that of the consumer. Personal consumption expenditures claimed approximately the same percentage of the GNP in 1952 and in 1972, 62.7 and 62.9 percent respectively. According to the national income accounts government purchases for nondefense goods and services increased by 7.3 GNP percentage points (from 8.3 to 15.6 percent) and government transfer payments by 4.5 GNP percentage points (from 5.5 to 10.0 percent) for a combined total increase in government nondefense of 11.8 GNP percentage points (from 13.8 to 25.60 percent). Defense purchases were meanwhile cut by 6.9 GNP percentage points (from 13.3 to 6.4 percent).[11] In other words, about three-fifths of the expansion in public spending for domestic purposes was financed by cutting the share of national defense.

---

[11] Basic data from *Economic Indicators*. Transfer payments are not a separate and identifiable item in GNP accounting. Most of them are included in personal consumption expenditures.

Whether this leaves military funds at a level where they provide an adequate defense establishment and preparedness is highly controversial and argued among experts. Some of our top military leaders believe and have warned that current appropriations are insufficient and that a continuation of these spending trends may lead to disaster. Spokesmen for the social services, however, are no less firm in their insistence that the United States is still spending too much on the military and ought to cut Department of Defense appropriations even farther. History may some day have the answer to which side was right in this battle for a bigger slice of the tax dollar.

A few years ago, Senator Frank Church expressed an opinion that is widely held and voiced frequently: "Big Government on the Potomac is chiefly the product of warfare not of welfare."[12] The statement as made is historically correct. Government revenues climbed to new heights in World War II and could not have risen to equal 30 percent or more of the GNP save in a war emergency. Congress would not have passed, and the American taxpayers would not have tolerated, tax boosts of that size except for purposes of national defense. Subsequently, however, after the public had become accustomed to an exorbitant tax burden, tax rates were reduced only slightly as military spending dropped and the savings were applied to the expansion of social services and benefits. When the demands of the forces clamoring for still larger programs continued to multiply and intensify, further cuts in defense became the only politically feasible method of raising the required funds. Consequently, the past twenty years have seen a conversion in the United States from the "warfare state" to the "welfare state."

Senator Church has pointed out also that "the federal government is spending every year, for defense, more than treble the cost of all the educational programs in the country—including the school buildings themselves, the salaries of teachers and administrators, the books and supplies and lab equipment, the janitorial and upkeep services . . . "[13] Actually, defense spending then equaled less than twice the outlays for education (not "more than treble") and in recent years it has amounted to *less* than the cost of education.[14]

---

[12] *Congressional Record*, March 7, 1963, p. S 3542. See also "What is a Liberal? A 'Liberal' Senator Answers," *U.S. News and World Report*, May 6, 1963.

[13] *Congressional Record*, March 7, 1963, p. S 3542.

[14] Expenditures for education totaled $29.4 billion in the school year 1961–1962, defense expenditures $51.1 billion. (Sources: U.S., Department of Health, Education and Welfare, *Digest of Educational Statistics, 1973*, 1974, p. 25; U.S., Bureau of the Census,

Numerous statements similar to Senator Church's could be cited. Most of this misleading information created a climate of opinion in this country that was favorable to augmenting social spending at the expense of national defense.. The fiscal relationship between defense and social purposes was clearly expressed by Kermit Gordon, president of the Brookings Institution, in 1968: "It is quite possible that the decisions of the new administration and the new Congress on the post-Vietnam defense budget will be the most important factor in determining the scale on which the nation attacks its internal social problems."[15] If attacking social problems is viewed only in terms of the amount of public money spent on them—and not in terms of effectively resolving problems—then Gordon's statement has certainly proven true.

Because the major increase in fiscal powers was generated in World War II for purposes of national defense, they were naturally located at the national level. When subsequently used for nondefense purposes, those powers served to strengthen the role and voice of the federal government in domestic affairs. Federal expansion in domestic public services, which traditionally and constitutionally had been a responsibility and a prerogative of state and local governments, was carried out largely by federal "grant-in-aid" programs under rather stringent conditions and close supervision by federal administrative departments. Usually the recipient governments had to raise matching funds.

Federal aid to state and local governments was insignificant prior to the 1930s and remained below $1 billion until 1946. Concern arose when it climbed steeply in the postwar disarmament period and reached $2.6 billion in 1952. In 1953 Congress created a Commission on Intergovernmental Relations, which was asked to submit recommendations that would help to reverse the centralizing trend in the power structure of American government. That at least was the intention and hope of the originators and sponsors of the commission. But political trends in the 1950s, particularly the 1954 elections, and the influence of major special interest groups caused the report of the commission—and the reports of its successor organizations—to follow pragmatic lines and support prevailing trends instead of trying to reverse them.

Historical Statistics on Governmental Finances and Employment, 1967 Census of Governments, 1969.)
In the school year 1973–1974 educational expenditures (public and private) were reported at $96.3 billion *(Digest of Educational Statistics, 1973,* p. 22) while national defense costs were reported at $80.6 billion in that fiscal year.

[15] Kermit Gordon, ed., *Agenda for the Nation* (Washington, D.C.: The Brookings Institution, 1968), p. 9.

Between 1952 and 1972 the number of federal grant programs multiplied from a few dozen to well over 500, and their amount jumped from $2.6 to $36 billion. They are estimated at $51.7 billion in the president's budget for FY 1975. In other words, federal aid multiplied twenty times in the past twenty-three years.

Federal aid programs have come to cover virtually every function of state and local governments and to encompass certain activities that used to be largely or wholly in the private sphere. Whereas several decisions by the United States Supreme Court that reinterpreted the United States Constitution have helped to shift power from communities and states to the central government, the various grant-in-aid programs are the main force in the concentration of decision making in Washington. They are popular with Congress because they enable is members to bestow benefits on their local constituents and get political credit for their munificence. Federal aid is no less cherished by governors, mayors, and other local officials because it makes it possible for these officers to advocate generous public programs that will presumably cost the local taxpayer only fifty cents on the dollar or less. That the taxpayer will have to foot the bill for the federal largesse sooner or later—through higher taxes or inflation or weakened national security—is seldom mentioned. Federal money, which to all appearances comes for free, has a Santa Claus type of appeal that is hard to resist.

It has well been said that states rights were first thought out, then fought out, and finally bought out. The issue at stake is of course not so much the rights of states as the rights of individuals to make their own decisions through their communities and local and state governments, without being overruled by an all-powerful central government and its bureaucracy. Freedom is indivisible and seldom maintained for a long time by individuals if it is denied to communities and local units of government.

It is the broad political appeal of federal aid that accounts largely for the spectacular growth of federal aid programs, even during incumbent administrations that by their ideology and announced goals are committed to local autonomy and responsibility.

Reordering National Priorities?

As we have seen earlier, the share of national defense in the tax dollar and in the national economy has been cut to less than half since 1952. This shows the impact of a concerted and powerful movement to "reorder priorities": to shift public funds from national security to domestic services.

In the Brookings Institution's *Setting National Priorities: the 1973 Budget* the authors suggested that "defense spending for the most part has not been subject to partisan politics. . . . Of the four general considerations affecting the defense budget, domestic factors are quantitatively the least important. . . . "[16] The authors admit though that "the pressure of competing domestic requirements now exercise greater restraint on increases in defense spending than at any time since the end of the Second World War."[17]

That partisan politics is not a major factor in setting defense policies is literally true because the division is not drawn strictly between the political parties but along ideological lines that cross party boundaries. But domestic and political considerations have become the main factors in setting the size of the defense budget. There simply is no way in which some of the favorite schemes for expanding domestic benefits can be financed except by cutting it out of the hide of the military. Nor is this a novel phenomenon.

Over a decade ago Samuel P. Huntington of the Institute of War and Peace Studies at Columbia University wrote in a carefully documented study of postwar budget policy formation:

> In both the Truman Administration before the Korean War and in the Eisenhower Administration after the war, the tendency was:
> 1. to estimate the revenues of the government or total expenditures possible within the existing debt limit;
> 2. to deduct from this figure the estimated cost of domestic programs and foreign aid; and
> 3. to allocate the remainder to the military.[18]

This finding may have been true at the time when the size of the federal debt had barely changed since the close of World War II. But the federal debt has been raised by $200 billion since 1962 (which in turn pushed inflation to high rates). Within the past dozen years the restraining budgetary influence of prospective revenues has been considerably weakened by a readiness to recommend and approve ever higher debt ceilings. But even so there is a limit, economic or political, to how much the debt ceiling can be boosted in any one year—except during wartime.

When Huntington wrote his report, congressional sentiment still favored national security. In the average of the years 1961–1963 Congress

---

[16] Charles L. Schultze et al., *Setting National Priorities: The 1973 Budget* (Washington, D.C.: The Brookings Institution, 1972), p. 38.

[17] Ibid.

[18] Huntington, *The Common Defense.* See also Schilling, Hammond, and Snyder, *Strategy, Politics and the Defense Budgets,* Taylor, *The Uncertain Trumpet.*

increased defense appropriations an average of $1.5 billion above the president's request. But the sentiment in the country and in the Congress has changed since the dilatory conduct and inconclusive outcome of the long, drawn-out Vietnam war divided the American people and generated general frustration and negative feelings toward the military establishment. In the fiscal years 1968–1973 Congress *reduced* the president's defense budget every year, for an annual average of $3.8 billion.

At a time when manpower, reduced as it is, accounts for 56 percent of the defense budget, there is an inevitable squeeze on development and procurement of advanced weapons systems. Yet they are the core of an adequate defense preparedness against the threat of the sustained Soviet military effort.

Most of the controversies focus on initiation and authorization of new strategic systems and the timetable for their deployment. The most urgent goals are: accelerated replacement of the Polaris-Poseidon fleet by 4,000 mile-range Trident I missile submarines and 6,000 mile-range Trident II submarines in the early 1980s; substitution of the B-1 manned bomber for the ancient B-52's; availability of a sufficient transport fleet, whether C-5 A's or modified wide-bottomed Boeing 747's; new fighter aircraft— the navy's F-14 and the air force's F-15; improved missile accuracy and multiple independently targeted reentry vehicles MIRV's); the army's SAM-D missiles and Minuteman III missiles; an attack aircraft carrier force; and nuclear attack submarines.

Stretch-outs of strategic development are a clear signal to the Soviets that they need not make many concessions on bilateral arms limitation as long as we are already slowing down our preparations on a unilateral basis. That explains to some extent the inability of President Nixon to conclude significant agreements at the Moscow summit talks in July 1974.

The advocates of sharply increased domestic spending know well that sizeable federal tax boosts for their purposes are politically unacceptable (except for social security contributions) and that the defense budget is the natural quarry from which to mine the gold. This is evident in the National Urban Coalition's study, *Counterbudget*, which proposed defense outlays that were $37 billion lower in FY 1975 than the president's budget recommended and domestic services that were $70 billion higher.[19]

Battle lines over the reordering of national priorities are drawn along philosophical lines. Those who believe that a further redistribution of income and expanded social services rate prime and overriding consid-

---

[19] Benson and Wolman, eds., *Counterbudget*, pp. 12–13.

eration demand that the trend of a decided shift from military to domestic expenditures be continued and strengthened. On the other hand, those who question the desirability or efficacy in resolving our internal problems by continuing such a course and who are troubled by a steady weakening of our national security position believe that the trend of the past two decades ought to be reversed and that national priorities be reordered from social objectives of doubtful value and attainability to reenforced national defense.

Can the Budget Be Controlled?

There is a curious ambivalence in the American attitude toward governmental spending. The public harbors a generalized preference for keeping public budgets low while they cheer officeholders and office-seekers who promise to increase funds for their favorite programs. This often causes political leaders to assume a paradoxical position of advocating restraint in general while pushing for enlarged appropriations for the major public programs.

President Eisenhower sought and won office on the premise of governmental austerity and did, in face, reduce federal expenditures by $10 billion between FY 1953 and FY 1955.[20] This turned out to be the result of a $10 billion cut in defense—and in nothing else. To have kept nondefense costs stable for two years, however, reveals an extraordinary effort of that administration in its early years.

Under President Kennedy, who as a young congressman had warned of the dangers of an expanding state, federal spending went up. But President Johnson in his first budget message in January 1964 pointed out with pride that his recommendation "calls for a reduction from the preceding year in total administration budget expenditures" and was "only the second budget in nine years to do so." Expendiitures did turn out to be $1.2 billion lower in FY 1965 than they had been in FY 1964; this consisted of a $4.0 billion cut in defense and a $2.8 billion increase in everything else.[21] Needless to say, this was not only the first time that President Johnson mentioned a spending cut in a budget message but also the last time, although the subject of cost reduction came up occasionally and was referred to in his last budget message in January 1969.

---

[20] In the administrative budget, which was then in use.

[21] In the administrative budget.

President Nixon entered office with a program of government frugality and recommended a $2.4 billion reduction in the FY 1970 budget submitted by his predecessor. But when the final accounts were in, outlays in FY 1970 were $1.3 billion higher than President Johnson had originally recommended.

Altogether, between FY 1969 and FY 1971 federal spending went up $27 billion—which consisted of a $4 billion cut in defense and a $31 billion increase for everything else.

While President Nixon's budgets recommended substantial boosts year after year, there is considerable evidence of White House efforts to stem the tide of federal outlays and to resist pressures for an even faster growth. The loud and consistent outcries of special interest groups among liberal members of Congress about the low level of the president's programmatic and budgetary recommendations suggest that his aims were usually on the frugal side. In most of President Nixon's battles with Congress over spending he was on the side of lower expenditures except on national defense. Spending ceilings recommended by him were either not adopted or shot so full of loopholes that they were largely ineffective. He vetoed few appropriations but tried to impound funds and was in this at least partially or temporarily successful.

The practice of impounding funds, that is, not spending moneys appropriated by Congress, had been used occasionally by earlier presidents but not as extensively as by President Nixon, whose impoundments in his first term have been estimated to total $40 billion. As of June 30, 1973 impoundments then in effect stood at $7.7 billion according to a report to Congress by Roy Ash, director of the Office of Management and Budget. Whether the president has the power to withhold funds appropriated by Congress has been questioned and about four dozen law suits were filed in federal courts, with most decisions going against the administration. Thus impoundment often delayed but did not prevent the spending of the controversial amounts.

It is not widely known that there is a huge carry-over of budget authority, that is, of funds that have been appropriated by the Congress but not yet spent—estimated at $311 billion at the end of FY 1974.[22] Moreover, there are sizeable outlays outside the budget, totaling $15.6 billion in FY 1974.[23] They are mostly for government enterprises such as

---

[22] *The Budget of the United States Government, Fiscal Year 1975*, p. 40.
[23] Ibid., p. 32.

the FNMA (Fanny May), the Federal Home Loan Banks, the Federal Land Banks, the Export-Import Bank, the United States Postal Service, etc.

The fact is that only a part—and only a minor part—of the buget is subject to control by the president or review by the congressional appropriations committees. Some of the largest federal programs are open-ended and expenditures are controlled by the authorizing legislation, thus exempt from the normal budget process. Nearly three-fourths of all budget outlays in FY 1975 are labeled "relatively uncontrollable," the percentage having gone up from 59.3 percent of the total budget in FY 1967 to 73.5 percent in FY 1975.[24]

The 1975 budget shows only 27.7 percent of the proposed spending to be "relatively controllable."[25] Two-thirds of the defense outlays are shown as "controllable"; only military retirement pay and obligations from prior year contracts are uncontrollable. Of the nondefense outlays, mostly for domestic purposes, only 12 percent are reported to be "relatively controllable." The major items among the 88 percent of nondefense outlays in FY 1975 that are listed as "uncontrollable" are:[26]

Social security and railroad retirement	$ 67.2 billion
Net interest	22.0
Medicare and medicaid	20.8
Public assistance	14.1
Civil federal retirement and insurance	7.1
Veterans benefits	9.6
Unemployment assistance	7.5
General revenue sharing	6.2
Prior year contracts and obligations	28.6
Other	11.2
Total uncontrollable nondefense outlays	$194.3

[24] Ibid., pp. 318-19.

[25] Percentages of controllable and uncontrollable items add up to slightly more than 100 percent because of a minus amount of 1.2 percent for "undistributed employer share, employee retirement."

[26] *The Budget of the United States Government, Fiscal Year 1975,* pp. 318-19. In September 1974 the Office of Management and Budget released a new presentation of the budget for FY 1975 in which it distinguished between "mandatory" and "discretionary" spending. Mandatory spending (on contractual obligations, entitlement programs, legislative and judiciary programs) accounted for 73.7 percent of all outlays; 62 percent of "discretionary spending" was for defense. The same release showed that between FY 1968

With 67 percent of proposed defense expenditures controllable but only 12 percent of the nondefense items controllable, it is understandable that efforts to cut the budget usually concentrate on defense. Most major nondefense items are beyond the reach of would-be budget cutters. It is obvious that efforts to control federal expenditures must start long before the budget process because most federal expenditures are fixed by statutes which neither the president nor the appropriations committees can change. Many benefits are set by law—such as social security and retirement pay, medicare, veterans benefits, revenue sharing; interest is set by contracts. Public assistance, medicaid, and unemployment assistance are reimbursements to states under statutory formulas.

Though public attention focuses on the budgetary process, the real decisions on the bulk of federal spending are made months or years earlier through substantive legislation. The submission of estimates by the departments, review and pruning by the Office of Management and Budget and by the president, the president's formal recommendations to the Congress in the *Budget of the United States Government,* appropriations hearings and deliberations in committees of both Houses, and finally votes on appropriations bills determine the spending limits for hundreds of bureaus and programs. But they are in the aggregate only a minor factor in setting the magnitude of spending by the federal government—and by state and local governments stimulated and aided by federal grants—in a particular year.

To be sure, all of these expenditures—except for prior existing obligations and contracts—are controllable by the Congress. But except for defense most of them can be controlled only to a small extent in the formation of the budget. They are basically set when programs are adopted, revised, or expanded, when benefit amounts or reimbursement formulas are determined. The die is cast when the program itself is adopted, although outlays may be small in the beginning. While the president and his Office of Management and Budget appear to play a dominant role in each year's budget, the extent of the decisions they can make is limited, once a program is anchored in the statute books. This is also true of appropriations committees. It is a congressional practice of long standing to place liberals on substantive committees dealing with

---

and FY 1975 (estimated) expressed in *constant* (1975) dollars, defense spending dropped from $134 to $88 billion (i.e., one-third), interest and other nondefense dropped from $78 to $52 billion (i.e., one-third), while payment to individuals and grants nearly doubled, from $89 to $166 billion.

social programs and conservatives on appropriations committees. As a consequence it happens sometimes that appropriations are set at lower amounts than the basic legislation authorizes. When appropriations committees doubt the justification or effectiveness of a program, they recommend to their respective Houses that they "underfund" it or not fund it at all. In particular, the Elementary and Secondary Education Act of 1965 and its Title I have for years been consistently underfunded because of the substantial evidence that the spending of additional funds has been ineffective in raising the achievement levels of so-called disadvantaged children.

Many members of Congress have long felt that current budget procedures, devised over three decades ago, do not enable them to evaluate the president's budget adequately and that they have to depend too much of the chief executive's judgment and on reports prepared by his Office of Management and Budget. Appropriations are reviewed by Congress on a piecemeal basis, in individual bills (about thirteen of them each year), amended up or down and finally approved. For many years, most of those bills have not passed Congress until well into the fiscal year to which they apply. Though appropriations committees keep score of approvals, many individual members believe that they do not get an adequate overall picture of their actions, as they go along. So a demand and movement arose for congressional budget reform, which was adopted as H. R. 7130 by overwhelming majorities in both Houses in the spring of 1974 and signed into law in July 1974.

The new law that will go into effect in 1976 establishes a budget committee in each House and a Congressional Budget Office to do the staff work and act as a counterpart to the Office of Management and Budget. A change in the fiscal year to October 1 through September 30 is intended to give Congress more time to consider budget requests. Congress will by an early resolution establish target figures for total appropriations. Last but not least, presidential impoundment of funds will be subject to congressional approval so that the president can be forced to spend funds appropriated by Congress.

Whether this new budgetary procedure will provide a tighter or more effective control is, to say the least, questionable. It leaves undisturbed the fact that the major items of expenditure for domestic purposes are set by program legislation and immune to budgetary review. Nor does the new law help to resolve the basic conflicts between the forces that want higher spending and those that want less spending; those conflicts are ideological and political, not procedural. The new procedure may help each side to bolster its arguments with more background data. This budget reform is, however, likely to accomplish its real purpose: to shift more power from the White House to the Congress ("the spirit of '74"). Whether that will make for tighter expenditure control is highly doubtful.

Evaluating Public Expenditures: The Planning, Programming, and Budgeting System and Cost Effectiveness

Efforts to improve the review of spending proposals and to bring about a better understanding of the return on investment in public programs gained momentum about a quarter century ago when it was suggested to change from line-item budgets (by items of expenditure) to program or performance budgets (by purpose or goal of expenditure). Commercial business can measure the effectiveness of its investments and return thereon by an objective and conclusive yardstick: profits. No such all-inclusive or ultimate gauge is available for governmental outlays. But approaches can be developed along similar lines by relating input to output, holding the magnitude of the resources employed against the product, and comparing the hopes and promises of the sponsors with the tangible results.

Program or performance budgeting was much talked about when it gradually developed into the Planning, Programming, and Budgeting System (PPBS)—particularly at state and municipal levels, and gained wide acceptance, among theoreticians more than among practitioners, among academicians writing about it or acting as consultants more than among responsible officials or politicians. It gained ascendancy in the early 1960s when Robert McNamara and his whiz kids—who had come from big business corporations and consulting firms—introduced in the Department of Defense cost effectiveness as the guiding principle by which to make rational choices among expensive weapons systems. In a memorandum to the heads of all federal departments and agencies on August 25, 1965, President Johnson ordered them to establish PPBS and asked them to "begin at once to develop plans for the creation of your program and planning staffs." His budget director, Charles L. Schultze, expressed confidence that "it will provide the information and the analyses needed by government managers as the basis for an improved ability to make rational choices among the alternatives offered."[27] A new era seemed to dawn in

---

[27] David Novick, ed., *Program Budgeting: Program Analysis and the Federal Budget*, (Washington, D.C.: Government Printing Office, 1965), p.iii.

which scientific methods in the formation of public programs and budgets would supplant instinct, guessing, and political horse trading. Top executives would now be able to measure government output and allocate public funds accordingly.

Seldom has an idea gone so fast from the Great White Hope to disillusion and abandonment. In but a few years from its inception PPBS had a great future behind it. Why did PPBS fail? Because the output of many major public programs is not as objectively measurable as industrial and commercial goods and cannot be adequately gauged by slide rule or computer. It often depends on imponderables and, above all, on human judgment, which in turn is governed by a person's set of values and political ideology. This is why PPBS, initially hailed as a breakthrough in the decision-making process, could not even penetrate major decision making in the Department of Defense where it had the widest acceptance and its strongest supporters at the top.

When PPBS was first proposed, conservatives, who generally like a cost-accounting, productivity-measurement, profit-and-loss statement approach, were somewhat apprehensive that PPBS would be turned by the administrators into a more sophisticated means of justifying ever larger spending for social purposes. Liberals viewed PPBS as a new method of documenting what they had known by instinct right along: that expanded or multiplied public spending for social purposes would yield high returns in education, welfare activities and social work, community development, health, and similar "investments in people." But after a few years of PPBS its input-output and cost-benefit studies were unable to deliver positive proof of the effectiveness of such programs, findings frequently were inconclusive or showed negative results, and outcomes often seemed to suggest that the programs did not or could not deliver on the promises of their sponsors. Thus liberals soon became disillusioned and concluded that rhetoric and appeals to compassion and envy were still more effective tools to accomplish their aims than such cumbersome and insipid analyses.

Top administrators, policy makers, and special interest groups were commonly not looking at PPBS for getting answers to policy questions but for material proof to support policies in keeping with their leanings and goals. When little "helpful" material was forthcoming, liberals became disenchanted; conservatives, as usual, rarely bothered to wade through voluminous records for evidence that might help their case.

The abandonment of PPBS still leaves us with these crucial questions: How productive are public expenditures, particularly in fields in which they have experienced exponential growth rates within the past two decades and in which demands are strong for further enlargement? How worthwhile are those huge outlays and what does the taxpayer get in return?

Tangible Returns on Investment in Education?

A large literature has developed over the past fifteen years on cost-benefit relationships in public programs.[28] Many of the studies deal with efficiency, with the mechanical or "paper shuffling" aspects of governmental operations; others deal with the innate social desirability of certain activities and with the problem of measuring valuable but intangible outputs and developing impartial and valid yardsticks for the final product. At this point, the literature does not offer very much that is of practical value in the formation of decisions on major government programs.

It is one thing to show a high correlation between the number of years of an individual's formal schooling and the size of his income, as Paul C. Glick and Herman P. Miller first did from data in the 1950 census and as many have done since.[29] It is another thing to prove that the higher income was the *result* of the additional years of schooling rather than both the length of schooling and the high income being the result of personal drive, persistence, and intelligence. If the first assumption were true it would be good policy to have *everybody* participate in formal full-time schooling for more years. But it would not be true if the size of income were determined by each person's traits, which also cause him or her to stay in school longer.

---

[28] See the good bibliography in W. D. Wood and H. F. Campbell, *Cost-Benefit Analysis and the Economics of Investment in Human Resources*, (Kingston, Ontario: Industrial Relations Center, Queen's University, 1970). See also the most recent in several symposium volumes published by the Joint Economic Committee of Congress, *Benefit-Cost Analyses of Federal Programs* (Washington, D.C.: Government Printing Office, 1973)

[29] Paul C. Glick and Herman P. Miller "Educational Level and Potential Income," *American Sociological Review*, June 1956. The latest such study shows that a family head of twenty-five years or older had a median cash income of $8,341 in 1972 if he had finished eight years of school, an income of $12,163 if he had finished high school, and an income of $17,270 if he had finished college (U.S., Bureau of the Census, *Money Income in 1972 of Families and Persons in the United States*, Current Population Reports, series P-60, no. 90. December 1973). The question is whether this proves the monetary advantage of school attendance or the differences of ability and attitudes among human beings.

Educational institutions are now the largest item of governmental expenditure, for an estimated total of $79 billion in the school year 1973–74.[30] Aggregate public and private expenditures for education were placed at $97 billion in 1973–74 and at $108 billion in 1974–75 by the Office of Education (in a release dated September 2, 1974) which is nearly ten times the corresponding figure for 1951–52 of $11.3 billion. But the existence of a relationship between the magnitude of expenditures and educational quality has yet to be proved. No systematic analysis has ever been attempted although voluminous material is available.

Over the twenty-year period 1952–1972, expenditure per student in public education jumped from $301 to $1,294, an increase of 330 percent during a period when the general price level increased 58 percent.[31] No one, to our knowledge, has tried to find out whether the learning of students has improved over that period with rising costs, though millions of test results are available from many school systems. For a few major city school systems data have been published on pupil achievements and costs or cost factors on a school-by-school basis. Other cities have such information but do not care to disclose it. In the New York City schools there exists a clear-cut and strong *negative* correlation between expenditures per pupil and pupil achievements.[32] A study of the Oakland city schools (which did not compute expenditures on a school-by-school basis) shows that there is a strong *negative* correlation (as there is in New York City schools) between class size (which is the main determinant of school costs) and pupil achievements.[33]

Students in the 30 elementary schools in New York City with a per pupil expenditure in 1967–1968 of $1,100 or more (average $1,330) scored half a year or more *lower* on reading and arithmetic tests in fifth and sixth grades than students in the 101 elementary schools with an expenditure below $600 (average $551). The teacher-pupil ratio in the former schools averaged 1:12.3, in the latter 1:25.9. The 62 Oakland elementary schools showed a clear inverse relationship between the staffing level and

[30] U.S., Office of Education, Department of Health, Education and Welfare, *Digest of Educational Statistics, 1973,* 1974, p. 22.

[31] Expenditures for public education increased from $8.4 to $67.5 billion (table 23); the number of students went from 27.9 to 52.2 million. Sources: U.S., Office of Education, Department of Health, Education and Welfare, *Statistical Summary of Education, 1951–52,* 1955; *Digest of Educational Statistics, 1973.*

[32] Gittel, ed., *New York City School Fact Book.*

[33] Research Department, Oakland Public Schools, *Achievement Test Results, 1970–71,* 1971.

reading, arithmetic, and language scores. To be sure, no analytical tables or summaries appear in the New York City or Oakland reports to show these facts. Only the raw materials, that is, the basic data for each school, are published and the New York City report simply expresses surprise at the absence of a positive relationship between the size of expenditures and pupil achievements, even in the 21 schools in the *More Effective Schools* program, where per student costs are twice those of other schools.

It has always been deemed axiomatic in educational circles that there exists a strong and positive cost-quality relationship in education.[34] In fact, it has become customary to treat per student expenditures and other input factors as being synonymous with and expressing educational quality. The National Education Association declared after summarizing 150 research studies that "the most powerful of all the factors which influence the quality of the schools is the level of financial support."[35]

It has only been in recent years that such statements have been questioned when research evidence suggested the absence of evidence to support them. The head of the most extensive survey of American schools ever undertaken (*Equality of Educational Opportunity*, 1966), James S. Coleman has concluded that "the evidence revealed that within broad geographic regions, and for each racial and ethnic group, the physical and economic resources going into a school had very little relationship to the achievements coming out of it."[36]

Although public educational expenditures multiplied eight times between 1952 and 1972 (see table 23) while enrollment less than doubled, and although school enrollments after a long period of growth are now declining, complaints about inadequate financial support and demands for sharp boosts are still being advanced in pleas to Congress, state legislatures, school boards, and the taxpaying public.

In the Brookings Institution's *Agenda for the Nation* the president of the National Academy of Education, Ralph W. Taylor, wrote the following in a chapter entitled "Investing in Better Schools," in a paragraph dealing with quality education: "Adequate financial resources to meet the great demands placed on the schools are not now available and urgently needed."[37]

---

[34] See, for example, Paul R. Mort, "Cost-quality Relationships in Education," in R. L. Johns and E. L. Morphet, eds., *Problems and Issues in Public School Finance* (New York: National Conference of Professors of Educational Administration, 1952), pp. 9-10.

[35] National Education Association, *Does Better Education Cost More?*, 1959, p. 40.

[36] James S. Coleman, "Toward Open Schools," *The Public Interest*, Fall 1967.

[37] Gordon, ed., *Agenda for the Nation*, p. 233.

We may wonder: if multiplying funds *per student* four times within twenty years leaves schools inadequately financed, how much would be enough? At this point no evidence is available to show that the extraordinary increases in educational funds have raised educational quality to a higher level—or that further increases are likely to do so.

One of the most widely publicized attempts to prove that extra money and special efforts could improve the learning achievements of lagging children was "performance contracting." It was introduced in 1969–1971 under the sponsorship of the Office of Economic Opportunity (OEO) and involved eighteen cities and twenty-three thousand students. The project turned the task of raising the educational level of the students over to private contractors who were to be paid on a sliding scale, according to progress as measured on standard achievement tests. "We'll educate your kids—or your money back." In most cases payment was to be made only for a student who gained one school year of growth between the fall pretest and the spring posttest.

The OEO staff "saw great promise in performance contracting as a means to help poor children achieve the same results from classroom effort now achieved by nonpoor students."[38] OEO, contractors, and the schools "really believed that the lagging pupils were disadvantaged only in their prior experience; that the public schools were terribly ineffective teachers; and that the application of the usual psychological principles would cause extraordinary leaps in achievement."[39]

But the results were devastating: there was no detectable effect of the experiments. The OEO reported: "In half of the 10 cases there was no difference between the gains of the experimental and control groups. In four of the cases there was a difference of as much as two-tenths of a grade level. These overall differences are so slight that we can conclude that performance contracting was no more effective in either reading or math than the traditional classroom methods of instruction."[40] OEO abandoned the project forthwith. Even the contractors lost their enthusiasm—and their money; most went out of business.

The governor and legislature of Michigan were even more ambitious when in 1969 they adopted, with great fanfare, an assessment program that

---

[38] U.S., Office of Economic Opportunity, *Performance Contracting: An Experiment in Accountability,* 1971, p. 3.

[39] Ellis B. Page,"How We All Failed in Performance Contracting," *Educational Psychologist,* May 1972.

[40] U.S., Office of Economic Opportunity, *An Experiment in Performance Contracting: Summary of Preliminary Results,* February 1972, p. 17.

included financial incentives and rewards for educational improvement. It introduced the principle of accountability in the state's school system. Michigan's state superintendent of schools declared that the state should guarantee a basic education to all of its children; he felt that failure to learn was always the fault of the schools, not the children. But it soon became apparent that additional resources and the offering of rewards had no positive influence on the students' learning; in fact, there seemed to be an inverse relationship. If the program had been carried out as originally designed, the districts intended to be benefited would have lost money.

The program was changed every year and made increasingly complicated by a veritable avalanche of information required and supplied. Reports became so involved that in the end few could understand what it was all about. But one fact became clear: the injection of additional funds brought no tangible educational results.[41]

Nowhere has it been more clearly shown that the infusion of large amounts of money does not by itself improve the quality of education than in the compensatory education programs for so-called disadvantaged or deprived children—Title I of the Elementary and Secondary Education Act of 1965 and project Headstart. Title I has been financing between fifteen and twenty thousand projects every year at a federal cost of about $1 billion in the early years and $1.8 billion more recently. But in city after city, from New York to Berkeley, from Syracuse to St. Louis and Los Angeles, results have been disappointing. Summarizing the results in his Education Reform Message, President Nixon wrote on March 3, 1970:

> . . . *the best available evidence indicates that most of the compensatory education programs have not measurably helped poor children catch up.* (Emphasis added.) Recent findings on the two largest such programs are particularly disturbing. We now spend more than $1 billion a year for educational programs under Title I of the Elementary and Secondary Education Act. Most of these have stressed the teaching of reading, but before-and-after tests suggest that only 19 percent of the children in such programs improve their reading significantly; 13 percent appear to fall behind more than expected; and more than two-thirds of the children remain unaffected—that is, they continue to fall behind. In our Headstart Program where so much hope is invested, we find that youngsters enrolled only for the summer achieve almost no gains, and the gains of those in the program for a full year are soon matched by their non-Headstart classmates from similar poor backgrounds.

Subsequent evidence has not materially changed those findings.

---

[41] See Jerome T. Murphy and David K. Cohen, "Accountability in Education—The Michigan Experience," *The Public Interest,* Summer 1974.

Two years after President Nixon's Education Reform Message *Newsweek* conducted a survey of the new programs in school districts throughout the country and reported on April 3, 1972 that "despite the expenditure of billions of federal dollars in the nation's largest school systems, compensatory education—designed to offset the cultural disadvantages of ghetto children—has been widely judged a failure." The article mentioned that "as recently as the mid-1950s big city schools were almost universally regarded as centers of academic excellence in the U.S." Achievements in those same school systems from New York City to San Francisco are now at the bottom of all schools, and slipping further year after year. What has changed? Billions of federal, state, and local dollars have been added, per student costs have been mounting, but the type of children who attend those schools has changed. There is now ample experience to show that differences in pupils' traits cannot be offset by any amount of money. It is the children more than the schools that determine the educational outcome.

Although for several decades all American children between the ages of seven and fifteen have been enrolled in school, 19 million adults—about 12 percent of the adult population—were reported to be totally or functionally illiterate in a release of the United States Office of Education on August 14, 1974. Such findings do not necessarily mean that schools make no difference. They do—sometimes. A study of two otherwise similar inner schools, released in April 1974 by the New York State Office of Education Performance Review, showed that in school *A*, which placed great emphasis on reading, 25 percent of the students scored at or above grade level on national norms for the Metropolitan Achievement Test, and more than 50 percent above the minimum acceptable competency levels set for each grade by the State Education Department; the comparable figures for school *B* were 10 and 16 percent respectively. School *A* had thirty-three pupils per teacher, and operated at 103 percent of capacity; school *B* had twenty-eight pupils per teacher and operated at 76 percent of capacity.[42] What seemed to make at least some difference in the outcome was not the magnitude of physical and manpower resources of each school, but the methods applied.

But such discouraging results did not stop Congress from boosting funds for compensatory education on several occasions and from extending the program again in 1974. Ten years ago better education for the children of the poor was intended to be a keystone in the War on Poverty. Many

[42] Office of the Governor, Albany, New York, *A Case Study of Two Inner City Schools.* Cited from *Bulletin of the Council on Basic Education,* May 1974.

believed that better education offered a final solution to the problem of the low-income population ("Education—An Answer to Poverty"). A Brookings Institution study by Thomas Ribich severely questioned the assumption—so widely held despite the absence of any proof—that education and training are effective means of generating the earning ability needed to lift people out of poverty.[43] No amount of evidence has been able to shake the confidence of the policy makers in the omnipotence of the dollar or belief in the unlimited malleability of the brain and the ultimate perfectability of man. The program's protagonists and supporters were unwilling to accept the fact that there is a law of diminishing returns in social programs and that increased input does not yield a greater output from a certain point on—a point that was reached in most American public schools long ago.

The social engineers who fashioned these and related programs were emotionally unable to face the fact that there is a limit to the extent to which inequalities in the endowment of individuals can be overcome by governmental action. They preferred to accept what Daniel Bell called the "two simplistic notions in the American temper: that all problems are soluble, and that the way to solve the problem is to pour men and money into it."[44]

It was hoped that equal educational opportunities would narrow socioeconomic differences—but it did not work that way. Gifted individuals with drive take greater advantage of educational opportunities than those who are less endowed; thus the differences between them may widen. When it was realized that equal opportunities may produce greater inequality in results rather than less, the demand shifted to opportunities that were more than equal. Since nothing can be more than equal the call turned into one for *unequal* opportunities to produce equal—or more nearly equal —results. It did so where direct governmental action was all that was needed, that is, in income distribution or hiring and promotion. It tried and failed, as it had to, in fields where action could only be indirect, most spectacularly so in education.

Direct action was the main goal of the War on Poverty, of which compensatory education was but a minor if important part.

---

[43] Thomas Ribich, *Education and Proverty* (Washington, D.C.: The Brookings Institution, 1968).

[44] Cited from Robert Cassidy, "How We Got from 'Equal Opportunity' to 'Equal Results'," *Planning,* February 1974.

Success in the War on Poverty?

If it was the goal of the War on Poverty to distribute huge amounts of public money among the low-income population, then it must be rated an unqualified success. Federal outlays for "income security" have multiplied four times in the ten years since the initiation of the War on Poverty, from $25.7 billion in 1965 to an estimated $100 billion in FY 1975. A substantial part of this was for contributory social security, old age and survivors, and disability programs for retirement pensions.

But public assistance and social service programs multiplied almost six times—from $3.3 to $17.9 billion—during that period of high prosperity and rising incomes. The number of children on AFDC multiplied five times between 1961 and 1969, while the total child population (under eighteen years of age) grew only by one-third. This was not because there were more poor people around (there weren't), and only partially because more of the poor people went on welfare. The growth in AFDC can largely be traced to the fact that the number of "absent fathers" quadrupled from 590,000 in 1961 to 2,482,000 in 1973.[45] Six out of seven absent AFDC fathers paid no support whatsoever for their children and many of them—or possibly most—may have abandoned their families because the AFDC program had made it attractive and lucrative to do so.

A nationwide study by the staff of the congressional Joint Economic Committee in the summer of 1974 concluded that welfare encourages family break-up and childbearing, and offers a disincentive to work. Here are some of the report's findings:

Does Welfare Encourage Family Breakup?
· · ·

This analysis found sizable financial incentives for family-splitting; the amounts generally exceed the extra costs of maintaining separate households. Weighted by AFDC caseload, the county figures revealed these national income differentials:

If an unemployed father deserted, the average gain in cash and food benefits varied from $1,004 for the one-child families to $1,318 for families with three children, a gain of about one-third in family income;

If the deserting father worked full time at $2 an hour, the average gain ranged from $1,806 to $2,358, a gain of nearly one-half in family income;

---

[45] U.S., Department of Health, Education and Welfare, *AFDC Studies,* 1961 and 1973.

Adding in housing benefits raised these averages by as much as $400; and

If medicaid were counted, many of the female-headed families would become newly eligible for free health care after the fathers left home, adding another several hundred dollars to the gain from splitting.

Since the above figures are national averages, the family-splitting incentive in specific situations can be lower, or it can run much higher. . . .

Does Welfare Encourage Motherhood?

The county data show a sizable financial incentive for a woman to have her first child in order to receive AFDC and medicaid benefits. The gain, both relatively and absolutely, declines for subsequent children, although the childbearing incentive for a middle-aged woman whose youngest child is age 18 or over is the same as that for a woman having her first child. The county data, when weighted for AFDC caseload size, show the following:

An unemployed, childless woman can almost double her benefits with an additional $1,159 in cash and food benefits by having her first child;

Adding in the value of public housing raises her gain to $1,447 on average, and medicaid would add nearly $400 more based on the cost of the care provided;

If this woman has a second child, the average gain in cash and food benefits is $756, an increase in income of 31 percent; and

The average gain for having a third child is $628, which is a 20 percent rise in cash and food benefits. . . .

How Much Incentive Is There to Work?

Since welfare benefits must be reduced in some way when recipients go to work, the return from working is measured by subtracting from wages the taxes paid, the expenses incurred because of work, and the welfare benefits lost. It has long been argued that this net gain from working is quite small and is, therefore, a factor in recipients' decisions about whether to work or how much to work.

The belief that work disincentives are high is supported by this study. Weighted by the AFDC caseload distribution, the county data show the following:

Due to the way income is counted, AFDC and food stamp benefits do not decline very rapidly as earnings rise, but net income left after work expenses for working mothers on AFDC and food stamps averages as little as 20 cents per dollar earned;

For such women who live in public housing, the average gain drops to as low as 11 cents for some cases;

For cases ineligible for regular AFDC benefits, other benefit losses, coupled with taxes and work expenses, hold down the net return from each dollar earned. Average gains run around 30 cents for singles and couples, 33 cents for two-parent families on AFDC-UF, and 50 cents for two-parent families in non-UF States; and

Fathers on AFDC-UF who go to work full time at the old ($1.60) or new ($2.00) minimum wage face net losses in discretionary income, because the AFDC benefits lost generally exceed the smaller net wage. A man with a wife and three children who finds a full-time job at $1.60 an hour has an after-tax income of $3,034, but loses AFDC-UF benefits of $3,840 a year in San Francisco and $3,588 in Portland, Ore.

The most striking of these findings is that low-wage workers now excluded from AFDC still may face high disincentives to work due to the combination of taxes, work expenses, and benefits lost from GA, food, and housing programs. In fact, taxes alone averaged 14 percent of wages for single people earning $4,000 a year, and 10 percent for couples with no children.[46]

The Family Assistance Plan (FAP) that President Nixon recommended to the Congress in 1969 would have somewhat reduced the perverse incentives of our welfare system. But it would have immediately more than doubled the number of recipients and lifted welfare outlays to new heights. The House of Representatives passed FAP twice but the Senate rejected it in 1972. Efforts continue to enact FAP or a similar system of guaranteed annual income.

The incidence of poverty declined dramatically in the United States between 1952 and 1972. The percent distribution of families with a cash income under $3,000 (in *constant* 1972 dollars) fell from 18.3 percent of the population in 1952 to 7.2 percent in 1972, of those with an income under $5,000 from 36.8 to 16.6 percent.[47] Similarly, the percent distribu-

---

[46] Subcommittee on Fiscal Policy of the Joint Economic Committee (Staff Study), *Welfare in the 70's: A National Study of Benefits Available in 100 Local Areas,* Studies in Public Welfare, Paper no. 15, 93d Cong., 2d sess., July 22, 1974, pp. 6-8.

[47] U.S., Bureau of the Census, *Money Income in 1972 of Families and Persons in the United States,* Current Population Reports, series P-60, no. 90, December 1973. It is now widely recognized that the annual income surveys of the Bureau of the Census materially underreport income and that cash (money) income omits income in kind. Many employees

tion of unrelated individuals with a cash income under $1500 (in constant 1972 dollars) dropped from 38.2 percent in 1952 to 17.9 percent in 1972, of those with an income under $5,000 from 80.2 to 62.4 percent.

The number of persons below the official *low income* or *poverty* level dropped from 39.5 million or 22.0 percent of the United States population in 1959 (earliest year available) to 24.5 million or 11.7 percent of the United States population in 1972.[48]

Much of this progress—cutting the percentage of the population designated "poor" into half within the span of thirteen years—was due to improved earnings from higher wages, but a sizeable share came from transfer funds distributed under public programs.

When the Economic Opportunity Act and related poverty legislation were introduced in the mid 1960s, their sponsors proclaimed poverty to be at the root of most social ills and the cause of the high and rising incidence of crime.

Some critics questioned that proposition because Americans enjoy the highest incomes in the world—yet suffer from the highest crime rates and disproportionate incidences of social ills and unrest. There were plenty of warnings that good intentions and lots of public money did not necessarily produce the desired results.

New York City's Mayor Robert F. Wagner, a leading liberal of long

---

receive free (or below-market priced) housing, food, and other benefits. Low-income persons get food stamps, housing subsidies, medical benefits, etc., none of which are counted as income in the Bureau of the Census surveys; this makes income appear lower than it actually is. Numerous persons and families have a low income or no income—or a negative income—in a year in which they suffered sizeable losses. Income in a particular year therefore does not adequately reflect their true long-run economic circumstances. They may have had a low income because their earning life began or ended during the course of the year, they may have taken time off for leisure, study, travel—paying current outlays from savings or the income of earlier years, or they may have been ill part of the year.

In other words, an unknown number of persons and families have a money income below the official poverty level in a particular year but may not be poor in any meaningful sense of the word.

If we assume for purposes of calculation—and on no factual basis—that 5 percent of the households are classified "poor" although they are really not poor, the percentage of all persons who are poor would be reduced from 22.0 to 17.0 percent in 1959 and from 11.7 to 6.7 percent in 1972.

[48] U.S., Bureau of the Census, *Characteristics of the Low Income Population 1972,* Current Population Reports, series P-60, no. 91, December 1973. The bureau reported in July 1974 that the "poverty population" had shrunk another 1.5 million in 1973. The incidence of low income (or poverty)—defined as an income of less than $4,540 for a four-person nonfarm family in 1973—had shrunk from 16.5 percent in 1959 to 6.9 percent in 1973 among whites and from 56.2 to 29.6 percent among nonwhites (Bureau of the Census, *Characteristics of the Low-Income Population: 1973 (Advance Report),* Current Population Reports, series P-60, no. 94, July 1974).

standing, said in 1962, two years before the passage of the Economic Opportunity Act:

> Once upon a time we thought that if we could just bulldoze the slums and build shiny new public housing for low-income people, all social problems involving these people would virtually disappear. This has turned out to be not so.
>
> Once we thought that if we built enough playgrounds and other recreational facilities, juvenile delinquency would disappear. This turned out to be not so.
>
> Once we thought that having discovered a magic bullet to kill the microorganisms that cause veneral disease, we had conquered veneral diseases. That turned out to be not so.[49]

But wishful thinking and blind hope carried the day when the component parts of the New Frontier and Great Society programs were enacted into law. With family income up 35 percent (in *constant* dollars) over the past ten years and 81 percent in the past twenty years, and education of the average person lengthened by two years, with racial differences in school attendance sharply reduced, and the simultaneous improvement in housing and other living standards we would have expected a commensurate lessening of social tensions. If lack of material possessions—necessities, amenities, conveniences—is the basic cause of unrest, we might have looked forward to an increase in contentment, happiness, social peace and domestic tranquility, a decline in crime, welfare dependency, conflict, and general restlessness among wide sections of the population.

But this is not what has happened. The number of crimes and other social ills kept on climbing fast, as incomes improved and poverty, measured by any standard, diminished.

After nearly ten years of the most expensive governmental War on Poverty ever, significant tangible results ought to be in evidence but they are conspicuous in their absence.

The authors of the Brookings Institution's budget review for 1973 raised a weighty point, as others had before: ". . . the public is asking harder questions about federal programs, both new and old. It is asking whether they work. It is no longer enough for politicians and federal

---

[49] "The Social Welfare Forum," *Proceedings of the Eighty-ninth Annual Forum, National Conference on Social Welfare, May 27–June 1, 1962,* New York City, pp. xv-xvi.

officials to show that they have spent the taxpayers' money for approved purposes; they are now being asked to give evidence that the programs are producing results."[50] There was a clear implication that social reform by way of government spending programs had not worked—a sharp contrast to the spirit that pervaded the Brookings Institution's 1969 volume *Agenda for the Nation.* In a masterpiece of understatement the 1973 report found: "It is hardly surprising that the major new programs of the 1960s did not achieve instant success."[51]

Between 1964 and 1972 federal spending for domestic services tripled, from $45 to $131 billion. Expenditures for domestic purposes of all governments, federal, state, and local, meanwhile soared from $101 to $257 billion. This means that it took only 8 years to increase those outlays by $156 billion, while it had required 175 years (from 1789 to 1964) to reach a spending level of $101 billion (tables 24 and 25). Is the American taxpayer not entitled to demand a reasonable return on an investment of such astronomical proportion?

Outlays for social welfare—education, income maintenance, health, labor, housing, and community development—accounted in 1952 for 20 percent of the expenditures of all governments (federal, state, and local; see table 23). By 1972 they claimed 48 percent or nearly one-half of the total. The doubtful results of multiplying educational expenditures eightfold and welfare expenditures fourfold between 1952 and 1972 have been discussed above (pp. 134 ff).

Increased spending in other social welfare fields was no more productive. Federal health expenditures multiplied fifteen times in those two decades, and outlays for housing and community development twenty times. But the complaints about inadequate health care have never been as vocal nor has criticism of public housing programs been as sharp—and amply justified. But this has so far not led to an objective review of the effectiveness with which public moneys have been spent for those purposes.

Congress, in a frantic attempt to accelerate medical research and find miracle cures for cancer and other illnesses, has showered so much money on the National Institutes of Health that they jocularly became known in Washington as the National Institutes of Wealth.

In a recent searching article in *Science* two researchers stated that neither the medical literature nor our data provide substantial clues as to

---

[50] Charles L. Schultze et al., *Setting National Priorities,* p. 449.
[51] Ibid., p. 453.

whether spending six times more for electrocardiograms or seven times more for laboratory services results in greater improvement in health for persons age 65 and over than does a lesser expenditure."[52]

Columbia University economist Eli Ginzberg pointed out that the need is not necessarily for more money and doctors but rather for structural changes in the system of health care delivery if medical care is to be effectively delivered to all, including the poor. He concluded that the heavy infusion of funds into the medical care system in recent years has chiefly raised costs for the same amount of health care.[53] The death rate in the United States did not change between 1952 and 1972, although public health expenditures multiplied six times.

Prices increased faster for medical services than for virtually anything else between 1952 and 1972 due, to a large extent, to the inflation of demand with public funds.[54] Yet, the current debate seems to focus on the choice between several new health schemes which would add between $6 and $60 billion a year from federal sources.

Federal housing and urban redevelopment programs, intended to help cure urban decay, have created numerous "instant slums" and in the process destroyed far more dwellings than they have built. In a survey of urban renewal in a number of cities the General Accounting Office found in 1970 that the program had resulted in:

1. A significant reduction in hoursing, especially for low- and moderate-income families, in project areas nationally
2. A significant reduction in the land area used and scheduled for use for residential purposes in project areas
3. The demolition in 324 of the cities of about 88,000 more dwelling units than were constructed for low- and moderate-income families under all HUD housing programs in those cities (about 126,000 units were built and about 214,000 units were torn down)[55]

---

[52] John Wennberg and Alan Gittelsohn, "Small Area Variations in Health Care Delivery," *Science*, December 14, 1973.

[53] Eli Ginzberg and Miriam Ostow, *Men, Money and Medicine* (New York: Columbia University Press, 1970).

[54] Between 1952 and 1972 the consumer price index went up 58 percent, the price of medical care 123 percent. Source: U.S., Department of Commerce, Office of Business Economics, *1971 Business Statistics, Biennial Supplement to the Survey of Current Business,* October 1971; U.S., Department of Commerce, Bureau of Economic Analysis, *National Income Issue,* Survey of Current Business, July 1973.

[55] U.S., Department of Housing and Urban Development, Comptroller General's Report to the Congress, *Opportunity to Improve Allocation of Funds to Better Meet National Housing Goals,* B-118754, pp. 17-19.

In each of the four cities discussed in some detail in the report, the office found that urban renewal had contributed to a shortage of housing for low- and moderate-income families. Altogether the federal government accounted for a net loss of 315,000 housing units in the twenty years ending December 31, 1968—after spending $7 billion for the ostensible purpose of rehabilitating big-city slums. For every unit put up the federal bulldozer leveled 3.5 others.[56]

Similar to what happened in medical care we find that the government, by pouring vast amounts of money into housing, pushed up construction costs faster than the general price level, thereby driving large numbers of moderate-income families out of the housing market.[57]

The more money the federal government channels into the housing market, the faster wages and other costs in construction move up. In consequence, fewer people can afford to buy new homes and the well intentioned policy becomes self-defeating. The resulting slack in housing construction then causes Congress to appropriate more money—and the spiral continues.

One of the urban renewal program's glamor exhibits, Pruett-Igoe in East St. Louis, deteriorated so quickly that some of the buildings had to be dynamited about a dozen years later to eliminate a social and environmental hazard. Protagonists for urban renewal seem unable to comprehend that slums are not decaying buildings but people and that it is far easier to construct gleaming apartment complexes and to move people to another section of town than to change their behavior. Though slums may often be the breeding grounds of crime, it is hardly the condition of the buildings that spawns it.

Rural programs have proven no more effective than urban renewal. The Appalachian plan initiated by President Kennedy to undertake the greatest regional economic recovery scheme ever attempted in the United States left the area ten years later largely untouched and unchanged, after spending $7 billion in public investment.[58]

---

[56] Similar findings had been reported some years earlier by Martin Anderson, *The Federal Bulldozer* (Cambridge, Mass.: M.I.T. Press, 1964), but the program went on regardless of its devastating results.

[57] Between 1952 and 1972, the consumer price index went up 58 percent, construction prices 102 percent. Source (construction prices): U.S., Department of Commerce, *Construction Statistics 1915–1964, A Supplement to Construction Review,* January 1966; U.S., Department of Commerce, *Construction Review,* December 1970 and April 1974.

[58] "Years of Vast Aid Bring Scant Relief to Appalachia," *New York Times,* November 29, 1970.

With many of these programs we must again ask, Are you helping to solve the problem or are you part of the problem?

Government Money and Social Reform

The failure of certain programs of the past ten to twenty years are gradually making an impact on scholars in the social sciences, many of whom had been in the forefront of reform movements not so many years earlier. Columbia University sociologist Amitai Etzioni offered an agonizing reappraisal:

> We have come of late to the realization that the pace of achievement in domestic programs ranges chiefly from the slow to the crablike—two steps backward for every one forward—and the suspicion is growing that there is something basically wrong with most of these programs. A nagging feeling persists that maybe something even more basic than the lack of funds or will is at stake. Consequently, social scientists like myself have begun to reexamine our core assumption that man can be taught almost anything and quite readily. We are now confronting the uncomfortable possibility that human beings are not very easily changed after all.[59]

In a *Fortune* article entitled "The Social Engineers Retreat Under Fire," Tom Alexander concluded that "the disappointing results of government ventures into social reform have cast doubt on some widely held theories and thrown the social sciences into an uproar."[60] He summarized:

> Like good empiricists faced with unexpected results many (sociologists, psychologists and anthropologists whose theories provided designs for so many ill-fated attempts at "social engineering") have come to question their previous assumptions. The orthodox view of environment as the all-important influence on people's behavior is yielding to a new awareness of the role of hereditary factors; enthusiasm for schemes to reform society by remolding men is giving way to a healthy appreciation of the basic intractability of human nature.

Even some of the architects and sponsors of the new programs in health, education and welfare have bared their self-doubt. Alice Rivlin, the former assistant secretary for planning and evaluation in the Department of Health, Education and Welfare, and now Director of the Congressional budget staff, wrote:

---

[59] Amitai Etzioni, "Human Beings Are Not Very Easy To Change After All," *Saturday Review,* June 3, 1972.

[60] *Fortune,* October 1972.

. . . the liberals have lost their innocence. By the end of the 1960s it was evident that merely spending more federal money was not necessarily going to produce results. Money for education would not automatically teach children to read. . . . More money for health might only escalate the price of health care, or put more people in hospitals who need not be there. . . . More money for welfare would only perpetuate a badly constructed system. . . .[61]

It may be well to remember that health, education and welfare accounted in 1972 for almost half of all expenditures of all governments—to be exact $172 billion or 47 percent of total government spending—and that they equaled well over half of the *increase* in all public outlays between 1952 and 1972 (see table 23). To put this in the right perspective, expenditures for health, education and welfare increased 833 percent between 1952 and 1972 while the aggregate of all other governmental costs went up only 164 percent. Eventually even some of the former enthusiasts of spending boosts for social programs began to have second thoughts.

As Robert Cassidy has written: "What is more striking, however, is that many so-called conservative arguments regarding social welfare programs are being taken seriously by the government and even by die-hard liberals."[62]

It is certainly true that some arguments long used by conservatives are now being given earnest consideration by liberals or former liberals. Recent writing by such eminent social scientists as Nathan Glazer, Sidney Hook, Daniel Patrick Moynihan, Daniel Bell, Irving Kristol, Seymour Martin Lipset, and others give living proof that ideas which not so long ago would have been ignored or ridiculed as reactionary and hopelessly out of date have acquired a new respectability.

Although some leading liberal intellectuals have in recent years modified their attitudes on governmental spending and social reform—or, for that matter, on concentration of power in the presidency—it may be questioned whether "government" is really giving serious thought to conservative ideas, as Robert Cassidy has suggested. Some officials undoubtedly do. The then director of the Office of Management and Budget and now Secretary of Health, Education and Welfare, Caspar W. Weinberger, for example, was quoted as saying in 1972: "It has become

---

[61] "Why Can't We Get Things Done?," *Brookings Bulletin,* Spring 1972.

[62] Cassidy, "How We Got from 'Equal Opportunity' to 'Equal Results'," *Planning* (American Society of Planning Officials), February 1974.

increasingly clear that money is not the essential element in improving social conditions throughout the country."[63]

But most liberals in the executive and legislative branches of government as well as our highest courts do not yet seem to have gotten the word. They still deal with the nation's major domestic troubles as if they had learned nothing from the experience of the past ten to twenty years. They still talk and act as if the spending of additional billions were the only true key to the solution of our problems.

Michael Harrington, whose book *The Other America: Poverty in the United States* helped give Presidents Kennedy and Johnson the idea and impetus for the War on Poverty, wrote recently that "the failures of the welfare state in recent years are the result of its conservatism, not of its excessive liberalism, or, more preposterously, of its radicalism."[64] He denied the egalitarian trends of the welfare state in the 1960s and, not surprisingly, blamed the ineffectiveness of most of its programs on "penny pinching." He recognized, however, that "the failures of the welfare state in the sixties have served as a stimulus for, and rationale of, the rise of neoconservative thought in the seventies."[65]

There is as yet little evidence that the social profitability of proposed programs, the tested and proven effectiveness on a smaller scale of new major schemes, and the relationship between the social cost of resources and the social value of the product play a significant role in the deliberations of the Congress and in its decisions on the authorization and funding of domestic services. The proponents of social spending schemes seem to say, as Ben Wattenberg and Richard Scammon expressed it: "the liberal battle-cry has become, 'We have failed; let us continue!' "[66] This suggests that the underlying thought and overriding goal in much of the tax and spending decisions is not so much social reform *per se* as redistribution of income, from those who have more to those who have less. That meets a deep-seated desire which is widespread, if not universal, and is at the core of almost all conflict in this world: the yen or appetite of some people for what other people possess. Historically much of the redistribution of

[63] "Cut Outlay, Don't Increase Taxes—Weinberger," *Los Angeles Times,* June 5, 1972.

[64] Michael Harrington, "The Welfare State and its Neoconservative Critics," in Lewis A. Coser and Irving Howe, eds., *The New Conservatives: A Critique from the Left* (New York: Quadrangle, 1974), p. 53.

[65] Ibid., pp. 29, 39, 46, 57, 108.

[66] Ben J. Wattenberg and Richard J. Scammon, "Black Progress and Liberal Rhetoric," *Commentary,* April 1973.

property, between nations or within nations, has been accomplished by violence—robbery, revolution, or war. Progressive taxation and social spending through cash transfers and public programs appear now to have become a more popular and more widely used method of accomplishing by the legislative process what previously could be obtained only by individual productive effort or through dispossession by force.

Redistribution of income and property is increasingly viewed as the prime purpose and task of government and this, more than anything else, explains the spectacular growth in domestic public expenditures over the past two decades. To redistribute through the political process the rewards and punishments of the market has become the foremost goal of those who do not believe that a man is entitled to the value of his product, who feel that the allocation of natural talent—of intelligence, inventiveness, judgment, drive, aspiration, persistence—is basically unfair to those less endowed and must be overruled and revised in a more egalitarian direction. Since talent as such cannot be redistributed among persons, at least the product of such talent and effort should be. The record of the past few decades suggests that those who so feel are having their way.

—5—

Issues and Prospects

Viewing the record of governmental finances between 1952 and 1972, the most striking fact appears to be the exponential growth of expenditures for domestic purposes, primarily for social programs—income maintenance, education, health, housing, and community development. Those outlays multiplied seven times in those two decades, from $35 to $257 billion, while the nation's output of goods and services only slightly better than doubled.[1]

The enormity of this change is even more clearly apparent in the federal picture. After a gradual growth over 163 years, federal expenditures for domestic purposes reached a level of $12 billion in 1952; they then jumped to $131 billion within the succeeding twenty years (table 21). To bring the most recent trends into sharp focus, federal spending for domestic purposes soared from $72 billion in FY 1969 to $167 billion in the budget for FY 1975. This means that it increased in each of the past six years by more than the total it had reached in 1952 as the result of a development of more than a century and a half.

This amounts to nothing less than a revolution in the nature of government in the United States during the third quarter of the twentieth century. Domestic programs accounted for one-sixth of all federal spending in 1952; by 1972 they claimed more than one-half of the total and were still heading steeply upward, in absolute as well as in relative terms. To be sure, the significant change in recent years has not been the growth of government as such. In terms of the size of its revenues and expenditures governmental growth has not expanded much faster than the nation's economy. The overpowering fact is the sudden and unprecedented explosion of governmental and particularly federal activities in the broad field of social welfare.

---

[1] By national income account definitions; see table 23. According to Bureau of the Census definitions, expenditures for domestic purposes increased from $41 to $283 billion; see table 4a.

Had this been financed by equivalent boosts in taxes, the American people would inevitably have been fully aware of what was happening because such an increase in the tax burden could not have taken place without their implicit consent. State and local taxes, to be sure, did rise steeply and taxpayers are painfully aware of that fact. However, federal taxes were reduced several times, which partially offset the higher state and local taxes and gave the public the impression that the growing federal largesse was coming for free. But the primary methods of financing the multiplication of social benefits and services, to the extent to which it exceeded the automatic growth of revenues from economic advance were *(a)* budgetary deficits, that is, inflation, and *(b)* a cut to less than half in the share of resources allocated to national security.

To many individuals and organizations in all walks of life—in government and politics, in academe, in labor and business—the expansion of social services to meet emerging needs was a point of pride. It seemed to prove that the United States was finally entering the twentieth century, later than most of Europe's industrial nations, but deliberately, purposely, and forcefully. If the American public was so backward that it would not willingly increase its taxes sufficiently for those ends, then this had to be done by indirection, when an opportunity arose through an emergency such as the depression of the 1930s or after the end of a war when taxpayers had become accustomed to bearing a heavy load. To its protagonists and supporters the new programs were and are only the harbingers of greater things to come, downpayments on a fair and just and therefore great society.

Opponents watched those trends with apprehension as part of an age-old struggle between man and his government. They viewed the line between public and private spending as the dividing line between the areas of coercion and freedom and tried without much success to keep the decision makers from expanding the former at the expense of the latter.[2]

William Henry Chamberlain once expressed the issue well: "The level of government spending is perhaps the most clear-cut battlefield between American conservatives and liberals." Mr. Chamberlain then recounted a statement by Senator Robert Taft in the 1952 election campaign: "General Eisenhower emphatically agrees with me in the proposal to reduce drasti-

---

[2] Gerhard Colm, in his "Theory of Public Expenditures" *(The Annals of the American Academy of Political and Social Science,* 183, [January, 1936]), defined the difference between coercion and freedom as follows: "The public realm is distinguished by the fact that it rests on authority and, if necessary, even on compulsion, while private relations rest on contract."

cally over-all expenses. Our goal is about $70 billion in fiscal '54 and $60 billion in fiscal '55.''[3] As it turned out, administrative budget expenditures hit a low of $64.6 billion in FY 1955—with *all* of a $10 billion reduction since FY 1953 taken in national defense; they then resumed their inexorable steep climb to new heights.

To be sure, the dividing line between public and private activities and expenditures is not always clear-cut. Irving Kristol offered a useful definition:

> The terms "public sector" and "private sector", as commonly used, are summary answers to the question: Who spends the nation's money? Not: For what purpose? Not: With what consequences? Merely: Who?—government or private associations and individuals?[4]

Concepts and practices differ on what should or should not be included in public, that is, governmental, expenditures. But by and large, all of the leading statistical data on governmental outlays—whether by the Bureau of the Census, or according to national income accounts, or from the federal unified budget, or even the now abandoned consolidated cash budget—are valid and helpful means of identifying magnitude and trends in public spending. The most widely used measure of the magnitude of governmental action is the percentage which governmental spending is of a national economic total—gross national product, net national product, national income, or personal income. All of these, if employed consistently, are useful.

Some regard that percentage as an inverse measure of the extent of freedom that exists in a country. It expresses the share of an individual's income that is directly or indirectly taken and controlled by government so that he can control only the remainder. That is probably an over-simplification. But crude as it may be, that percentage is an easy if imprecise way of quantifying the division of power between the citizen and his government, at least on a historical basis. Its use for comparisons among countries may be subject to question. In many less developed countries such as India, government extracts a smaller share of the GNP than it does in industrial nations, yet it controls economic activities more tightly.

---

[3] William Henry Chamberlain, "State vs. Individual," *Wall Street Journal,* March 11, 1960.

[4] Irving Kristol, "Is the Welfare State Obsolete?," *Harper's,* June 1963.

Bigger government, expressed in terms of employee numbers or dollars spent or as a percentage of the GNP, is not in itself the ultimate goal of many or most of those who argue and work for it. Nor are bigger domestic public programs. Nor is the size of government and its programs the true and final reason for the opposition of those who fight them.

Michael Harrington, a liberal opinion leader, made it clear that he demanded a larger role for the public sector not for its own sake but as a means to an end. He believes that only government can raise the resources and enforce the correct priorities to wipe out slums, find jobs for the underemployed, provide efficient mass transportation, and reconstruct large cities as livable communities.[5]

Proponents do not really aim at big government as such, nor do opponents fight it. They aim at the *results* of big government, at what greatly enlarged public domestic programs will produce:

1. *a redistribution of income* from those who have more to those who have less in order to reduce or eliminate economic differences and to approach, if not necessarily attain, an egalitarian status among all Americans and among all mankind. This is to be accomplished by a progressive tax structure and by expenditures that allocate benefits and services mostly to low-income persons
2. *a shift of power* in decision making from the individual to organized society, that is, government, and from smaller units of government to larger ones, thence to the central government, and eventually to an international body encompassing all countries

In other words, big government is largely a means to the ends of money and power, to a more equal distribution of the former, to a concentration of the latter. Resistance to big government basically attempts to retain claim to what one earns and possesses and to personal freedom.

A Built-in Growth Trend?

There is something in the American tradition that views big government with suspicion. The saying that "the government that governs the least governs the best" may be obsolete but has left some indelible marks. To a Gallup Poll in August 1968 asking "which of the following do you think will be the biggest threat to the country in the future—big business,

---

[5] Michael Harrington, *Toward a Democratic Left: A Radical Program for a New Majority* (New York: Macmillan, 1968).

big labor or big government?'', 46 percent, or nearly half, answered by pointing at government, 26 percent at labor and 12 percent at business, with 16 percent voicing no opinion. The sentiment among all major groups, both political parties, and independents was clearly on the side that big government was the chief threat; there were two exceptions: blacks and persons with an annual family income under $3,000.[6] In other words, except for those two widely overlapping groups, which are the intended main beneficiaries of public social programs, most Americans fear big government, they do not favor it.

Gunnar Myrdal observed that "it is fairly generally recognized by those who have studied the problem that there is a serious and irrational bias against public investment and consumption in America."[7] Yet he predicted that:

> At the same time there is bound to be a bigger government in the sense that the government will have to take increased responsibility for organizing public consumption in the fields of education and health. It will have to redistribute incomes on a large scale by its taxation, social security schemes and agricultural policies. It will have to invest much more in slum clearance and low-rent housing and, indeed, in the complete renewal of the cities and their transport systems, as well as more generally in resource development. It will generally have to increase its responsibilities for a larger part of consumption and investment and, consequently, for employment and production.[8]

That Americans generally dislike big government is most clearly apparent from the fact that presidents have regularly promised to reduce governmental expenditures and tried to point with pride at some actual or claimed temporary successes, even though spending soared during their administrations.

It is now seldom remembered that Franklin D. Roosevelt campaigned in 1932 by denouncing President Hoover for his "reckless and extravagant" deficit spending and socialistic schemes and for pouring out relief. Roosevelt asserted that federal expenditures could be cut 20 percent.[9] As it turned out, federal expenditures more than doubled between 1932 and 1940.

---

[6] "Big Government Is Feared in Poll," *New York Times,* August 18, 1968.

[7] Gunnar Myrdal, *Challenge to Affluence* (New York: Pantheon, 1968), p. 64.

[8] Ibid., p. 93.

[9] See Frank Freidel, *Franklin D. Roosevelt: The Triumph* (Boston: Little, Brown, 1956).

One of President Eisenhower's main themes before and after assuming office was frugality in government. He promised in his budget message in January 1954: "We will reduce the share of the national income which is spent by the Government."[10]

He kept that promise. Federal expenditures, as a percentage of national income, dropped from 25.2 percent in 1953 to 22.4 percent in 1960, his last year in office (see table 24). That reduction of 2.8 percentage points consisted of a 5.2 percent point *decline* in national defense and a 2.5 percent point *increase* in domestic expenditures (domestic expenditures doubled while national income rose only 36 percent). In this case, as so often, a rise in social expenditures was offset by a reduction in defense. Representative Adam Clayton Powell, a liberal leader and sponsor of much progressive legislation as chairman of the House Education and Labor Committee, commented in 1957 on President Eisenhower's policies: "Mr. Eisenhower's middle of the road today is left of Mr. Roosevelt's left of 25 years ago."[11]

John F. Kennedy, as a young Congressman from Massachusetts wrote in 1950:

> Every time that we try to lift a problem from our own shoulders, and shift that problem to the hands of the government, to the same extent we are sacrificing the liberties of our people.[12]

After he had been in the White House for over two years, President Kennedy, at a news conference on April 24, 1963 stated that "in nearly every case, the percentage of expenditures and employment have gone down" and that "federal expenditures in relation to the population, non-defense expenditures, are declining."[13] Budget Director Kermit Gordon remarked simultaneously that federal civilian expenditures had increased proportionately *less* than the GNP. After correcting for the omission of $28 billion in expenditures excluded from the administrative budget, the record shows that federal nondefense spending, on a per capita basis,

---

[10] Eisenhower added: "We are convinced that more progress and sounder progress will be made over the years as the largest possible share of our national income is left with individual citizens to make their own countless decisions as to what they will spend, what they will buy, and what they will save and invest."

[11] U.S., Congress, House, Committee on Education and Labor, *Federal Aid to States for School Construction,* 85th Cong. 1st sess., 1957, p. 395.

[12] *Boston Post,* April 23, 1950.

[13] *Wall Street Journal,* April 22, 25, 1963. See also a reply, "Putting a Myth to Rest," *Wall Street Journal,* May 29, 1963.

increased faster than the GNP, not more slowly. But what is important here is that the president and his budget director found it advisable to claim that they had been successful in cutting federal expenditures. This suggests that they believed the general public to be in favor of such policy which, by all appearances, probably was a correct assessment.

President Johnson pursued the same line. In a speech on November 19, 1964, he said: "I believe that, barring massive changes in defense spending, your federal government does not have to grow in size relative to the size of the economy. . . . Federal spending in 1965 will be the lowest in fourteen years in terms of our Gross National Product. Non-defense spending will be lower than it was thirty years ago in terms of our Gross National Product."[14] In his budget message in January 1965 President Johnson said that "We have good reason to expect that government expenditures in the years ahead will grow more slowly than the gross national product, so that the ratio of federal spending to our total output will continue to decline." The fact is, however, that during the eight years of the Kennedy-Johnson administrations, between 1960 and 1968, federal domestic spending increased 134 percent, the GNP only 72 percent (defense outlays meanwhile went up 76 percent) (see table 24).

Both before and after entering office, one of President Nixon's favorite themes was economy in government spending. Listening to the large number of those who criticized his policies as miserly, starving vital public services, and reversing the trend toward social progress, one would think that President Nixon succeeded in drastically cutting federal nondefense spending. He did recommend in his budgets—as other presidents had— smaller amounts for some programs than their protagonists had demanded; he impounded, or at least tried to impound, some appropriated funds and issued a few vetoes. He also proposed extremely expensive programs, some of which were not adopted by the Congress.

But for whatever reason, federal expenditures for domestic purposes increased at a faster rate in President Nixon's administration than they had during the administrations of Presidents Eisenhower, Kennedy, and Johnson (see p. 119). In fact, the rise between FY 1969 and FY 1975 as proposed in the president's budget, and subsequent actions, suggest that a new record of domestic spending growth may be set during the Nixon-Ford administrations. This could conceivably but does not necessarily mean that President Nixon, or President Ford, once in office, did not carry out, or at least try to carry out, what they had repeatedly promised they would aim

[14] *Saturday Review,* January 9, 1965, pp. 28–29.

for: a slow-down in the growth rate of federal spending. More likely it means that an incumbent president's plans and wishes, particularly when he is faced with a Congress of the opposite political party, do not control spending trends. As imposing as the institutional presidency looks, and as ax-swinging as its budgetary arm is commonly pictured, they may in the end not wield as much power over expenditure policies as it seems from the outside. Other forces may influence the attitude and sentiment of the Congress more powerfully and thereby set long-range trends more decisively than the temporary occupant of the Oval Office.

Many would trace the growth trend in domestic spending to the New Deal of the 1930s but Solomon Fabricant has shown that it dates back at least to the beginning of the century and M. Slade Kendrick ran it back to the early days of the Republic.[15]

The German socialist economist Adolf Wagner first pronounced the "law of the increase of state activities," which has since been known as "Wagner's law":

> Comprehensive comparisons of different countries and different times show that, among progressive peoples, with which alone we are concerned, an increase regularly takes place in the activity of both the central and the local governments. This increase is both extensive and intensive: the central and local governments constantly undertake new functions, while they perform both old and new functions more efficiently and completely. In this way the economic needs of the people to an increasing extent and in a more satisfactory fashion, are satisfied by the central and local governments. The clear proof of this is found in the statistics which show the increased needs of central governments and local political units.[16]

Wagner's law did not attract much attention at the time—and even less support. But the record of the near century that has since passed certainly proved him to be correct. The trend goes back much farther in history and we find criticism of growing fiscal spending in ancient Egypt, Rome, and in Greek city-states.[17] Aristotle warned:

> Where there are revenues the demagogues should not be allowed after their manner to distribute the surplus: the poor are always receiving and always wanting more and more, for such help is like water poured into a leaky cask.[18]

---

[15] Fabricant, *The Trend of Government Activity in the United States*; Kendrick, *A Century and a Half of Federal Expenditures*.

[16] Adolf Wagner, *Grundlagen der Politischen Oekonomie* (1893), as cited by Charles J. Bullock, *Selected Readings in Public Finance*, 3d ed. (Boston: Ginn, 1924), p. 32.

[17] *Panem et circenses*, the pyramids and the acropolis may have been WPA or Great Society projects of their day.

[18] Benjamin Jowett, trans., and W. D. Ross, ed., *The Works of Aristotle* (Oxford: Clarendon Press, 1921), vol. 10, *Politics* 6. 5. 1320a.

Few would dare write so bluntly in the 1970s.

We might assume that with incomes rising and the extent of poverty shrinking the need for government intervention on behalf of the poor or low- to middle-income population might gradually decline. It would seem that in countries in which most people are comparatively well off—as they are in the United States—and many not truly poor, individuals and families could take care of their own requirements more adequately and would have to depend less on support by the government. But it has not worked that way. As prosperity grew so did the demands on government and the action of politicians to meet them, with leaps forward during periods of actual or claimed economic stagnation or decline. There is always a recession for those who produce little or nothing.

The foundation for the spectacular expansion in expenditures for social purposes in the United States was laid in the days of the Great Depression and the New Deal. To be sure, federal spending for domestic purposes never exceeded $7 billion a year during the 1930s and still stood at a mere $12 billion in 1952.

Public spending was small during the 1930s when considered in terms of today's magnitudes. New Deal policies aimed more at restoring predepression conditions than at remaking society.

Thus we might have expected the force of the drive to diminish when economic conditions improved. But it was between 1952 and 1972, when the GNP in *constant* dollars expanded by 100 percent, when per capita income in *constant* dollars increased 70 percent (from $2,641 to $4,492 in 1972 dollars), and when the percentage of families with an income under $3,000 (in 1972 dollars) fell from 18.3 to 7.2 percent, and of those with an income from $3,000 to $4,999 from 18.5 to 9.4 percent of the United States population that the big jump occurred in federal spending for domestic purposes—from $12 billion in 1952 to $131 billion in 1972 and to an estimated $167 billion in FY 1975. It was obviously not greater need that caused the spectacular expansion in social programs.

If it was not greater need, what was the force that powered the big government trend? It was the minds of the young intellectuals of the 1930s whose ideologies were formed during the depression days, who later became the shapers of public opinion and the makers of public decisions. The seeds of the 1930s bore a rich harvest in the 1950s, 1960s, and 1970s.

This shift to the left does not seem to have greatly affected the great mass of the American people. In a nationwide Gallup Poll published on May 6, 1974, 59 percent of those who expressed a preference declared themselves to be conservatives and only 41 percent chose a liberal label.[19] That does not differ much from earlier polls which showed 53 percent conservative in 1936 and 51 percent in 1962.

Successful politicians are usually cognizant of the ideological leanings of the majority of the voters and it is probably because they intuitively knew of the conservative persuasion of their constituents that the presidents whom we quoted earlier (as well as other officeholders) promised to economize in their expenditures policies or prided themselves on having held down spending. The decisive issue that still divides liberals and conservatives is the magnitude of governmental activity in the domestic field.

In 1972 Charles Kadushin of Teachers' College, Columbia University, conducted an opinion poll among what he called the country's intellectual elite, the eight thousand or so persons who had contributed to the top twenty-two intellectual journals during the five-year period 1964–1968.[20] Here are his findings:

> Given their background and position where do elite intellectuals stand politically in comparison to everyone else? To the left. The American intellectual elite is more liberal on any issue of public policy than the American public at large, more liberal than any other segment of the American elite, and generally more liberal than the elite university professors surveyed in the Carnegie study.[21]

Most of those listed among the top group as the most prestigious intellectuals are known to be strongly on the left, though usually not members of the radical ("new") left.

Intellectuals may be small in numbers but their influence on public policy is enormous and, in the long run, decisive. The students and instructors of the 1930s became the professors, heads of departments, and textbook writers of the 1950s and 1960s, the editors, authors, reporters,

---

[19] However, 64 percent of those who expressed a partisan preference labeled themselves Democrats, only 36 percent Republicans.

[20] The list of those journals, to be sure, was biased on the left and did not include *National Review* or any other journal that could be called even moderately conservative. Few of the journals listed would carry an article by a conservative or with a conservative bent. It is, however, a fact that there are far more intellectual journals on the left than on the right. Individuals who are conservatively inclined have not done as much writing—and apparently not as much intellectual reading—as liberals. Conservative journals therefore could not and did not develop to the extent to which liberal journals did.

[21] Charles Kadushin, "Who Are the Elite Intellectuals?," *The Public Interest*, Fall 1972.

commentators, the members and staffs of legislative bodies, the technical and policy officials in executive departments, the leaders of professional associations, presidents, board members and staffs of grant-giving foundations, top attorneys in public affairs cases, protagonists and organizers of civic causes and, last but not least, the law clerks and judges of our courts. Many of them worked with a dedication rarely equaled elsewhere and their efforts produced tangible results in due time.

What became of the intellectually gifted with conservative leanings, those who did not absorb and assimilate the anticapitalist, egalitarian spirit of the 1930s? Most entered business careers to become financially more successful but politically less interested or effective. Many of the rest who chose academe soon learned on which side the bread was buttered.

The majority of intellectuals were and are attracted to ever-growing government because it affords an opportunity to exercise power over the affairs of state in planning, influencing, and directing the fate of men, the action and fortunes of the nation. To wield such power is a most basic instinct and desire of ambitious individuals. The average academician as one of hundreds or thousands on a campus is but a tiny wheel with little direct authority, often frustrated beyond endurance in his ideas and aims. He can become the governing force of immense power while working in or advising government—if he develops or promotes plans to expand and exercise that power and participate in it. And the greater the authority concentrated in government, whether expressed in percentage of the GNP channeled through it or in regulation or other legal power, the greater the academician's satisfaction in money and stature.

Moreover, while men in leading industrial, commercial, and financial positions possess greater economic power than the academician or writer, the academician or writer finds that his best chance to overrule them, to reduce their strength and add to his own, is to increase the size and force of government. He can thus prove that the pen is mightier than the dollar.

It is the intellectuals whose ideas germinated in the spiritual climate of the 1930s, who became the pacesetters and formed the "establishment" of the 1950s and 1960s. The small group of intellectuals in academe who differed, who warned of the dangers of big government and opposed it—men such as Friedrich von Hayek, Wilhelm Roepke, Ludwig von Mises—were ignored, or ridiculed, or viewed and treated as outsiders who could not grasp the spirit of the times.

It was only when some of the gargantuan programs failed to produce the hoped-for and promised socially wholesome results that a few of the keener observers among the liberal intellectuals began to have second thoughts and to voice doubts about the effectiveness of the tools chosen or even about the attainability though not necessarily the desirability of the announced goals (see pp. 149–151). The number of those critics is still small and as of this writing they are voices crying in the wilderness of academe.

Galbraith and His Disciples

The drive for the expansion of domestic public activities was largely suspended during World War II and resumed soon afterwards in President Truman's Fair Deal, in the form of campaigns for specific social programs such as national health insurance, public housing and urban renewal, federal aid to education, etc. The issue of big government as such came to the forefront later with the publication in 1958 of John Kenneth Galbraith's *The Affluent Society*. It still is the most widely known and effective treatise in its field.

In his brilliant writing style Galbraith advanced the thesis that government is too small and private consumption too big, that public services are being starved while the consumer luxuriates.

> The community is affluent in privately produced goods. It is poor in public services. The obvious solution is to tax the former to provide the latter. . . . By making private goods more expensive, public goods are made more abundant. . . .[22]

> The line which divides our area of wealth from our area of poverty is roughly that which divides privately produced and marketed goods from publicly rendered services.[23]

That *The Affluent Society* was able to gain such wide popularity is truly amazing. Its proposition that taxes are too low and that the average man has too much money left to spend according to his own whims is out of step with generally held beliefs and is, if understood, not likely to attract much following among the American people. Which politician would want to run on a platform that proposes a boost in taxes because consumers have more money than they know what to do with and "excess" money should therefore be taken from them?

---

[22] Galbraith, *The Affluent Society*, p. 315.
[23] Ibid., p. 251.

But Galbraith's thesis that public goods are scarce while private goods are abundant, has a ring of truth to it and merits further study. Why is it that public facilities and services always appear to be inadequate or scarce —space for driving and parking, hospitals and medical care, schools and teachers, public parks and sanitation, police, and dozens of others, while there is no shortage of automobiles, television sets, houses, clothing, powerboats, cosmetics, or camping equipment?

The answer is simple: because there is no limit to human wants or desires for things that are free. Our appetite for private goods is disciplined by the necessity of paying for them. There can be no shortage of goods in a free market for people willing to pay a fair price except under war or emergency conditions or when the government interferes with the market by price control or other regulations. When an effective demand rises in a free market, supply will soon catch up with it, with price acting as a balancer.

But most public services are not paid for by the user directly. They seem to come "for free," with the cost borne by someone else or by that distant abstraction, "the government." If the cost of public services is defrayed from business taxes that are supposedly borne by the corporation and its stockholders (though they are actually included in the price to consumers), or paid from state or federal "grants-in-aid," users are given the illusion that the services cost nothing. So, they like them and want more. As long as goods and services can be had gratis or at a fraction of their cost, demand will always exceed supply. That is why public goods will always be scarce.

Balance between demand and supply will be achieved only if the would-be purchaser foots the bill. In public services this is possible only in direct-charge services, for earmarked revenues such as those in programs for old age, medical care or disability, in road construction financed from highway-user charges, or in various local programs financed by a tax levy for a specific and identified purpose. The balance between supply and demand is disturbed when large sections of the population are freed from tax liability—as has been the case increasingly in the federal income tax—though they can enjoy public benefits at someone else's expense and retain the right to vote for candidates who promise to support greater benefits for them. Unless those who make the decision must weigh the pleasure of getting the service against the pain of having to pay the cost, decisions will be unbalanced with a perpetual bias to increase public spending. It was H. L. Mencken who once called an election an advance auction of stolen goods.

When Galbraith talked about the consumer luxuriating while government is being starved and about the imbalance between public and private spending, he conveniently ignored the fact that government spending for nondefense purposes has been rising consistently faster than personal consumption spending.

GOVERNMENTAL NONDEFENSE EXPENDITURES AND PERSONAL
CONSUMPTION EXPENDITURES, 1929, 1952, AND 1972

	Governmental Nondefense Expenditures (in billions)	Personal Consumption Expenditures (in billions)	Ratio Between Public and Private Consumption
1929	$ 9.6	$ 77.2	1:8.04
1952	47.8	216.7	1:4.53
1972	296.5	726.5	1:2.45
Multiplier:			
1929 to 1972	30.9	9.4	
1929 to 1952	5.0	2.8	
1952 to 1972	6.2	3.4	

SOURCE: *Economic Indicators,* June 1974; Supplement to *Economic Indicators,* 1967.

Between 1929—the earliest year for which these data are available —and 1972, governmental nondefense expenditures multiplied 30.9 times, personal consumption expenditures only 9.4 times. The ratio between public and private spending was 1:8.04 in 1929, 1:4.53 in 1952, and 1:2.45 in 1972. In other words, public nondefense spending grew three times faster than private spending in this forty-three year period. Table 26 shows that between 1952 and 1972 personal consumption increased 235 percent—food, clothing, and housing 190 percent, everything else 350 percent. Governmental expenditures for domestic purposes meanwhile went up 645 percent—832 percent for social welfare (education, social security and public welfare, health, hospitals, and sanitation), 414 percent for everything else.

This record does suggest an imbalance or bias. But it is hardly in the direction of private consumption as Galbraith asserted while he scorned the vulgar manner in which the consumer spends his earnings on trivia. Some of Galbraith's disciples and followers such as Seymour Melman, Kenneth

Boulding, Robert Heilbronner, and others aimed their criticism more at the imbalance between public spending for defense and nondefense purposes. National defense dropped from 50 percent of all governmental expenditures in 1952 to 21 percent in 1972 (see table 23). Whether it should drop further will remain controversial.

The publication of *The Affluent Society* in the late 1950s made a deep impact in intellectual and political circles and spawned many other books and articles advocating a similar approach and voicing hope that those ideas would be put into practice. As Henry Steele Commager predicted in 1959:

> It is inevitable that there will be an immense growth of the welfare state. Government and particularly the national government, will necessarily take on ever larger responsibilities in the realm of conservation, education, science, public health, urban rehabilitation, hydroelectric power, communication and so forth. The dividing line between "private" and "public" and between "local" and "general," already blurred, will become all but meaningless.

> Finally, an affluent society, universal education, the welfare state, and a growing awareness of and respect for world opinion should go far to bring about a truly classless society in the United States. That has always been an American ideal, and in the nineteenth century the Western world looked to the United States as exemplar and model of equalitarianism. But our progress toward true equality has been slower than anticipated, and today some Old World societies are more truly equalitarian than is the American.[24]

This added to the Galbraith thesis another thought that was needed to give the "salvation-through-government-spending" drive a broader appeal to make it politically more attractive: egalitarianism, or, in action terms, redistribution of income.

Redistributing Income

"Many people regard inequalities of income as a clear case of the tyranny of the strong and fortunate over the weak and poorly endowed," wrote University of Wisconsin economist Harold Groves a dozen years

---

[24] Henry Steele Commager, "Brave World of the Year 2000," *New York Times Magazine,* November 1, 1959.

before the appearance of *The Affluent Society*.[25] Demands for economic equality, or at least a narrowing of differentials in income and wealth, are of course age-old and have been at the core of many political movements—socialism, communism, populism. Progressive taxation and public expenditures to or for the benefit of low-income persons have been the main instruments of carrying out those aims, at least in countries that did not resort to outright expropriation.

University of Chicago economist Henry C. Simons wrote more than a third of a century ago: "The case for drastic progression in taxation must be rested on the case against inequality—on the ethical or aesthetic judgment that the prevailing distribution of wealth and income reveals a degree (and/or kind) of inequality which is distinctly evil or unlovely."[26] The case for reducing or eliminating income inequality rests in Simons's words on another ethical precept: "At any rate it may be best to start by denying any justification for prevailing inequality in terms of personal desert."[27]

A recent and widely acclaimed work by the Harvard social theorist, John Rawls, *A Theory of Justice,* presents other current trends in egalitarian thought. Rawls asserts that a social order is just and legitimate *only* to the degree that it is directed to the redress of inequality:

> There is no more reason to permit the distribution of income and wealth to be settled by the distribution of natural assets than by historical and social fortunes. . . . No one deserves his greater natural capacity, nor merits a more favorable starting place in society. . . . All social primary good—liberty and opportunity, income and wealth and the basis of self-respect—are to be distributed equally unless an unequal distribution of any or all these goods is to the advantage of the least favored.[28]

Reviewing Rawls's theory, Daniel Bell called it "the most comprehensive effort in modern philosophy to justify a socialistic ethic" and added: "It is striking that Rawls, like Jencks, does not discuss either 'work' or 'effort'—as if those who had succeeded, in the university, or in business or government, had done so largely by contingent circumstances or fortune or social background."[29] Some feel that the denial of any merit

---

[25] Harold C. Groves, *Financing Government* (New York: Henry Holt, 1946), p. 31.

[26] Henry C. Simons, *Personal Income Taxation* (Chicago: University of Chicago Press, 1938), p. 18.

[27] Ibid.

[28] John Rawls, *A Theory of Justice* (Cambridge, Mass.: Harvard University Press, 1971), pp. 74, 102, 303.

[29] Daniel Bell, "On Meritocracy and Equality," *The Public Interest,* Fall 1972, pp. 57 and 58. Christopher Jencks also attributes economic success to luck or fortuitous circumstances and therefore not a matter of personal merit that would justify a reward in the form of

in economic success is based largely on envy and jealousy[30] and even Rawls admitted that "none of these remarks is intended to deny that appeal to justice is often a mask for envy. What is said to be resentment may really be rancor."[31] In light of such complex questions, some authors have expressed amazement that egalitarian theories have become so widely accepted and that for some people the issue is no longer even considered controversial.[32]

Some regard redistribution of income from the top down as a clear case of the tyranny and exploitation of a productive but vote-weak minority by a greedy and vote-strong majority, and feel that rewards for effort are still necessary. University of Chicago law professors Walter J. Blum and Harry Kalven, Jr. have argued: "Whatever we may think in moments of tranquility, we do not live from day to day without the help of the assumption that those around us and we ourselves deserve in some way the praise and blame, the rewards and the punishments, we all dispense and receive."[33] Blum and Kalven referred to the ever-present danger that tax legislation may be turned into (or is) "class legislation in its most naked form."[34]

Income used to be distributed in the shape of a pyramid: a mass of low-income people at the bottom, sidelines narrowing to a peaked top. In much of the world it still is. But in the United States and other industrial countries it has changed to the shape of a diamond: the great bulk in the middle with a narrow base and a narrow top. (See table p. 170)

This remarkable upward movement and the steady reduction in the low-income segment of the American people has only helped to strengthen the drive for increased government action as the following three quotations suggest:

M.I.T. economist Lester C. Thurow summarized an income distribution study for the Joint Economic Committee of Congress: "One of the prime functions of government is continually to redistribute market incomes so that incomes are in accordance with our social or collective

---

higher income or status. "Economic success seems to depend on varieties of luck and on-the-job competence that are only moderately related to family background, schooling, or scores on standard tests" (Christopher Jencks et al., *Inequality*, p. 8).

[30] Helmut Schoeck, *Envy, A Theory of Social Behavior* (New York: Harcourt, Brace and World, 1970).

[31] Rawls, *A Theory of Justice*, p. 540.

[32] See Irving Kristol, "About Equality," *Commentary*, November 1972.

[33] Walter J. Blum and Harry Kalven, Jr., *The Uneasy Case for Progressive Taxation* (Chicago: University of Chicago Press, 1953), p. 82.

[34] Ibid., p. 20.

judgments as to what constitutes a just distribution of economic resources."[35]

Harvard economist Wassily Leontief warned that "the distribution of income is clearly emerging as the issue that will dominate the American political scene in the closing quarter of this century."[36]

Daniel P. Moynihan wrote: "This seems to be happening in 1972, at least on domestic matters. Both parties are putting primary emphasis on income redistribution, the issue likely to dominate the 1970's."[37]

DISTRIBUTION OF MONEY INCOME AMONG FAMILIES, 1952 AND 1972
(In *Constant* 1972 Dollars)

Families with money income:	1952	1972
under $5,000	36.8%	16.6%
$5,000 to $14,000	58.2	53.1
$15,000 and over	5.1	30.3
	100.0	100.0

SOURCE: U.S., Bureau of the Census, *Money Income in 1972 of Families and Persons in the United States,* Current Population Reports, series P-60, no. 90, December 1973.

NOTE: Money income excludes food stamps, public housing, medicare, medicaid and many other types of in-kind income. It also is substantially understated and should not be confused with "personal income" as defined in the national income accounts.

The demand for redistribution of income has converted the historic American principle of equality of opportunity to a claim for equality of results. It equates equity with equality and basically denies a person's right to the fruits of his labor, aiming to take from those who are productive and give to those who are unproductive or nearly so. It regards such action not as charity but as a basic precept of social justice regardless of whether lack of productivity is the result of voluntary action and personal attitude or brought about by insuperable forces and misfortune.

---

[35] U.S., Joint Economic Committee, *The American Distribution of Income: A Structural Problem,* 92d Cong., 2d sess., March 17, 1972, p. 1.

[36] Wassily Leontief, in "Debate 72," *Life,* June 30, 1972,

[37] Daniel P. Moynihan, "Emerging Consensus," *Newsweek,* July 10, 1972.

H. L. Mencken once wrote:

> All government, in its essence, is a conspiracy against the superior man: its one permanent object is to oppress him and cripple him. If it be aristocratic in organization, then it seeks to protect the man who is superior only in law against the man who is superior in fact; if it be democratic, then it seeks to protect the man who is inferior in every way against both. One of its primary functions is to regiment men by force, to make them as much alike as possible and as dependent upon one another as possible, to search out and combat originality among them.[38]

Redistribution of income promises to reduce social tension and social conflict. But it has not done so nor is it likely to do so, because more often it only whets the appetite. Most conflict in this world, strife among individuals, social struggles and wars among nations, as well as most crime, is caused by the desire of some people for what other people have. That desire is often clothed in a pseudoethical justification of envy—reasons why other people are not entitled to that which they possess and why those who have not should have it.

As long as law and order, personal property rights, and inviolability of boundaries, among nations and among individuals, are maintained, the extent of violence is likely to remain small. But once those fences are broken, when official justifications are given and laws are imposed that take from some and give to others, action is encouraged and demands are raised beyond limit, because no amount of "remedy" will satisfy those who feel that they are entitled to what others have. The move toward egalitarianism may lie at the root of much violent upheaval. In all likelihood it was probably no coincidence that the wave of redistributive legislation in the 1960s was shortly followed by unprecedented outbursts of civil disturbances that rocked the country from end to end and left deep scars that may not heal for many years.

War on Poverty?

The big government goal of *The Affluent Society* was not a saleable commodity in the political market. But when seasoned with "alleviation of poverty" it turned attractive and became the focal theme of action in the

---

[38] H. L. Mencken, *A Mencken Chrestomathy* (New York: Alfred A. Knopf, 1949), p. 145.

1960s. The efforts of dedicated individuals and groups toward that goal during the early and middle 1950s bore fruit in the 1960s.[39]

President Kennedy was strongly influenced by Michael Harrington's *The Other America: Poverty in the United States*, which was followed by several dozens of similar books, not to mention streams of articles in magazines and newspapers, and television reports and debates. But few of President Kennedy's New Frontier proposals were enacted into law. It took President Johnson's political genius to conceive a War on Poverty as a road to the Great Society and thereby as a means to establish his role in history and to maneuver the program's major parts through the Congress: Economic Opportunity Act, Civil Rights Act, Elementary and Secondary Education Act, Medicare and Medicaid, and many changes in existing laws on minimum wages, housing, etc., in addition to a sizeable tax cut.

The new programs would, it was expected, revolutionize the United States.[40] They may have done just that in some unintended respects. The riots that followed came at least close to it.

The theory that underlies the poverty war programs is that poverty is a deficiency which is bound to perpetuate itself through generations unless eradicated by governmental action of the type instituted in the 1960s. If that hypothesis were true, most of America's 212 million inhabitants would still be poor, ignorant and unemployed, as their ancestors were when they landed on these shores. It seems that the history of the United States, and its strong economic mobility upward—and downward—stands as living proof of the fundamental error in this theory. The American record suggests that the condition of poverty is not so much a cause but a result, and that it can best be remedied—in those cases where it *can* be remedied—by the individual.

Upon signing the Economic Opportunity Act on August 20, 1964 President Johnson declared it to be "the policy of the United States to eliminate the paradox of poverty in the midst of plenty." Is "poverty in the midst of plenty" truly a paradox? It is, in the same sense that the presence of shadows is a paradox when the sun shines. If there were no sunshine, there would be no shadows.

That a money income of $4,540 for a four-person nonfarm family constitutes poverty[41] is due only to the high income levels prevailing in the

---

[39] See James L. Sunquist, *Politics and Policy: The Eisenhower, Kennedy and Johnson Years* (Washington, D.C.: Brookings Institution, 1968).

[40] "Revolutionizing the U.S.," *U.S. News and World Report,* July 26, 1965; "LBJ's Revolution," *U.S. News and World Report,* October 11, 1965.

[41] U.S., Bureau of the Census, *Characteristics of the Low-Income Population 1973 (Advance Report).*

United States that have lifted the average family income to $12,051 in 1973.[42] In many other industrial countries $4,540 is regarded as a respectable medium income and in the majority of the world's 138 countries it represents a status of affluence which only a small minority enjoys.

Until such time as we learn how to abolish the lowest 10 or 20 percent from our income scale, there will be persons at the lower end of that scale who may be called poor—by comparison. The fact is that productivity, that is, the value of the output of goods or services, varies more widely among individuals in the United States than income. The question is how far government should go and can go in "abolishing poverty" and how it should go about it.

To abolish poverty is a noble idea but certainly not a new idea. The American people have long been engaged in the most effective anti-poverty campaign the world has ever seen. They have changed the historical distribution of income from the shape of a pyramid to the shape of a diamond. Can the low end be completely wiped out?

To those who believe "there are no great problems in the alleviation of poverty that the direct disbursement of money to the poor will not tolerably remedy,"[43] the poverty war was an unquestioned if limited success. It multiplied various forms of income-support payments. But a prime idea in the program had been that by spending *more* on school education, as well as on youth and general manpower training, *less* would have to be spent later on for welfare, crime fighting, and the cost of social ills. But most of those programs did not produce the promised results and turned out to be failures.

Nowhere is this more clearly apparent than in education. It was then widely believed—and still is contended by many—that millions of children were unable to master the three Rs because their schools were starved for funds and that the solution was to appropriate more money. The money was spent, but academic achievements as measured on standard tests declined. The intensive study of American schools conducted by James Coleman and his associates found that for the groups studied "by far the largest part of the variation in student achievement lies *within* the same school, and not *between* schools."[44]

---

[42] U.S., Bureau of the Census, *Money Income in 1973 of Families and Persons in the United States (Advance Report),* Current Population Reports, series P-60, no. 93, 1974. If the family head was a year-round full-time worker, family income averaged $14,614 in 1973; if the wife was also in the paid labor force, family income averaged $17,292.

[43] Robert L. Heilbronner, "Priorities for the Seventies," *Saturday Review,* January 3, 1970.

[44] Emphasis added. James S. Coleman et al., *Equality of Educational Opportunity,* p. 297.

In his restudy of the Coleman findings, Christopher Jencks reported:

> In the short run it remains true that our most pressing political problem is the achievement gap between Harlem and Scarsdale. But in the long run it seems that our primary problem is not the disparity between Harlem and Scarsdale, but the disparity between the top and bottom of the class in both Harlem and Scarsdale.[45]

There are vast achievement differences among the schools in New York City though they are funded on the same tax base; and, as mentioned earlier (p. 135) the high-achievement schools spend much less per pupil than the low-achievement schools.[46] Christopher Jencks summarized his findings:

> There is no evidence that school reform can substantially reduce the extent of cognitive inequality, as measured by tests of verbal fluency, reading comprehension, or mathematical skill. . . .
>
> These findings imply that school reform is never likely to have any significant effect on the degree of inequality among adults. . . .
>
> Our research suggests, however, that the character of a school's output depends largely on a single input, the characteristics of the entering children. Everything else—the school budget, its policies, the characteristics of the teachers—is either secondary or completely irrelevant, at least so long as the range of variation among schools is as narrow as it seems to be in America.[47]

Yet for ten years billions of dollars were poured into a program that did not produce what its sponsors promised it would—and Congress extended the law for another four years in the summer of 1974. Many persons are emotionally unable to accept the fact that differences in achievement are largely differences between individual children and not between schools.[48]

---

[45] Christopher Jencks et al., *Inequality*.

[46] This does not mean that children learn less because the schools they attend spend more. It does mean that the school administrators tried to overcome the learning deficiencies of children who lag one or more years behind national norms, that is, behind the average performance of all children, by pouring in more money, lowering class sizes, etc. That this has proven to be as ineffective as rain dances or the incantations of witch doctors has had no deterrent impact on the proponents of such plans. They are emotionally unable to accept the fact that children with innate capacity and aspiration to learn show high achievement—ahead of their grade level, that is, age—despite large class sizes and low expenditures per pupil, whereas low-capacity children continue to fall behind regardless of the multiplication of funds.

[47] Mary Jo Bane and Christopher Jencks, "The Schools and Equal Opportunity," *Saturday Review of Education,* October 1972, pp. 40–41.

[48] For example, Kenneth B. Clark, who still feels that schools have failed children from low-income backgrounds and that urban schools are inadequately funded. See his *Pathos of Power* (New York: Harper and Row, 1974).

Public assistance, especially AFDC, was vastly expanded and the number of children on AFDC multiplied threefold between 1960 and 1970. But social ills that were supposed to be ameliorated, such as illegitimacy and abandonment, simultaneously soared—and not just coincidentally—and the crime rate kept going up steeply.[49]

The failure of the Community Action Program was described by Daniel P. Moynihan in *Maximum Feasible Misunderstanding: Community Action in the War on Poverty.*[50] The number of examples could be multiplied in many programs which did not produce what their sponsors had promised.

Within not too many years after the enactment of the War on Poverty, people were beginning to ask whether this was a *Great Society* or a *Sick Society.*[51] Wrote Peter Drucker in 1969:

> There is mounting evidence that government is big rather than strong; that it is fat and flabby rather than powerful; that it costs a great deal but does not achieve much. There is mounting evidence also that the citizen less and less believes in government and is increasingly disenchanted with it. Indeed, government is sick—and just at the time when we need a strong, healthy, and vigorous government. . . .
>
> The greatest factor in the disenchantment with government is that government has not performed. . . . But the greatest disappointment, the great letdown is the fiasco of the Welfare State. . . .[52]

The plight of the cities is receiving growing attention and is widely regarded as mainly a problem of getting more money from the federal government. But financial troubles—growing demand for public services and an inadequate tax base—are only the symptoms of the disease. As is so often the case, they are the result of the illness, not its cause. The middle- and upper-income classes that historically provided the cities' economic base and resources as well as civic leadership have been engaged in a mass exodus and are being replaced by new residents who have little or nothing to offer in support, contributions, or leadership, but need and demand

---

[49] See the statement by Roger A. Freeman in U.S. Senate, Committee on Finance, *Social Security Amendments of 1971,* 92d Cong., 2d sess., part 3: 1511 ff.

[50] New York: The Free Press, 1969.

[51] "Is There a Sick Society in the U.S.: Riots, Crime, Youth Revolt," *U.S. News and World Report,* August 28, 1967.

[52] Peter F. Drucker, "The Sickness of Government," *The Public Interest,* Winter 1969; see also "The Sickness of Government," *New York Times,* February 9, 1969; and more extensively in Peter F. Drucker, *The Age of Discontinuity* (New York: Harper and Row, 1969), pp. 212, 217–18.

vastly expanded public services. The trend appears to be intensifying and signals more trouble for cities in the years ahead.

The flight from the cities is not necessarily a natural phenomenon like the weather or earthquakes. It is of course partially due to rising affluence, which enables more people to live in suburbia. But to a large extent it can be traced to perverse public policies. To be sure, city policies are not designed with the intent or for the purpose of driving out the high- and middle-income families and attracting the poor—but they could not be much different if they were. Some of those policies are the result of federal influence, mandates, or court orders. Many are city-made. So, city residents vote with their feet—to escape to a more congenial jurisdiction from a government whose course of action they found unbearable but beyond their power to influence.

There is no sign that policies affecting cities are likely to be changed to reverse the trend of migration—to attract middle- and upper-income families and to discourage low-income families from coming in and taking over. Most of the programs that have been adopted—or that cities are asking the federal government to institute and finance—are unlikely to reverse existing trends and some major cities seem to be headed for increasingly precarious conditions.

A national survey on the hopes and fears of the American people, conducted in 1971 by the Gallup organization for Potomac Associates found: "Traditional optimism about the nation's steady progress has faltered. The average American feels that the United States has slid backwards over the past five years."[53] When asked about unrest in the country and ill-feeling between groups, nearly half—47 percent—expressed their belief that it would lead to a breakdown.

Whatever the promise and high expectations of the Great Society legislation when it was proposed, adopted, and carried into practice, it must be regarded as a failure; within a few years it led to increased tension, to fear, and to a feeling of having fallen back.

In a review of seven books on related subjects, Elizabeth Drew found:

> It is widely believed that we tried the items on our national agenda, and they did not work. We spent a lot of money on our problems, and we don't feel better. We entrusted the government to the brightest in our midst, and they appear to have fouled up.[54]

---

[53] Elizabeth Drew, "Contemplating the National Navel," *New York Times Book Review*, June 4, 1972.

[54] Ibid.

Ms. Drew added that the "great legislative outburst occurred after Lyndon Johnson's overwhelming election victory in 1964. Within two years, the Congress had grown weary of the President, his programs and his prodding. . . . [1967] was not a good year for federal programs. But in 1968 it was smart to say that they had not worked."[55]

Once in a blue moon an error in public policy is admitted and subsequently corrected. The Eighteenth Amendment (Prohibition) is an outstanding example of a well-intentioned government administering a cure that was worse than the disease. So it was repealed fourteen years later, with the bootleggers the main losers.

But in the welfare programs of the past decade or two there are millions of people with a personal stake and vested interest, people who either receive various forms of regular cash or in-kind benefits for free or were given and hold jobs at a salary and with a power they never could have obtained otherwise. Others serve as advisors or consultants to government or foundations and hold fat contracts. But as far as members of Congress are concerned, they have solved the problem by appropriating billions of dollars; they feel this is all that can be expected of them.

The expansion of federal activity to many hundreds of domestic benefit and service programs, however, had grave consequences beyond mere cost. The blunder at the Bay of Pigs can be charged, at least in part, to the fact that President Kennedy devoted only little time to an advance study of the proposed action and had to rely mostly on others because he was preoccupied with his New Frontier programs. President Johnson became so deeply involved in Vietnam not because he had so planned. Quite the contrary. His primary interest was focused on domestic affairs and he aimed to devote his undivided attention to the pursuit of the Great Society. In consequence he gave inadequate time to the study of the extremely complicated Vietnam situation, acted rashly—and it blew up in his face with a vengeance. That ruined his chances to achieve what he had wanted above everything else: an honored role during his incumbency and fame in the history books.

Domestic matters now consume most of the time of the president and Congress and leave insufficient hours for the study of national security and foreign affairs, which only our highest national officials can properly weigh and decide. Governors, state legislatures, mayors, city councils, county commissioners, and school boards could resolve domestic service

---

[55] Ibid.

problems, with some fiscal aid from the national government, if necessary. This would leave the president and Congress free to concentrate on matters that inevitably are their responsibility.

The issue was clearly presented some years ago by W. Glenn Campbell, Director of the Hoover Institution on War, Revolution and Peace at Stanford University:

> The core of the problem is that the President who is called upon to make decisions on which hang the very existence of the nation and lives of many millions, decisions which require more study than there are hours in the day, must cut short his consideration of foreign policy and national security to deal with aid for sewage treatment plants, to round up an extra five or ten votes for a Department of Urban Affairs or for public works acceleration, to worry in whose district he should place some of the added public works projects, or to figure out how to make some discredited and unpopular aid-to-education bills acceptable to a Congress which has concluded after examining the evidence on innumerable occasions that they are unnecessary, and has rejected them time and again.
>
> A review of the *Congressional Record* shows that most of the time of Congress is spent on approving numerous types of local benefits and not on the most vital and urgent business at hand—national security. There may not have been too much harm in engaging in politically more rewarding pursuits than national security in a simpler world, when the nation was not so gravely threatened. But today it is intolerable to have the President and Congress devote so much of their time to domestic affairs which can as well or better be handled by others.
>
> There are no objective yardsticks, no scientific criteria, and no hard and fast formulae by which anybody can measure the needs of defense and of a hundred other services in order to assign relative priorities. Former Budget Director Bell testified, "It is plain that considering the national security in this broad sense requires the President—and the Congress—to make a difficult series of choices for which we do not have a satisfactory set of criteria." Nor is it possible to solve such choices with an automatic calculus. They require wisdom, and human wisdom of the highest order. If the President and Congress are to concentrate on them we must devise a better division of labor in regard to governmental functions than we have at the present time.
>
> *It would seem, therefore, that the first and foremost priority for national security rests, not on money, but rather on the brains of our top officials–on their adequate time for study, for deliberation, for decision.* They should not be called upon to deal with hundreds of local services and benefits which can be adequately judged by officials who are closer to the scene and can devote their whole time and talents to these tasks.[56]

---

[56] W. Glenn Campbell, "Assuring the Primacy of National Security," in David M.

Concentration of Power and Loss of Freedom

By its massive entry over the past two decades into the field of domestic public services, the national government has decisively altered the nature of the American federal system. In establishing a federal structure with an intricate system of checks and balances the founding fathers had aimed to disperse authority so widely that no one branch or level of government —and no one man—could prevail over the others. They concluded from history that concentration of power corrupts and sooner or later leads to abuse and tyranny. Whenever the wisdom of the age-old lesson is disregarded, its truth is brought home to the nation sooner or later with a brutal shock.

Constitutionally and traditionally, the federal government held responsibility and authority only over certain specified and delegated functions such as national security, foreign affairs, the postal service, and a few others. Most of the domestic public services were within the realm of the states and their local subdivisions. So when the Congress decided to establish a federal presence in some of those areas it usually did so through federal grants-in-aid to the states that were not only earmarked but conditioned on an operation under closely specified federal rules and a tight supervision by federal administrators. Only a few domestic programs, such as social security, are operated directly by departments of the national government.

The number of federal grants multiplied from a few dozen in the immediate post-World War II period to well over 500—according to some counts, close to 1,000—in recent years. Their amount jumped from $2.6 billion in 1952 to $36 billion in 1972 and an estimated $52 billion in FY 1975. The concurrent shift of power to the national government diminishes not just historic states rights but individual rights because freedom is indivisible.

When the right of citizens is restricted to run public services in their communities and states according to their own concepts—which may and do differ widely—the freedom of those citizens is adversely affected. A central government that holds sway over local governments thereby also controls the individuals who live in those jurisdictions. Most residents of the United States are increasingly dependent upon the national government

---

Abshire and Richard V. Allen, eds., *National Security: Political, Military, and Economic Strategies in the Decade Ahead* (Stanford, Calif.: Hoover Institution on War, Revolution and Peace, and New York: Praeger, 1963), pp. 976–77.

in some form—for wages, promotions, grants, subsidies, orders, or pensions, or are subject to favors or harassment by regulatory or tax enforcement agencies.

Few can afford to oppose policies of the federal bureaucracy; few have a chance to succeed if they do and dare stand up for their rights. Enforced consensus and conformity have become the rule because the penalty for deviation is too severe. Extension of federal grants into every nook and cranny of local services smoothed the road and conditioned public attitude toward increasing federal regulation and interference by new laws, administrative rules, practices of dedicated and power-hungry bureaucrats, and orders of ambitious judges who shifted from interpreting the law to policy making and amending the meaning of the constitution. There are few if any activities or practices left to local governments, business firms, associations or individuals that are not governed or can be governed and often drastically changed by federal authorities under the sanction of law.

While ample lip service is being lavished on the precept of home rule, particularly by those who are busy digging its grave, and a facade of local autonomy is being maintained—because the architects of centralization "wisely refrained from tampering with the Ark of the Covenant," preserved the symbols, and respected the rituals—the substance of self-government has been drained.

As long as local diversity is maintained, citizens who find themselves in the minority in their home areas can move to jurisdictions whose policies or governments are more appealing to them. When national uniformity is imposed, by federal law or regulation or by federal courts, the individual's choice and the right of communities to exercise home rule and local autonomy come to an end.

The multiplication of federal grants for domestic services has led to the formation of a vertical functional autocracy which supersedes the self-government of local communities that used to characterize the American scene. If grants were intended to aid states and local governments, as is often asserted, they could be given without conditions, to be spent at the discretion of local authorities.

That was in fact tried when revenue sharing was enacted in October 1972. It was done on federally specified conditions and with several controls attached. Currently there is a drive underway to tighten those controls and introduce further earmarking when the present authorization for revenue sharing expires.

Until just a few years ago most political scientists—and particularly those who were inclined toward bigger government—favored a stronger shift of power from state and local governments to the national government and to the presidency. Events of recent years have caused many of the former enthusiasts of greater concentration authority to have second thoughts.

The expansion and intensification of domestic public services has had a direct and negative impact on personal freedom. Again, if we define freedom as the ability of the individual to make meaningful choices among known alternatives, then it follows that the extent of his freedom depends on the range of decisions which he can make for himself and his family as opposed to those being made for him. The larger a share of an individual's product or resources government takes *from* him and spends *for* him, the less an individual can allocate to his manifold needs and wants—for housing, education, health, recreation—according to his own judgment, desire or preference. The heavier his taxes are for public schools, the less able is he to send his children to a private school of his choice.

When a government expands and intensifies its activities and tightens the rules under which its residents must live, it always does so in the name of the people and for their presumed benefit. It may retain established rituals and honored traditions by which it hides the change and stakes out a seemingly respectable claim to legitimacy. Hitler, Mussolini, and Stalin claimed to be governing in the long-range interest and for the good of their citizens, many of whom (and at times a majority of whom) believed, at least temporarily, that it was all done for their own "liberty and pursuit of happiness." Nearly half a century ago, Mr. Justice Brandeis, one of the leading liberals of his day, warned that

> experience should teach us to be most on our guard to protect liberty when the government's purposes are beneficent. Men born to freedom are naturally alert to repel invasion of their liberty by evil-minded rulers. *The greatest dangers to liberty lurk in insidious encroachment by men of zeal, wellmeaning but without understanding.*[57]

It is the nature of government to continually try to extend the range and intensity of its functions and to penetrate deeply into affairs which used to be regarded as being in the private sphere, thereby narrowing and endangering individual freedom. "Liberty has never come from the government," Woodrow Wilson wrote, reminding us that "a history of liberty is the history of limitations of governmental powers, not the increase of it."

---

[57] Olmstead v. United States, 277 U.S. 438 (1927), at 477. Emphasis added.

It is for good reason that the recognized leader of the behavioral scientists, B. F. Skinner—who has been called "the most influential of living American psychologists"—came to the conclusion in his book, *Beyond Freedom and Dignity,* that we can no longer afford freedom, and so it must be replaced with control over man, his conduct, and his culture.

Prospects for the Last Quarter of the Twentieth Century

Forecasting the future is an ancient art, once highly honored, but a most hazardous undertaking. Some wise statistics professors used to teach their students never to make a projection or prediction for less than fifteen years so they could keep their jobs for fourteen. The target in this chapter is twenty-five years away, the turn of the century, which at this writing is about as far ahead as the midcentury lies behind.

There is a seemingly irresistible attraction to pin our dreams and hopes and expectations on a millennial year which, over the source of history, so many have visualized as the realization of the romantic notion of *the millennium.* It was so a thousand years ago when huge masses waited and prepared themselves for the Second Coming or the Thousand Year Reich and it is so again when there is much speculation about the year 2000. Of course, most of the scholarly studies that have been undertaken are more down to earth and some are outright disappointing to those who harbor great hopes. Herman Kahn and Anthony Wiener wrote in 1967: "We would be willing to wager small sums, at even odds, that the next third of a century will contain fewer surprises than either of the preceding thirds (i.e., that in this respect the world is more like 1815 than 1914)."[58] Nor does the comprehensive study of the Commission on the Year 2000, sponsored by the Carnegie Foundation, foresee many fundamental or spectacular changes or developments.[59]

In fact, as we are moving closer to the magical year, utopian expectations of the millennium seem to be increasingly transformed into an attitude that can more properly be termed *fin de siècle.* It is what Lance Liebman called "the negativist reaction to the Promethean fallacy . . . the new pessimism that exists concerning the human capacity to achieve social ends"

---

[58] Herman Kahn and Anthony J. Wiener, *The Year 2000: A Framework for Speculation on the Next Thirty-Three Years* (New York: Macmillan, 1967), p. 38.

[59] Daniel Bell, ed., *Toward the Year 2000: Work in Progress* (Boston: Houghton Mifflin, 1967).

because of "the failure of domestic reform in the 1960s."[60] It is what Herbert Gans diagnosed as "The American Malaise," as the consequence of a "recent widening of the gap between these expectations and their achievement."[61] Surveying the country in 1972 and looking ahead the editors of *Changing Times* found that "fear seemed to be the mood of the land."[62] Andrew Hacker warned that "only a few decades remain to complete the era America will have known as a nation." He called his book *The End of the American Era.*[63]

Even if forecasters are able to set aside their personal values or biases, their hopes and fears, their record of being right is rather poor. Around 1960 some of our leading newspapers and magazines carried predictions for the decade ahead, many of which had been prepared by leading experts in the various relevant disciplines. As it turned out, most of those predictions of things to come were wide off the mark.

As a rule, they tended to overestimate the size of the population, they slightly overrated economic growth, and they were overly optimistic regarding the tranquility that would pervade the nation and the rest of the globe. Most foresaw correctly that there would be no worldwide conflagration but some minor wars, though none expected the deep involvement of the United States in the decade's most troublesome armed conflict in Southeast Asia. They did not predict the crime explosion, the youth and drug revolt, and the campus, urban and racial riots, and few, save those with a special interest, expected the tidal wave of social legislation. Where they went wrong the farthest: none predicted inflation to be as steep, persistent, and worldwide as it has been and still is and few thought that government spending would grow as much or that the comparative standing of the United States in many fields would decline as sharply as it did. No economist predicted in 1972 the worldwide wave of high-rate inflation in 1973 and 1974 and the doubling or tripling of the prices of many major commodities on the world's markets. That experience, not the first of its kind, should caution us on quantitative forecasts for the years ahead. But we might at least try to identify trends that appear to be of a long-range nature.

---

[60] Lance Liebman, "Social Intervention in a Democracy," *The Public Interest,* Winter 1974.

[61] Herbert J. Gans, "The American Malaise," *New York Times Magazine,* February 6, 1972.

[62] "The Storm 70's—Big Changes Still to Come," *Changing Times,* August 1972.

[63] Andrew Hacker, *The End of the American Era* (New York: Atheneum, 1970).

Prospects: Zero Population Growth?

One of the safest predictions in recent yeas has been that the next population projection of the Bureau of the Census would be scaled down from the preceding one. The customary four population projections (under four alternative assumptions) for the year 2000 ranged from 283 to 361 million in 1967, from 271 to 322 million in 1971, and from 251 to 300 million in 1972. In February 1975 the Census Bureau issued new projections which varied from 245 to 287 million.[64] The birthrate stood at 18.1 per 1000 population in 1971 and has since dropped by 17 percent to 15.0 in the twelve months ending with December 1974, the lowest rate in the history of the United States.[65] With death rates maintaining a remarkable long-term stability at 9.4 per 1000, births are the main determinant of changes in population size. The birthrate has fluctuated with wars and economic fortunes but shown a secular downward trend. It hit a postwar high of 25.3 per 1000 in 1957 and 1959 but has since been sliding with only a mild sign of bottoming out late in 1974. The number of births fell from an all-time high of 4.3 million in 1957 to a total of 3,166,000 in 1974.

The fertility rate, that is, the number of children an average woman bears during her lifetime slid from 3.8 in 1957 to 2.4 in 1970, to 2.0 in 1972, and to 1.9 in 1973. The lowest projection in the 1975 estimate for the year 2000 is based on a rate of 1.7. The replacement level, that is, the fertility rate at which the population would replace itself within about seventy years, is 2.1. This means then that, disregarding immigration, the United States population would at this rate become stationary in due time—*zero population growth*—and then start to decline. For the next few decades, however, the United States population will keep growing, carried by the momentum of the postwar baby boom. The fourteen to thirty-four-year-old population (birth years 1940–1960) was 47 percent higher in 1974 than it had been in 1960. Immigration, which has been running at about 400,000 net per year, will postpone zero population growth to about the year 2015. No one, of course, can or dares predict whether or when the birthrate will flatten out or turn up again.

A fertility prospects survey of the Bureau of the Census in June 1974 showed that the number of lifetime births expected by wives eighteen to

---

[64] U.S., Bureau of the Census, *Population Estimates and Projections*, Current Population Reports, series P-25, nos. 381, 470, 493, and 541.

[65] U.S., Department of Health, Education and Welfare, National Center for Health Statistics, *Monthly Vital Statistics Report*, vol. 23, no. 12, February 28, 1975.

thirty-nine years old dropped 18 percent between 1967 and 1974 (from 3118 per 1000 wives to 2550).[66] Child population (under fourteen years of age) in the United States declined 3.5 million (−6.4 percent) between April 1970 and July 1974, and was smaller in 1974 than it had been in 1960.[67] The implication for future school and college enrollment—and in due time for the size of the United States population—is obvious.

If we suppose that the lowest of the 1975 projections materializes, the United States population will grow from 208.8 million in July 1972 (and 212.8 million in January 1975) to 245 million in the year 2000, an increase of 17 percent in the span of twenty-eight years, compared with a 33 percent growth in the twenty-year period 1952–1972. This means that the rate of population growth, including immigration, will be cut into half: from 1.4 percent per annum between 1952 and 1972 to 0.7 percent between 1972 and 2000. Over the twelve-month period ending January 1, 1975, the United States population increased 1.6 million or 0.76 percent.[68]

Slower growth in population suggests less need for public services to expand over the period under review. But changes in population composition are no less significant.

Prospects: Sustained Economic Growth?

One of the major demographic factors affecting the capacity of the economy to sustain welfare services is the dependency ratio, that is, the ratio between persons in the productive ages (twenty to sixty-four) and the nonproductive or dependent ages (under twenty, and sixty-five and over). In 1900 there were in the United States 100 persons in dependent ages for every 107 persons in the productive ages, a ratio of 1:1.07. Declining birthrates lifted the ratio gradually to 1:1.38 in 1950, which facilitated more ample support for the aged and the young. The postwar wave of babies pushed the ratio down to 1:1.10 in 1960. It stood at 1:1.18 in 1974 but, assuming a fertility rate of 1.7, will be at 1:1.58 in the year 2000 according to the abovementioned projections. With the number of persons in the productive age groups projected to grow by 31 percent between 1974

---

[66] U.S., Bureau of the Census, *Prospects for American Fertility: June 1974,* Current Population Reports, series P-20, nos. 269 and 277.

[67] U.S., Bureau of the Census, *Estimates of the Population of the United States by Age, Sex and Race: July 1, 1974 and April 1, 1970,* Current Population Reports, series P-25, no. 529.

[68] U.S., Bureau of the Census, *Population Estimates and Projections,* Current Population Reports, series P-25, no. 542.

and 2000 while the dependent age group will decline 2.5 percent, support to the aged and the young should require a smaller share of the total economic product.[69] That contrasts with the situation in the earlier period: between 1950 and 1972, the dependent age group grew 54 percent, the productive age group only 8 percent.

Declining labor force participation of men—from 87.2 per 100 men age sixteen and over in 1952 to 79.7 in 1972—has been more than offset by sharply higher participation of women—from 34.8 in 1952 up to 43.9 in 1972, running at 46 per 100 in 1975, so that there was a slight increase in total labor force participation. With the rate of childbearing on the downgrade and opportuniities for women steadily widening there is a chance that aggregate labor force participation may not be lower by the year 2000—and could even be higher. An offsetting factor, however, is the tendency toward earlier and better paid retirement as well as the trend toward other and increasingly more generous types of transfer payments.

Weekly hours of work have been slowly but steadily declining, about 2.5 hours over the past twenty years, mostly in retail and other services that provide an increasing share of the total employment. The trend appears to be continuing.

To predict the rate of unemployment for a year or even half a year ahead is a rash undertaking. To try and project it for a decade or two would be idle. The unemployment rate has been averaging 5.3 percent of the civilian labor force in the 1970s, slightly up from the 4.5 percent of the 1950s and the 4.8 percent of the 1960s. Considering the looseness of definition of unemployment in United States practice—quite different from the usage in most European countries—our general antibusiness and anticapital-formation bias in tax and other public policies, our uniquely high minimum wage laws and general wage scales, and the ever-increasing unemployment and welfare benefits that make gainful employment unattractive to many low-productive persons, a rate of 5 percent—and possibly more —does not seem higher than might be expected. Nor do the prospects appear promising that the public policies which cause those unemployment rates to run in the neighborhood of 5 percent or more will be significantly changed—except possibly in directions that would add to inflationary pressures.

Looking ahead, and considering rising minimum wage rates and growing demands to further liberalize unemployment compensation under

---

[69] The number of persons sixty-five and over is projected to increase by nine million, which will be more than offset by an 11 million decline of persons below the age of twenty. The average age of the American population will rise from 28.6 to 37.0 years.

national standards, the unemployment rate is likely, in the long run, to move at higher levels than those that prevailed in 1972.

School-age population (ages five to seventeen) is likely to decline by 16 percent, from 51 to 43 million, between 1974 and 2000, under the abovementioned low-fertility projections. College age population (ages eighteen to twenty-four) will shrink 15 percent (from 26.9 to 22.8 million). That should make it far easier to finance education, compared with the 1952–1972 period when enrollments nearly doubled. The past twenty years have seen a steep rise in the percentage of young people attending college, to a point where some of the major job markets for college graduates are now amply supplied or even overloaded.[70] With the vast majority of the sixty million job openings projected between 1972 and 1985 available to persons who have not completed college, the percentage of high school graduates proceeding to college is not likely to increase. It is more likely to decline, having fallen from 55 percent in 1968 to 49 percent in 1972, according to the U.S. Education Commissioner's annual report for 1974. In an October 1973 survey the Bureau of the Census found that the percentage of high school seniors who intend to enter college dropped from 45.4 percent in 1972 to 42.1 percent in 1973.[71] The period of expansion in colleges and universities may be over for a long time. Enrollment is expected to rise only slightly in the second half of the 1970s and to shrink substantially after 1980.

There are, however, some factors that suggest rising demands on government. The number of persons age sixty-five and over will increase 40 percent—from 20.8 to 30.6 million— and the average retirement age still seems to be lowering, all of which will put a severe strain on the social security system and most pension funds as well as on general medical, geriatric, and congregate care (nursing home) facilities and services.

Fertility seems to be inversely related to family income. This may partially be due to the fact that childless women are more likely to be gainfully employed. But a recent census study shows, for example, that the number of children ever born to wives of household heads averaged 2.66 at ages twenty-five to thirty-four, in family income brackets below $3000 and 2.8 between $3000 and $4999 but only 1.8 in income brackets between $15,000 to $24,999 and 1.7 in brackets of $25,000 and up.[72] Also,

---

[70] There is a question about the extent to which that condition may have been intensified by a widespread lowering of admission and academic standards.

[71] U.S. Bureau of the Census, *College Plans of High School Seniors: October 1973,* Current Population Reports, series P-20, no. 270, October 1974.

[72] U.S., Bureau of the Census, *Fertility Expectation of American Women: June 1973, Population Characteristics,* Current Population Reports, series P-20, no. 265, June 1974.

according to the same report, fertility rates are higher for wives of low-skilled and unskilled workers, for blacks and for women of so-called Spanish origin. Those categories constitute a disproportionately heavy share of the welfare load and this has potent implications for future demands on social and medical benefit and service programs, public housing and housing subsidies, special education, law enforcement, and other public servcies.

Inflation has been a perpetual if fluctuating fact of life for four decades and has recently advanced from the 5–6 percent level of the second half of the 1960s to two-digit status. Basically, inflation expresses the unwillingness or political inability of the decision makers to have government and the rest of the economy live within their means; it is an attempt to distribute and allocate more than 100 percent of the pie after promising each that he will get more than the slice he has been getting—as each has been demanding. To a considerable extent inflation is the result of a hypochondriac fiscal policy throughout the postwar period that has acted as if unemployment had been and were due to inadequate demand rather than to structural rigidities and other obstacles to market adjustment that are largely government imposed. Internationalization of inflation in recent years has made it more respectable and, though it may be the most critical economic issue facing the free world today, efforts seem to focus more on finding easier ways to live with it than to end it. ("If you can't lick 'em, join 'em.")

While there is a good chance that present double-digit inflation rates may moderate within a reasonable time, we cannot be optimistic about the long-range prospects, given the political climate that is likely to prevail during the last quarter of the twentieth century in the United States and in many other democratic countries. There is no inflation or unemployment in the Soviet Union. But neither is there a press that would report that inflation or unemployment do exist after the government decreed that they don't.

Consumer prices doubled in the past quarter century, which means that the dollar lost half of its purchasing power. It appears likely that prices will go up at a somewhat faster rate over the next twenty-five years. It is hoped, though, that Americans will not have to face the type of runaway inflation experienced in several European countries after World War I or II and in China, some Latin American countries, and Persia at other times in history. At least not yet.

What do these facts imply for economic growth? The GNP has been increasing at an average annual rate of about 3.3 percent (in *constant* dollars) for many decades and has approximately doubled every twenty years:

GNP GROWTH IN CONSTANT DOLLARS, IN TWENTY-YEAR PERIODS

	GNP *1958 dollars* *(in billions)*	*Percent* *Increase*
1929*	$203.6	
1952	395.1	94%
1972	790.7	100

SOURCE: *Economic Report of the President,* February 1974.

* Because 1932 was the depth of the depression, we are using 1929 as the last predepression year.

An annual growth rate of 3.3 percent is somewhat lower than the growth experiences of leading European countries and the Soviet Union but it is a respectable long-range rate, considering the political obstacles that private enterprise in the United States faces.

To some extent the future rate of economic growth will depend on events and developments all over the world, many of which are beyond the control or even influence of the United States. But by far the most powerful factor is the policies this country will pursue in the years ahead. In the continuing struggle over income and poverty the American people face a choice between concentrating on enlarging the economic pie as much as possible so that everyone can have a bigger piece or engaging in an ever more fierce struggle over splitting the same or only slightly enlarged pie.

Until not so long ago there seemed to exist a broad consensus among Americans that a bigger pie was the most desirable goal and should rate top priority. In recent years movements have sprung up that question the desirability or even the feasibility of continued growth and would prefer stability. Some forces that aim primarily at a division of the pie in line with their own beliefs of social justice seem much more bent on cutting the share of those who get the bigger slices than in enlarging the smaller slices.

If future tax and other economic policies will encourage capital formation and afford private enterprise the widest possible freedom, national income and product could well double again over the next twenty years, climbing from $1158 billion in 1972 to $2.3 trillion (in *1972* dollars) by

1992, and might approach the neighborhood of $3 trillion soon after the turn of the century.

If, however, redistribution of income from the most productive to the least productive segments of society continues or is reenforced as the guiding principle of public policy, if tightening regulation rather than liberation of enterpreneurship becomes the dominant rule, the GNP growth rates of 3.3 percent per annum or more may be impossible to maintain in the long run.

Money income per family rose 3.0 percent annually in *constant* dollars between 1959 and 1971, not much more slowly than the GNP, because more married women entered the labor force to augment their families' resources. *Median* family income stood at $10,281 in 1971 and was projected to reach $18,122 by 1990, assuming a 3 percent growth per annum.[73] Mean family income would rise from $11,583 to $20,289. Under the same assumptions, the proportion of families with an income under $4000 would decline from 13.0 percent of all families in 1971 to 4.9 percent by 1990, families with an income between $4000 and $9,999 from 35.2 to 16.9 percent. The proportion of families with an income of $15,000 and over (in *constant* 1971 dollars) would increase from 24.8 percent of all families to 61.3 percent.[74]

These income data and projections include of course welfare and other transfer payments by government. But even so, the rising level of productivity, earnings, and income suggest that the proportion of American families with so little income that they *need* public support will decline. This does not necessarily mean that the proportion or number of families that *receive* such support will shrink. That will depend more on the type and generosity of income maintenance and other social benefit programs that are in force at the time than on the number of families that are poor by today's standards. Those standards will probably rise as the number of poor families under existing definitions shrinks and earning levels go up. The sharp rise in the number of female-headed families—between 1970 and 1973 at more than twice the annual rate of the 1960s—is an ominous sign for prospects in welfare dependency.

---

[73] U.S., Bureau of the Census, *Illustrative Projections of Money Income Size Distributions for Families and Unrelated Individuals,* Current Population Reports, Special Studies, series P-23, no. 47, February 1974. At a 2 percent per annum growth rate, median family income would be $14,986 in 1990, at a 4 percent rate, $21,778.

[74] Ibid.

Governmental Growth to the Year 2000

Are conditions and forces at the three-quarter point sufficiently similar to those that existed at midcentury to suggest a continuation of apparent trends in government at comparable rates? Only in some respects. Some of the changes that have occurred will influence developments in opposite directions, thus partially offsetting each other. Population growth will be half of what it was or less, the number of young people will shrink, but the size of the aged group will expand. A greater proportion of the population may be gainfully employed, more people will have an income sufficient to give them a comfortable living, and more will be able to sustain themselves at minimum levels of existence without outside aid. But substantial income differentials will continue and could, in some respects, even widen. Will that growth in positive as well as negative factors create increased tensions powerful enough to lead to stronger attempts at income equalization and similar types of government intervention? That could very well be the case.

We have seen that trends in the funding of national security and domestic services ran in opposite directions between 1952 and 1972 and that, in fact, the sharp upward trend in the latter was made possible only by shrinking the share of the former. Therefore, prospects for development in domestic services cannot be properly weighed without considering the future allocation of resources to national defense.

No mortal can foresee whether the next twenty-five years will be a period of peaceful development or whether they will witness a nuclear holocaust which future historians—if there are any—will call World War III. Projections at this time must be based on the assumption that there will be no major war engulfing the superpowers but they should consider the probability of armed conflicts in several parts of the world *without* direct American military involvement (though probably as a supplier). If these assumptions prove to be wrong then all bets are off, and we have to draw other plans.

Prospects of a genuine détente between the superpowers are much harder to evaluate. Limited agreements reached in Vladivostok in the fall of 1974 do not suggest the proximity or likelihood of a comprehensive and genuine restriction on, or halt in, the armament development and deployment race. The United States has exercised great restraint for many years while the Soviet Union simultaneously pursued a strong expansion program, especially since the naval confrontation during the Cuban missile crisis. Under the impact of the disastrous conduct and frustrating conclusion of the Vietnam War, an antimilitary sentiment has pervaded the United States and has powerfully affected the allocation of financial and manpower resources for national security.

There are a few signs that attitude may be changing. The war in the Middle East in the fall of 1973 and subsequent events drove home the lesson that *(a)* the United States' ability to aid countries under an attack that is engineered and powered by the Soviet Union or some other hostile country depends on the state of United States preparedness and weapons availability, and *(b)* the Soviet Union can be counted on to be on the opposing side in a major international conflict and will use its ever advancing and expanding technology to counteract and endanger United States interests.

The fourth and latest war in the Middle East, in which Soviet support for one side brought United States support for the other, and a near confrontation, followed by mediation toward a settlement that could possibly prove more short-lived than earlier ones, served as a *demonstratio ad oculos* of the unfortunate fact of life that, détente or not, the cold war is not over but only conducted less obtrusively, that the world is not yet "safe for democracy," and that the spirit of Yalta II—and SALT II—could be as evanescent as the spirit of Yalta I or of Camp David.

Whether attitudes toward national defense are changing or will change during the balance of this century is anybody's guess. But a few facts can be stated with certainty. Some developments cannot be repeated: national defense was cut from 50 percent of total governmental expenditures in 1952 to 21 percent in 1972, and from 13.5 percent of the GNP to 6.8 percent (see table 23). Defense cannot be cut by another 6.7 percent of the GNP nor by another 29 percent of total government expenditures in the next twenty years.

Much of the expansion in domestic services between 1952 and 1972—from 10.0 to 22.3 percent of the GNP, from 37 to 69 percent of total governmental expenditures—was financed from reductions in the share of national defense. A second shift of the 1952–1972 magnitude is beyond possibility. If a further shift occurred, it would have to be on a smaller scale.

Another part of the domestic services expansion was "financed" by huge budget deficits and covered up by monetary expansion that helped to drive the rate of inflation to double-digit levels. Sentiment against inflation may now be aroused sufficiently to make a repetition or enlargement of this experience politically hazardous and counterproductive. While inflationary trends will probably continue for a long time, there will be attempts to control them. At times these attempts may be ineffective, as they have been since 1971. Projections by the Brookings Institution in 1973 suggested that the federal budget would be balanced in fiscal years 1975 and 1976 under full employment conditions.[75] Simultaneous projections under the auspices of the American Enterprise Institute showed similar results.[76] But the country is now far from full employment conditions and budgetary deficits are estimated to amount to $45 billion in FY 1975 and to $80 billion or more in FY 1976, the highest peacetime deficits in United States history. That not entirely novel experience with budgetary predictions should restrain us from being overly optimistic about the prospects for balanced federal budgets in future years. Decision makers may be well intended but they may not be able to resist political pressures which make for large budgetary deficits.

The succession of tax boosts at state and local levels that characterized most of the postwar period appears to have come to a halt. This stability could last for a while, although prospects are not overly favorable. California voters had an opportunity in November 1973 to adopt a constitutional initiative, submitted by Governor Ronald Reagan, to limit state taxes to a declining share of personal income. It failed after a massive counter campaign by special interest groups with a stake in ever-growing governmental spending. This suggests that a taxpayers' revolt, though often mentioned, is not now in the making and that state and local taxes may soon resume their upward trend.

Federal taxes were cut sharply in March 1975 and are not likely to be raised substantially for purposes other than social security or energy conservation, barring a national emergency.

The prospect of deriving sizeable revenues from a tightening of so-called loopholes in the federal income tax is not a hope but a mirage. Most of the over one-half of personal income which presently escapes federal income taxation accrues to persons in the low- and middle-income groups, and is unlikely to be made taxable (see chap. 3).

Congress' continuing policy emphasis, as demonstrated again in the March 1975 tax cut, appears to be to free more income in the lower brackets from taxation. The remainder of untaxed income—in the high

[75] Edward R. Fried et al., *Setting National Priorities: The 1974 Budget* (Washington, D.C.: The Brookings Institution, 1973), p. 414.

[76] David J. Ott et al., *Public Claims on U.S. Output: Federal Budget Options in the Last Half of the Seventies* (Washington, D.C.: American Enterprise Institute for Public Policy Research, 1973), p. 14.

brackets—is too small to yield large revenues. Moreover, action by Congress to make our tax system even more punitive of success than it is is apt to depress the rate of economic growth and thus defeat the goal of increasing public revenues.

Efforts to simplify the incredibly complicated structure of the federal income tax are not promising and, in any case, would have little impact on the amount of revenue. If all deductions, exemptions, exclusions, and credits were abolished and the tax were imposed on *all* personal income (as defined in national income accounts), the rates could be cut in half—from a range of 14–70 percent to a range of 7–35 percent. Alternatively, a flat rate of 21 percent of the present tax base or a 10.5 percent flat rate on *all* personal income would yield as much as the present 14–70 percent scale on the current base of 47 percent of the personal income. But such proposals are anathema to those who regard the income tax as a major instrument for the redistribution of income. Plans of that type may be fascinating subjects for intellectual exercise but do not stand a chance of enactment unless attitudes change drastically—of which there is no present sign.

The only practical possibility of substantially increasing federal revenues is the imposition of a consumption tax which in all industrial countries except the United States is a major contributor to national government receipts. In *The Affluent Society* John K. Galbraith chided his liberal friends for opposing the levying of sales taxes and thereby frustrating efforts to expand starved public services. But liberals did not then nor are they likely now to wax enthusiastic over consumption taxes because they regard them to be regressive and thereby counterproductive in terms of income redistribution. Whether they will at some point take to expenditure taxes, which can be shaped to be progressive, remains to be seen.

Some students of taxation have for some time advocated the adoption of a national value-added tax (VAT), which has now been generally adopted by most countries of the European Economic Community. However, liberal forces, with organized labor in the lead, oppose a VAT as smelling too much like a sales tax, while conservative groups, which favor VAT, would want to see it enacted only as partial or total replacement of the corporate profits tax. Conservative groups object to having it levied as an additional tax to swell government coffers and thereby to expand social benefits and services. A national VAT is therefore not likely to become a reality in the United States within the near future except in a war emergency. Within the next few decades discussions of and experiments with enactment of an expenditure tax or a VAT are likely.

What all this adds up to is that an expansion of domestic public services at the 1952–1972 rate may be difficult or impossible to finance in the balance of this century. It may, however, be worthwhile to see what a continuation of recent trends *would* produce.

A projection of governmental employment trends to the year 2000 would show these results: Governmental employment totaled 16.2 million in 1972; in the preceding twenty years it had declined 30 percent in national defense, increased 124 percent in the rest of government. If these trends were to continue for the balance of this century, defense employment would fall another 1.3 million, to 2.2 million, while all other governmental employment would triple from 12.7 to 39 million for an aggregate of 41 million in the year 2000. The entire labor force has been projected to rise from 89 million in 1972 to 112.6 million in 1990;[77] it may reach, and could possibly slightly exceed 120 million by the year 2000.

Assuming that 94 percent of the labor force were then gainfully employed—and this is of course purely a stab in the dark—there would be 113 million jobholders of whom, under the above projections, 41 million, or 36 percent, would be governmental. That would mean a ratio between public and private employees of 1:1.75, which is utterly absurd. In other words, governmental employment cannot possibly rise in the next twenty to twenty-eight years at as fast a rate as it did in the preceding twenty years. Nor is there any reason why it should. More than half of the increase in public nondefense employment between 1952 and 1972 occurred in education; student enrollment nearly doubled and the staff tripled. From this point on educational enrollment is projected to decline and there is no reason for educational employment to increase substantially or at all. The projection to 41 million of governmental employment was used merely to demonstrate the certainty that the upward trend of the 1952–1972 period cannot continue at that rate and must gradually flatten out. If the 4:1 ratio between public and private employees that existed in 1972 were to stabilize, the public payroll would equal about 22.6 million in the year 2000—which still is an increase of 40 percent during a period when population may increase 20 percent. Weighing the political strength of conflicting forces, a 40–50 percent growth in public employment between 1972 and 2000 appears to be well within the range of possibility.

A projection of governmental expenditures at rates of the recent past shows a similar picture. Between 1952 and 1972, national defense outlays

---

[77] Dennis F. Johnston, "The U.S. Labor Force Projections to 1990," *Monthly Labor Review,* July 1973.

increased 68 percent, domestic services 645 percent, and all other costs 180 percent (table 23). Adjusted to *constant* 1972 dollars by the use of the implicit price deflator for the GNP, national defense increased 1 percent, domestic services 346 percent, all other costs 68 percent. Extending those rates to the year 2000 would suggest domestic expenditures of slightly over $2 trillion (up from $257 billion in 1972) and other outlays (interest, space, etc.) of $70 billion (up from $35 billion). The projection for national defense and for other costs are well within the realm of possibility. The amount for domestic purposes is, of course, absurd. Expenditures for domestic purposes multiplied 7.5 times between 1952 and 1972 in current dollars, 4.5 times in *constant* dollars. They cannot possibly repeat this feat. Otherwise government expenditures might absorb about 70 percent of the GNP in the year 2000.

The purpose of this projection is simply to demonstrate that, despite complaints about the starvation of the government sector and the slow growth and inadequate funds for social services, the growth rate between 1952 and 1972 was so steep that, if projected into the future, the results would be ridiculous.

Thus, regardless of the economic developments or political trends in the remaining years of this century, the growth rate in services for domestic purposes is bound to decline materially, although the share those costs are taking of total government expenditures and of the GNP may continue to rise slightly. Total governmental expenditures equaled 27 percent of the GNP in 1952, 32 percent in 1972, and could well go higher by a few percentage points without reaching the level of Sweden or Holland. Assuming that the GNP multiplies 2.5 times between 1972 and 2000 (in *constant* dollars), governmental expenditures might expand close to threefold, reaching possibly $1 trillion (in 1972 dollars).

Although a straight projection to the year 2000 of 1952–1972 trends in governmental employment and spending would produce absurd results, it should be realized that the actual 1972 figures would have appeared just as preposterous in 1952. Concepts of what is possible, tolerable, or desirable have changed over the past quarter century, the period when big government in social programs first became a reality in the United States. Current demands by special interest groups for program enlargements are strong and, if granted, would lead to another explosion in governmental domestic expenditures.

A group of members of Congress submitted in the House on April 10, 1974 a compilation of over 450 pending bills that would cost $875 billion over the next four-year period.[78] To be sure, most of those bills will not be enacted; authorization amounts in those that will be approved may be cut back. But many of the proposals are seriously meant, pushed hard by determined, well organized, and powerful groups, and could well wind up on the statute books within not too many years.

National health insurance has been under review for about three decades and may soon become a reality. The cost of the pending bills varies from $6.5 billion a year for the Nixon Comprehensive Health Insurance Bill to an estimated $60 billion for the Kennedy-Griffith Health Security Bill. The plan that may be adopted within the next few years might be closer to the lower range. Experience with similar programs and in other countries, however, suggests that costs would soon multiply and could eventually exceed the present upper range of proposals.

Clamor for a nationally guaranteed annual income, though rejected by the Senate in 1972, continues and might succeed in the enactment of a huge program which, with the force of many millions of beneficiaries behind it, would probably multiply in numbers of recipients and amounts.

That social security, supplemental security income, unemployment and other welfare benefits will be increased beyond the present built-in price escalator is a foregone conclusion, as Congress has proven in the past—particularly in even-numbered years.

Teacher associations and allied forces have been amazingly successful over the years in pushing educational funds to stunningly high levels, mostly from state and local sources. They have so far not succeeded in realizing a goal they have pursued for well over a century: the authorization of a federal program of general financial support for public education. Less than 10 percent of the support of public educational institutions is now derived from federal sources. This does not mean that the protagonists of federal aid may not at some time be able to put through a program by which the national government would supply a substantial share of the current and capital costs of schools, colleges, and universities, and simultaneously assume much of the support of students.

Public housing and urban renewal are other fields for which vast public funds are demanded, where shining new projects become instant slums. Major cities, under the impact of federal policies and by their own actions, are increasingly turning into islands of poverty, crime, and decay, and other social ills, with a growing concentration of black and American Indian population—whether Spanish or English-speaking—who depend

---

[78] *Congressional Record,* April 10, 1974, p. H 2873.

increasingly on government sustenance while contributing little to their communities or to society. Environmental improvement and rapid transit are further examples from a long list of demands for steep boosts in multibillion-dollar governmental appropriations.

While each of the special interest groups pursues its own aims, they tend to band together when endangered by a common enemy, to form an unconquerable phalanx to defeat at the next election candidates who oppose limitless government expansion. The path is lined with the tombstones of legislators and chief executives who tried to stem the tide of gargantuan government and thereby incurred the fatal wrath of groups which seek more public funds for their purposes and more public aid or employment for their members.

To weigh over long periods ahead the relative influence of opposing political and ideological forces and to accurately appraise public sentiment or events that shape it is well-nigh impossible. The gift of prophecy is not given to man and respect for foresight has yielded in recent times to charity for those who don't exercise it. Who could have predicted but three years ago the events that are now known under the conglomerate term of *Watergate* or dared specify the profound consequences they may have upon this nation?

Experience with long-range fiscal projections should caution most students of the subject to restrict themselves to short-range considerations. The United States budget began in 1971 to include five-year projections which usually do not disclose any startling information. At the time of the upcoming presidential election of 1968, the Brookings Institution prepared its symposium volume, *Agenda for the Nation,* which attempted to chart for the new administration, for Congress, and for the general public what the participants regarded to be desirable policies for some time ahead. Most of its authors favored a further and significant expansion of the public services they covered, and those who addressed themselves to the question of financing visualized the defense budget as an obvious source of funds. This was even more true of a similar project by the National Planning Association three years earlier,[79] and of the National Urban Coalition's *Counterbudget* three years later.

The Brookings Institution followed up its Agenda with a review of the federal budget for FY 1971 and has been issuing similar volumes every

---

[79] Leonard A. Lecht, *Goods, Priorities and Dollars* (New York: Free Press, 1966). "The costs projected for full realization of all the goals are estimated to exceed the gross national product anticipated in 1975 by approximately $150 billion, or 15% of GNP" (p. 19).

year since, discussing significant trends in federal activity as they are reflected in the president's budget.[80] The review of the 1973 budget contained a few sentences that questioned the effectiveness of some of the new programs to accomplish what their sponsors had promised and what Congress and the public had expected or to make tangible inroads on the social problems at hand (see above, p. 145). They questioned only the choice of the particular method or program and did not raise broader questions regarding the general approach of the Great Society legislation.

Congress has been sincerely searching for a solution to serious and growing social problems but does not seem to have selected a proper corrective in most cases. This suggests that somehow Congress was unable to understand the nature of the problem and/or unwilling to face the facts as they are rather than as it would like them to be. Throwing huge amounts of public funds at a problem is the customary answer of some intellectuals, in and out of government, who aim to remake others in their own image and are loath to admit that they have not succeeded, and probably cannot succeed. Their usual answer is that there is nothing wrong with the programs under review that could not be cured by doubling or tripling the appropriation. Belief in the omnicompetence of government and in the omnipotence of the dollar die hard because both are so much more comfortable than the alternative. It is hard to accept the inherent imperfections in the nature of man, and the ineradicable differences between individuals and to take the often harsh and possibly unpopular actions necessary to protect the rest of society as well as the affected individuals themselves. In reviewing some of the new programs, we must often ask government: Are you helping to solve the problem or are you part of the problem?

There seems to have been a loss of spirit, a decline in the acceptance of individual responsibility, not only in the United States but in much of the rest of the western world. André Malraux perceived in 1949 that "western civilization has begun to doubt its own credentials,"[81] and James Burnham called the loss of spirit *The Suicide of the West*.[82] Arthur Krock, the *New York Times* Washington correspondent for many decades, described in his latest volume how a permissive liberal political philosophy is leading to national self-destruction and the decline and fall of American

---

[80] Charles L. Schultze et al., *Setting National Priorities: The 1971 Budget* (Washington, D.C.: The Brookings Institution, 1970); idem, *Setting National Priorities: The 1972 Budget* (1971); idem, *Setting National Priorities: The 1973 Budget* (1972); Edward R. Fried et al., *Setting National Priorities: The 1974 Budget* (1973); and B. M. Blechman et al., *Setting National Priorities: The 1975 Budget* (1974).

[81] André Malraux, *The Psychology of Art* (1949), quoted in Robert L. Bartley, "'Failure of Nerve': Message for Today?," *Wall Street Journal*, April 12, 1971.

[82] James Burnham, *The Suicide of the West* (New York: John Day, 1964).

democracy.[83] We find an interesting number of comparisons with the late stages of Greek and Roman civilization. Future historians may see in retrospect whether the America of today and tomorrow is to be compared more closely to the Rome of the second century A.D.—the Golden Age of the Antonines—or to the Rome of the fifth century A.D.—the time of the Goths, the Vandals, and the Huns. Whether the growing activity of government in social affairs is ushering in a new and glorious era or a *decline and fall* remains to be seen. The controversy will undoubtedly go on for a long time.

Decisions on the growth of governmental activities in the social field and on the magnitude of government as such will depend on the basic philosophical attitude of the American people and their representatives in Congress and in the other branches and levels of government. It will hinge on three major issues:

1. *Freedom vs. government:* As governmental activity expands, aiming to deal with and resolve major social ills by appropriation of funds and intensification of service programs, the freedom of the individual to make his own decisions and to rise and fall by his own actions gradually diminishes. Whether the positive value of the benefits that may at some time be derived from government will exceed the diminution of personal freedom and responsibility remains an open question.
2. *Rewards by the free market vs. redistribution of income:* Those who view the allocation of rewards by the market to be purely fortuitous, devoid of personal merit, and grossly unjust, push for a more effective redistribution of income—from those who earn it to those who yearn it. They may continue to succeed, as they have in recent decades. If so, government will play an increasingly powerful role in changing income distribution through tax, transfer, and social service programs.
3. *Strengthening or cutbacks in national defense:* An increasingly large number of Americans now believe that national defense is consuming too large a share of our national resources and that funds for the military can be cut further with impunity, because we already possess an "overkill" capacity and are not likely to be attacked by anyone, if we stay out of other countries' affairs. Others feel that this is an area where we cannot afford to incur risks because there would be no possibility of a "second chance" in case of a mistake and that existence of an adequate military preparedness and ability to inflict intolerable losses upon an

---

[83] Arthur Krock, *The Consent of the Governed* (Boston: Little, Brown, 1971).

aggressor—and awareness of this by a would-be aggressor—are the best and the only guarantors of national security and preservation of peace. In a recent speech, Secretary of Defense James Schlesinger said that

> democracies are suffering from their traditional problem that they need an overt manifest threat in order to bring about the appropriate allocation of resources within the society to maintain a defense establishment that continues militarily to deter rather than to rely upon the goodwill of potential opponents.[84]

It may well be that the ancient Roman proverb, *si vis pacem para bellum,* is as valid today as it ever was.

---

[84] Quoted in Leslie H. Gelb, "Schlesinger for Defense," *New York Times Magazine,* August 4, 1974.

TABLE 1
GOVERNMENTAL REVENUES IN THE UNITED STATES, 1902–1972
(By Level of Government)

Fiscal Year	All Governments (in millions)	Federal Government (in millions)	State and Local Governments (in millions)	All Governments (in percent of GNP)	Federal Governments (in percent of GNP)	State and Local Governments (in percent of GNP)
1902	$ 1,694	$ 653	$ 1,041	8.2%	3.2%	5.0%
1913	2,980	962	2,018	8.1	2.6	5.5
1922	9,322	4,261	5,061	12.8	5.9	6.9
1932	10,289	2,634	7,655	15.3	3.9	11.4
1942	28,352	16,062	12,290	20.4	11.6	8.8
1952	100,245	71,798	28,447	29.7	21.3	8.4
1962	168,062	106,441	61,621	31.0	19.6	11.4
1972	381,849	223,378	158,471	34.7	20.3	14.4

Multiplier			
1902–1952	59.2	110.0	27.3
1952–1972	3.8	3.1	5.6
1902–1972	225.4	342.1	152.2

SOURCES: U.S. Bureau of the Census, *Historical Statistics on Governmental Finances and Employment,* 1967 Census of Governments, 1969; *Governmental Finances in 1971-72,* December, 1973.

1902-1922 GNP from Raymond W. Goldsmith, *A Study of Savings in the United States,* vol. 2, (Princeton, N.J.: Princeton University Press, 1956).

1932-1972 GNP from U.S. Department of Commerce, Bureau of Economic Analysis, *National Income and Product Accounts of the United States 1929-1965,* Supplement to the *Survey of Current Business,* August 1966; *The Budget of the U.S. Government,* 1975.

TABLE 2
GOVERNMENT LABOR FORCE AND POPULATION,
1870–1972

	Government Labor Force (all governments) (in thousands)	U.S. Population (in thousands)	Ratio of Government Workers to Persons in Population
1870	265	39,818	1:150
1900	1,401	75,994	1: 54
1920	2,920	105,710	1: 36.2
1940	4,902	132,122	1: 27.0
1949	7,559	149,188	1: 19.7
1952	10,697	157,553	1: 14.7
1972	16,052	208,842	1: 13.0

SOURCES: 1870: Fabricant, *The Trend of Government Activity,* table B1, p.168 (this figure is not strictly comparable with later data).

1900, 1920, 1940, 1949: Ibid., table B14, p. 198 (the figure for 1940 does not include government emergency workers. If they are included, the total is 7,794,000 and the ratio 1:17.0).

1952, 1972: *Economic Report of the President,* 1974; U.S. Bureau of the Census, *Historical Statistics on Governmental Finances and Employment,* 1967 Census of Governments, 1969; and idem, *Public Employment in 1972,* 1973.

TABLE 3

GOVERNMENTAL EMPLOYMENT, PRIVATE EMPLOYMENT, AND POPULATION,
1952 AND 1972

	1952 (in thousands)	1972 (in thousands)	Percent Increase and Decrease
Governmental employment			
Total	10,697	16,052	+ 50.1%
National defense and international relations	4,934	3,561	− 27.8
All other (domestic services)	5,763	12,491	+116.7
Employment in private industry	53,646	68,412	+ 27.5
U.S. population	157,553	208,842	+ 32.6
Ratios to population			
Total	1:14.7	1:13.0	
National defense and international relations	1:31.9	1:58.7	
All other (domestic services)	1:27.3	1:16.7	
Ratios to private employment			
Total	1: 5.0	1: 4.3	
National defense and international relations	1:10.9	1:19.2	
All other (domestic services)	1: 9.3	1: 5.5	

SOURCES: Population, private employment and armed forces: *Economic Report of the President,*
1974. All other governmental employment: U.S. Bureau of the Census, *Historical
Statistics on Governmental Finances and Employment,* 1967 Census of Governments,
1969; and idem, *Public Employment in 1972,* 1973.

TABLE 4a
Governmental Expenditures in the United States, 1902–1972

Fiscal Year	Total Governmental Expenditures (in millions)	National Defense and International Relations (in millions)	Veterans Benefits and Services (in millions)	Interest on General Debt (in millions)	All Other (Domestic Services) (in millions)
1902	$ 1,660	$ 165	$ 152	$ 97	$ 1,246
1913	3,215	250	189	170	2,606
1922	9,297	875	516	1,370	6,536
1932	12,437	721	1,057	1,323	9,336
1942	45,576	26,555	610	1,591	16,820
1952	99,847	48,187	5,728	4,814	41,118
1962	176,240	55,172	6,120	9,173	105,775
1972	397,427	79,258	12,071	23,077	283,021

SOURCES: U.S. Bureau of the Census, *Historical Statistics on Governmental Finances and Employment*, 1967 Census of Governments, 1969; and idem. *Governmental Finances in 1971–1972*, 1973.

TABLE 4b
Governmental Expenditures in the United States, 1902–1972
(In Percentage of Gross National Product)

Fiscal Year	Total Government Expenditures	National Defense and International Relations	Veterans Benefits and Services	Interest on General Debt	All Other (Domestic Services)
1902	8.0%	0.8%	0.7%	0.5%	6.0%
1913	8.8	0.7	0.5	0.5	7.1
1922	12.8	1.2	0.7	1.9	9.0
1932	18.6	1.1	1.6	2.0	13.9
1942	32.7	19.1	0.4	1.1	12.1
1952	29.6	14.3	1.7	1.4	12.2
1962	32.5	10.2	1.1	1.7	19.5
1972	36.1	7.2	1.1	2.1	25.7

SOURCES: U.S. Bureau of the Census, *Historical Statistics on Governmental Finances and Employment*, 1967 Census of Governments, 1969; and idem, *Governmental Finances in 1971–1972*, 1973. GNP figures for 1902, 1913, and 1922 from Raymond W. Goldsmith, *A Study of Savings in the United States* (Princeton, N.J.: Princeton University Press, 1956), 2: 427.

TABLE 5a
FEDERAL EXPENDITURES, 1902–1972

Fiscal Year	Total Federal Expenditures (in millions)	National Defense and International Relations (in millions)	Veterans Benefits and Services (in millions)	Interest on General Debt (in millions)	All Other (Domestic Services) (in millions)
1902	$ 572	$ 165	$ 152	$ 29	$ 226
1913	970	250	189	23	508
1922	3,763	875	516	988	1,384
1932	4,266	721	1,057	582	1,906
1942	35,549	26,555	610	1,026	7,358
1952	71,568	48,187	5,728	4,262	13,391
1962	113,428	55,172	6,120	7,162	44,974
1972	242,186	79,258	12,071	17,114	133,743

SOURCES: U.S. Bureau of the Census, *Historical Statistics on Governmental Finances and Employment,* 1967 Census of Governments, 1969; and idem, *Governmental Finances in 1971–1972,* 1973.

TABLE 5b
FEDERAL EXPENDITURES, 1902–1972
(In Percent of Gross National Product)

Fiscal Year	Total Government Expenditures	National Defense and International Relations	Veterans Benefits and Services	Interest on General Debt	All Other (Domestic Services)
1902	2.7%	0.8%	0.7%	0.1%	1.1%
1913	2.6	0.7	0.5	0.1	1.3
1922	5.2	1.2	0.7	1.4	1.9
1932	6.4	1.1	1.6	0.9	2.8
1942	25.5	19.1	0.4	0.7	5.3
1952	21.2	14.3	1.7	1.3	3.9
1962	20.9	10.2	1.1	1.3	8.3
1972	22.0	7.2	1.1	1.6	12.1

SOURCES: U.S. Bureau of the Census, *Historical Statistics on Governmental Finances and Employment,* 1967 Census of Governments, 1969; and idem, *Governmental Finances in 1971–1972,* 1973. GNP figures for 1902, 1913, and 1922 from Raymond W. Goldsmith, *A Study of Savings in the United States* (Princeton, N.J.: Princeton University Press, 1956), 2: 427.

TABLE 6

AVERAGE ANNUAL EARNINGS PER FULL-TIME EMPLOYEE BY INDUSTRY
IN CURRENT AND CONSTANT DOLLARS, 1952 AND 1972

	1952		1972	*Percent Increase (Current Dollars)*	*Percent Increase (Constant Dollars)*
	Current Dollars	*Constant Dollars (1972=$100)*			
Total all government and government enterprises	$3,279	$ 5,168	9,264	182.5%	79.3%
Federal	3,345	5,272	10,223	205.6	93.9
Civilian	4,028	6,349	12,150	201.6	91.4
Military	2,879	4,538	8,438	193.1	85.9
Government enterprises	3,998	6,301	10,722	168.2	70.2
State and local	3,177	5,007	8,725	174.6	74.3
School	3,169	4,995	9,213	190.7	84.4
Nonschool	3,111	4,903	8,278	166.1	68.8
Government enterprises	3,675	5,792	8,036	118.7	38.7
Total all private industries	3,430	5,406	8,440	146.1	56.1
Manufacturing	3,832	6,040	9,232	140.9	52.8
Wholesale and retail trade	3,298	5,198	7,663	132.4	47.4
Services	2,489	3,923	6,742	170.9	71.9
Finance, insurance, and real estate	3,539	5,578	9,092	156.9	63.0
Contract construction	3,978	6,270	10,320	159.4	64.6
Agriculture	1,423	2,243	3,824	168.7	70.5

SOURCES: U.S. Department of Commerce, Bureau of Economic Analysis, *National Income and Product Accounts of the United States 1929-1965,* Supplement to the *Survey of Current Business,* August 1966.
U.S. Department of Commerce, Bureau of Economic Analysis, *Survey of Current Business, National Income Issue,* July 1973.
Consumer price index from *Economic Report of the President,* 1974.

NOTE: The consumer price index was 79.5 percent in 1952 and 125.3 percent in 1972; the percent increase was 57.6.

TABLE 7a
Governmental Employment by Level of Government, 1952–1972

	Total (in thousands)	Federal Total (in thousands)	Federal Civilian (in thousands)	Armed Forces (in thousands)	State and Local Total (in thousands)	State (in thousands)	Local (in thousands)
1952	10,697	6,175	2,583	3,592	4,522	1,060	3,461
1953	10,593	5,930	2,385	3,545	4,663	1,082	3,580
1954	10,582	5,723	2,373	3,350	4,859	1,149	3,710
1955	10,481	5,427	2,378	3,049	5,054	1,199	3,855
1956	10,542	5,267	2,410	2,857	5,275	1,268	4,007
1957	10,847	5,239	2,439	2,800	5,608	1,300	4,307
1958	10,933	5,041	2,405	2,636	5,892	1,408	4,484
1959	11,039	4,951	2,399	2,552	6,088	1,454	4,634
1960	11,322	4,935	2,421	2,514	6,387	1,527	4,860
1961	11,672	5,056	2,484	2,572	6,616	1,625	4,992
1962	12,216	5,367	2,539	2,828	6,849	1,680	5,169
1963	12,474	5,286	2,548	2,738	7,188	1,775	5,413
1964	12,803	5,267	2,528	2,739	7,536	1,873	5,663
1965	13,312	5,311	2,588	2,723	8,001	2,028	5,973
1966	14,511	5,984	2,861	3,123	8,527	2,211	6,316
1967	15,313	6,439	2,993	3,446	8,874	2,335	6,539
1968	15,877	6,519	2,984	3,535	9,358	2,495	6,864
1969	16,191	6,475	2,969	3,506	9,716	2,614	7,102
1970	16,216	6,069	2,881	3,188	10,147	2,755	7,392
1971	16,133	5,689	2,872	2,817	10,444	2,832	7,612
1972	16,052	5,244	2,795	2,449	10,808	2,938	7,870
Percent increase and decrease 1952–1972	+50.1%	−15.1%	+8.2%	−31.8%	+139.0%	+177.2%	+127.4%

SOURCES: 1952–1967: U.S. Bureau of the Census, *Historical Statistics on Governmental Finances and Employment, 1967 Census of Governments,* 1969. 1968–1972: U.S. Bureau of the Census, *Public Employment in 1968* (and annually for 1969–1972).

Armed forces: *Economic Report of the President,* February 1974, table C-24.

NOTE: Data are as of October, except for 1957 figures, which are for April.

TABLE 7b
GOVERNMENTAL EMPLOYMENT BY LEVEL OF GOVERNMENT, 1952–1972
(Per 1000 Population)

		Federal			State and Local		
	Total	Total	Civilian	Armed Forces	Total	State	Local
1952	67.9	39.2	16.4	22.8	28.7	6.7	22.0
1953	66.1	37.0	14.9	22.1	29.1	6.8	22.3
1954	64.9	35.1	14.6	20.5	29.8	7.0	22.8
1955	63.2	32.7	14.3	18.4	30.5	7.2	23.2
1956	62.4	31.2	14.3	16.9	31.2	7.5	23.7
1957	63.1	30.5	14.2	16.3	32.6	7.6	25.0
1958	62.5	28.8	13.7	15.1	33.7	8.1	25.6
1959	62.1	27.9	13.5	14.4	34.2	8.2	26.0
1960	62.7	27.3	13.4	13.9	35.4	8.5	26.9
1961	63.5	27.5	13.5	14.0	36.0	8.8	27.2
1962	64.8	28.5	13.5	15.0	36.3	8.9	27.4
1963	65.9	27.9	13.5	14.4	38.0	9.4	28.6
1964	66.7	27.4	13.2	14.2	39.3	9.8	29.5
1965	68.5	27.3	13.3	14.0	41.2	10.4	30.8
1966	73.8	30.4	14.6	15.8	43.4	11.3	32.1
1967	77.0	32.3	15.0	17.3	44.7	11.8	32.9
1968	79.1	32.5	14.9	17.6	46.6	12.4	34.2
1969	79.9	32.0	14.7	17.3	47.9	12.9	35.0
1970	79.1	29.6	14.1	15.5	49.5	13.4	36.1
1971	77.9	27.5	13.9	13.6	50.4	13.7	36.7
1972	76.9	25.1	13.4	11.7	57.8	14.1	37.7

SOURCES: 1952–1967: U.S. Bureau of the Census, *Historical Statistics on Governmental Finances and Employment*, 1967 Census of Governments, 1969. (U.S. Bureau of the Census, 1969);

1968–1972: U.S. Bureau of the Census, *Public Employment in 1968* (and annually for 1969–1972); idem, *Population Estimates and Projections*, Current Population Reports, series P-25, no. 499, May 1973.

Armed forces: *Economic Report of the President*, February 1974, table C-24.

TABLE 8a

GOVERNMENTAL EMPLOYMENT BY FUNCTION, 1952–1972

	Total	National Defense (in thousands)			Nondefense (in thousands)							
		Total	Armed Forces	Department of Defense and International Relations*	Total	Education	Postal Service	High-ways	Health and Hospitals	Police Protection	Natural Resources	All Other
1952	10,697	4,934	3,592	1,342	5,763	1,884	525	460	589	254	292	1,759
1953	10,593	4,752	3,545	1,207	5,841	1,960	500	467	626	263	282	1,743
1954	10,582	4,539	3,350	1,189	6,043	2,059	504	482	662	281	279	1,776
1955	10,481	4,250	3,049	1,201	6,231	2,181	509	478	690	295	287	1,791
1956	10,542	4,064	2,857	1,207	6,478	2,286	516	496	723	309	297	1,851
1957	10,847	4,022	2,800	1,222	6,825	2,470	524	479	750	316	289	1,997
1958	10,993	3,757	2,636	1,121	7,176	2,600	541	530	795	337	309	2,064
1959	11,039	3,673	2,552	1,121	7,366	2,756	554	522	821	347	308	2,058
1960	11,322	3,611	2,514	1,097	7,711	2,930	568	537	850	363	322	2,141
1961	11,672	3,694	2,572	1,122	7,978	3,062	580	545	879	367	334	2,211
1962	12,216	3,963	2,828	1,135	8,253	3,236	585	562	907	380	342	2,241
1963	12,474	3,853	2,738	1,115	8,621	3,448	590	568	939	390	365	2,321
1964	12,803	3,833	2,739	1,094	8,970	3,687	593	568	975	401	355	2,391
1965	13,312	3,843	2,723	1,120	9,469	3,974	610	582	1,002	420	372	2,509
1966	14,511	4,393	3,123	1,270	10,118	4,331	692	594	1,049	437	379	2,636
1967	15,313	4,797	3,446	1,351	10,516	4,568	705	600	1,089	458	386	2,710
1968	15,877	4,888	3,535	1,353	10,989	4,847	714	604	1,130	489	394	2,815
1969	16,191	4,828	3,506	1,322	11,363	5,079	728	602	1,162	514	393	2,885
1970	16,216	4,388	3,188	1,200	11,828	5,316	731	612	1,202	538	404	3,025
1971	16,133	3,982	2,817	1,165	12,151	5,501	716	613	1,231	557	417	3,116
1972	16,052	3,561	2,449	1,112	12,491	5,646	666	610	1,295	581	421	3,272
Percent increase and decrease 1952–1972	+50.1%	−27.8%	−31.8%	−17.1%	+116.7%	+199.7%	+26.9%	+32.6%	+119.9%	+128.7%	+44.2%	+86.0%

SOURCES: 1952–1967: U.S. Bureau of the Census, Historical Statistics on Governmental Finances and Employment, 1967 Census of Governments, 1969.
1968–1972: U.S. Bureau of the Census, Public Employment in 1968 (and annually for 1969–1972).
Armed forces: Economic Report of the President, February 1974, table C-24.
Data are as of October, except for 1957 figures, which are for April.

NOTE:
* Department of Defense civilian employment for 1952 and 1972, taken from the U.S. Civil Service Commission Annual Reports, was 1,337,000 and 1,083,000 respectively.

TABLE 8b
GOVERNMENTAL EMPLOYMENT BY FUNCTION, 1952–1972
(Per 1000 Population)

	Total	National Defense			Nondefense							
		Total	Armed Forces	Department of Defense and International Relations	Total	Education	Postal Service	High-ways	Health and Hospitals	Police Protection	Natural Resources	All Other
1952	67.9	31.3	22.8	8.5	36.6	12.0	3.3	2.9	3.7	1.6	1.9	11.2
1953	66.1	29.7	22.1	7.6	36.4	12.2	3.1	2.9	3.9	1.6	1.8	10.9
1954	64.9	27.8	20.5	7.3	37.1	12.6	3.1	3.0	4.1	1.7	1.7	10.9
1955	63.2	25.6	18.4	7.2	37.6	13.1	3.1	2.9	4.2	1.8	1.7	10.8
1956	62.4	24.1	16.9	7.2	38.3	13.5	3.1	2.9	4.3	1.8	1.8	10.9
1957	63.1	23.4	16.3	7.1	39.7	14.4	3.0	2.8	4.4	1.8	1.7	11.6
1958	62.5	21.5	15.1	6.4	41.0	14.9	3.1	3.0	4.5	1.9	1.8	11.8
1959	62.1	20.7	14.4	6.3	41.4	15.5	3.1	2.9	4.6	2.0	1.7	11.6
1960	62.7	20.0	13.9	6.1	42.7	16.2	3.1	3.0	4.7	2.0	1.8	11.9
1961	63.5	20.1	14.0	6.1	43.4	16.6	3.2	3.0	4.8	2.0	1.8	12.0
1962	64.8	21.0	15.0	6.0	43.8	17.2	3.1	3.0	4.8	2.0	1.8	11.9
1963	65.9	20.3	14.4	5.9	45.6	18.2	3.1	3.0	5.0	2.1	1.9	12.3
1964	66.7	20.0	14.3	5.7	46.7	19.2	3.1	2.9	5.1	2.1	1.8	12.5
1965	68.5	19.8	14.0	5.8	48.7	20.4	3.1	3.0	5.2	2.2	1.9	12.9
1966	73.8	22.3	15.9	6.5	51.5	22.0	3.5	3.0	5.4	2.2	2.0	13.4
1967	77.0	24.1	17.3	6.8	52.9	23.0	3.6	3.0	.5	2.3	1.9	13.6
1968	79.1	24.3	17.6	6.7	54.8	24.2	3.6	3.0	5.6	2.4	2.0	14.0
1969	79.9	23.8	17.3	6.5	56.1	25.1	3.6	3.0	5.7	2.5	2.0	14.2
1970	79.1	21.4	15.6	5.8	57.7	25.9	3.6	3.0	5.9	2.6	2.0	14.7
1971	77.9	19.2	13.6	5.6	58.7	26.5	3.5	3.0	5.9	2.7	2.0	15.1
1972	76.9	17.1	11.7	5.4	59.8	27.0	3.2	2.9	6.2	2.8	2.0	15.7

SOURCES: 1952–1967: U.S. Bureau of the Census, *Historical Statistics on Governmental Finances and Employment*, 1967 Census of Governments, 1969.
1968–1972: U.S. Bureau of the Census, *Public Employment in 1968* (and annually for 1969–1972); idem, *Population Estimates and Projections*, Current Population Reports, series P-25, no. 499, May 1973.

TABLE 9
AVERAGE NUMBER OF FULL-TIME AND PART-TIME EMPLOYEES
BY INDUSTRY, 1952 AND 1972

	1952 *(in thousands)*	1972 *(in thousands)*	Percent *Increase and Decrease*
Total all private industries	46,505	62,961	+ 35.4%
Agriculture, forestry, fisheries	2,236	1,367	− 38.9
Mining	919	627	− 31.8
Contract construction	2,707	3,704	+ 36.8
Manufacturing	16,752	19,039	+ 13.7
Transportation	2,922	2,652	− 9.2
Communication	789	1,146	+ 45.2
Electric, gas, and sanitary services	566	718	+ 26.9
Wholesale and retail trade	10,111	15,829	+ 56.6
Finance, insurance, and real estate	2,088	3,915	+ 87.5
Services	7,415	13,964	+ 88.3
Government and government enterprises	10,657	16,224	+ 52.2
Federal	6,204	5,290	− 14.7
State and local governments	4,453	10,934	+145.5
National defense	4,975	3,486	− 29.9
Domestic services	5,682	12,738	+124.2

SOURCES: U.S. Department of Commerce, Bureau of Economic Analysis, *National Income and Product Accounts of the United States, 1929-1965,* Supplement to the Survey of Current Business, August, 1966; idem, *Survey of Current Business, National Income Issue,* July 1973; and U.S. Civil Service Commission, *Annual Reports,* 1952 and 1972.

NOTE: Data in this table differ from the data in tables 3, 7, and 8 because they were taken from a different source. They show the same trends, however.

TABLE 10
Comparison of Federal Salary Ranges Under the
General Schedule, 1952 and 1972

General Schedule Grade	1952 Minimum	1952 Maximum	1972 Minimum	1972 Maximum	Percent Increase Minimum	Percent Increase Maximum
1	$ 2,500	$ 2,980	$ 4,564	$ 5,932	83%	99%
2	2,750	3,230	5,166	6,714	88	108
3	2,950	3,430	5,828	7,574	98	121
4	3,175	3,655	6,544	8,506	106	133
5	3,410	4,160	7,319	9,515	115	129
6	3,795	4,545	8,153	10,601	115	133
7	4,205	4,955	9,053	11,771	115	138
8	4,620	5,370	10,013	13,019	117	142
9	5,060	5,810	11,046	14,358	118	147
10	5,500	6,250	12,151	15,796	121	153
11	5,940	6,940	13,309	17,305	124	149
12	7,040	8,040	15,866	20,627	125	158
13	8,360	9,360	18,737	24,362	124	160
14	9,600	10,600	21,960	28,548	129	169
15	10,800	11,800	25,583	33,260	137	182
16	12,000	12,800	29,678	36,000*	147	181
17	13,000	13,800	34,335	36,000*	164	161
18	14,800	14,800	36,000*	36,000*	143	143

SOURCES: U.S. Department of Labor, Bureau of Labor Statistics, *Monthly Labor Review* vol. 81, no. 12, December 1958; U.S., Civil Service Commission, *Pay Structure of the Federal Civil Service, March, 1972,* 1973.

* The rate of basic pay for employees at these rates is limited by section 5308 of title 5 of the United States Code to the rate for level V of the Executive Schedule (as of this effective date, $36,000).

TABLE 11
COMPARISON OF FEDERAL EMPLOYEE AVERAGE SALARIES
BY GENERAL SCHEDULE GRADES, 1952 and 1972

General Schedule Grade	1952	1972	Percent Increase
Total All Grades	$ 4,149	$12,553	203%
1	2,600	4,669	80
2	2,886	5,385	87
3	3,126	6,403	105
4	3,401	7,459	119
5	3,703	8,431	128
6	4,123	9,476	130
7	4,503	10,318	129
8	4,949	11,521	133
9	5,349	12,506	134
10	5,769	13,935	142
11	6,220	15,060	142
12	7,344	17,853	143
13	8,634	21,114	145
14	9,855	24,776	151
15	11,180	29,256	162
16	12,130	33,796	179
17	13,089	35,799	174
18	14,800	36,000	143

SOURCES: U.S. Civil Service Commission, *Pay Structure of the Federal Civil Service, June 1952*, 1953; idem, *Pay Structure of the Federal Civil Service, March 1972*, 1973.

TABLE 12

GRADE DISTRIBUTION BY MAJOR GROUPS OF FEDERAL GENERAL-SCHEDULE EMPLOYEES, 1952 AND 1972

	1952	1972	Percent Increase	Percentage of Total 1952	Percentage of Total 1972
Total all grades	917,173	1,260,135	+37%	100.0%	100.0%
G.S. 1–3	337,507	128,005	−62	36.8	10.2
G.S. 4–10	467,405	699,598	+50	50.9	55.5
G.S. 11–12	79,836	267,235	+235	8.7	21.2
G.S. 13–15	31,844	160,947	+405	3.5	12.8
G.S. 16–18	581	4,350	+649	0.1	0.3

SOURCES: U.S. Civil Service Commission, *Pay Structure of the Federal Civil Service, June 1952,* 1953; idem, *Pay Structure of the Federal Civil Service, March 1972,* 1973.

TABLE 13

GOVERNMENTAL REVENUES AND EXPENDITURES AS A PERCENTAGE OF GROSS NATIONAL PRODUCT, NET NATIONAL PRODUCT, NATIONAL INCOME, AND PERSONAL INCOME, 1952 AND 1972

Measured by:	FY 1952 Total Governmental Revenues	FY 1952 Total Governmental Expenditures	FY 1972 Total Governmental Revenues	FY 1972 Total Governmental Expenditures
Gross national product	29.7%	29.6%	34.7%	36.1%
Net national product	31.9	31.7	38.1	39.6
National income	35.2	35.1	42.6	44.3
Personal income	38.1	37.9	42.5	44.3

SOURCES: Revenue and expenditure data: U.S. Bureau of the Census, *Historical Statistics on Governmental Finances and Employment,* 1967 Census of Governments, 1969; idem, *Governmental Finances in 1971–72,* 1973.

Gross national product, net national product, national income, personal income for fiscal year: U.S. Department of Commerce, Bureau of Economic Analysis, *National Income and Product Accounts of the United States, 1929–1965, Supplement to the Survey of Current Business,* August 1966; idem, *Survey of Current Business, National Income Issue,* July 1973; idem, *The Budget of the United States Government,* 1975.

TABLE 14
CURRENT GOVERNMENT RECEIPTS IN OECD MEMBER COUNTRIES IN 1972
(As a Percentage of Gross Domestic Product)
Average (mean) 34.6%

	Percentage of GDP
Sweden	50.1%
Norway	48.1
Denmark	44.6*
Netherlands	44.1†
Germany	39.0
United Kingdom	38.6*
France	38.0
Finland	38.0
Austria	37.0*
Canada	36.0
Belgium	35.8
Luxembourg	35.7†
Italy	34.7
Ireland	34.2*
Iceland	33.3§
United States	31.5**
Australia	29.3
Greece	27.4†
Switzerland	27.1‡
Portugal	24.0*
Turkey	23.8*
Spain	23.4
Japan	22.3*

SOURCE: *The OECD Observer*, February 1974.

    * 1971.

    † 1970.

    ‡ 1969.

    § 1968.

  ** The OECD report shows a 1971 figure of 30.5% for the United States; 1972 data were apparently not available when the report was prepared. The corresponding figure for calendar year 1972 was 31.5%. SOURCE: *Survey of Current Business* (July 1973).

TABLE 15

RATE OF REVENUE INCREASE AND DECREASE OF FEDERAL AND STATE-LOCAL
GOVERNMENTS IN PEACETIME AND WARTIME, 1902–1972

Fiscal Year	Federal Government	State and Local Governments (from own sources)	GNP
		Peacetime	
1902–1916	+ 53%	+ 188%	+114%
1920–1940	− 5	+ 170	+ 8
1945–1972	+314	+1,032	+421
		Wartime	
1916–1920	+640%	+ 33%	+ 99%
1940–1945	+671	+ 30	+122
Exhibit: Breakdown of post–World War II period			
1945–1950	− 19%	+ 65%	+ 25%
1950–1953	+ 71	+ 32	+ 36
1953–1972	+201	+ 419	+207

SOURCES: Basic data for years 1902, 1940, 1950, 1953, 1972(see table 1). Data for 1916, 1920, and 1945 are not available from the U.S. Bureau of the Census or from any other source and had to be estimated by using U.S. Treasury reports for those years and by interpolating state and local data.

TABLE 16
GOVERNMENTAL REVENUE, 1952 AND 1972

	FY 1952							FY 1972						
	Total	Federal (in millions)	State	Local	Percentage of GNP	Percentage of all Taxes	Percentage of all Revenue	Total	Federal (in millions)	State	Local	Percentage of GNP	Percentage of all Taxes	Percentage of all Revenue
Income taxes	$ 50,983	$49,147	$ 1,751	$ 85	15.1%	64.5%	50.9%	$146,556	$126,903	$17,412	$ 2,241	13.3%	55.8%	38.4%
Consumption taxes	15,689	9,332	5,730	627	4.6	19.8	15.7	57,589	20,101	33,250	4,238	5.3	21.9	15.1
Property taxes	8,652	—	370	8,282	2.6	11.0	8.6	42,133	—	1,257	40,876	3.8	16.1	11.0
Other taxes	3,743	1,264	2,006	473	1.1	4.7	3.7	16,255	6,729	7,951	1,575	1.5	6.2	4.3
All taxes	79,067	59,743	9,857	9,467	23.4	100.0	78.9	262,533	153,733	59,870	48,930	23.9	100.0	68.8
Social Security taxes	3,547	3,547	—	—	1.1		3.5	47,341	47,341	—	—	4.3		12.4
Other revenues	17,631	8,507	4,473	4,651	5.2		17.6	71,976	22,304	24,457	25,215	6.5		18.8
All revenues	100,245	71,798	14,330	14,117	29.7		100.0	381,849	223,378	84,327	74,144	34.7		100.0
Percent of GNP	29.7%	21.3%	4.2%	4.2%				34.7%	20.3%	7.7%	6.7%			
Percent of Total	100.0%	71.6%	14.3%	14.1%				100.0%	58.5%	22.1%	19.4%			
Exhibit:														
Individual income taxes	28,919	27,921	913	85*	8.6	36.6	28.9	109,974	94,737	12,996	2,241*	10.0	41.9	28.8
Corporation income taxes	22,064	21,226	838	—	6.5	27.9	22.0	36,582	32,166	4,416	—	3.3	13.9	9.6

SOURCES: U.S., Bureau of the Census, *Historical Statistics on Governmental Finances and Employment*, 1967 Census of Governments, 1969; idem, *Governmental Finances in 1971-1972*, 1973.

NOTE: Because of rounding details may not add to totals.

* Includes minor amounts of corporation income tax.

TABLE 17
Individual Taxes as a Percentage of GNP at Market Prices in OECD Member Countries
(Average 1968-1970)

	Taxes on Goods and Services	Taxes on Income and Profits Paid By: Households	Corporate Enterprises	Income and Profits Taxes (= columns 2+3)	Social Security	Other Taxes
Australia	7.9	8.8	3.7	12.5	—	4.0
Austria	13.5	7.4	1.7	9.1	9.2	4.0
Belgium	12.3	8.3	2.2	10.5	9.8	1.2
Canada	10.1	9.0	4.0	13.0	2.4	4.7
Denmark	15.5	16.5	1.0	17.5	3.1	3.6
Finland	14.1	11.3	2.3	13.6	4.3	0.8
France	13.0	4.0	1.8	5.8	14.5	3.0
Germany	10.4	8.7	2.2	10.9	10.8	1.9
Greece*	12.1	n.a.	n.a.	13.1	6.2	4.8
Iceland†	17.2	n.a.	n.a.	7.1	1.9	2.4
Ireland	15.8	5.3*	2.0*	7.7	2.4	3.9
Italy	11.5	3.4	2.0	5.4	11.0	2.2
Japan	4.7	4.3	3.9	8.2	3.6	2.9
Luxembourg*	8.0	7.7	4.6	12.3	9.5	2.6
Netherlands	10.5	10.5	2.9	13.4	14.2	1.6
Norway	14.2	11.5	1.4	12.9	9.2	2.2
Portugal	8.8	n.a.	n.a.	5.6	4.6	2.1
Spain	6.8	2.1	1.7	3.8	7.4	1.2
Sweden	12.8	19.0	2.0	21.0	8.2	1.0
Switzerland	6.5	7.9	1.8	9.7	3.2	2.2
Turkey	9.5	4.5	1.0	5.6	3.0	2.3
United Kingdom	10.9	11.5	2.7	14.2	5.0	6.5
United States	5.3	9.7	3.8	13.5	5.2	3.9

SOURCE: Organization for Economic Cooperation and Development, *Revenue Statistics of OECD Member Countries 1968-1970*, 1972.
* 1968 and 1969 only.
† 1969 only.

TABLE 18
INDIVIDUAL TAXES AS A PERCENTAGE OF TOTAL TAXATION IN OECD MEMBER COUNTRIES
(Average 1968-1970)

	Taxes on Goods and Services	Taxes on Income and Profits Paid By: Households and Institutions	Corporate Enterprises	Total Income and Profits Taxes	Social Security	Other Taxes
1.	Iceland† 60.1%	Sweden 44.1%	Japan 20.2%	Australia 51.1%	France 40.0%	Greece* 18.6%
2.	Ireland 53.0	Denmark 42.5	Australia 15.0	Sweden 48.8	Spain 38.4	Switzerland 17.7
3.	Turkey 46.7	Switzerland 36.6	Luxembourg* 14.2	U.S.A. 48.4	Italy 36.3	U.K. 17.6
4.	Greece* 46.1	Australia 36.1	U.S.A. 13.7	Denmark 45.1	Netherlands 35.8	Canada 17.0
5.	Finland 42.9	U.S.A. 34.4	Canada 13.0	Canada 43.0	Germany 31.7	Australia 16.5
6.	Portugal 41.7	Finland 34.7	Spain 8.8	Japan 42.1	Luxembourg* 29.3	Japan 15.3
7.	Denmark 40.2	U.K. 31.4	U.K. 7.4	Finland 41.5	Belgium 28.9	U.S.A. 14.1
8.	Italy 38.1	Norway 29.8	Netherlands 7.2	Switzerland 40.1	Austria 25.6	Ireland 13.0
9.	Austria 37.8	Canada 29.0	Finland 7.1	U.K. 38.8	Norway 23.8	Austria 11.4
10.	Norway 36.7	Netherlands 26.4	Ireland* 6.9	Luxembourg* 38.0	Greece* 23.6	Turkey 11.3
11.	Belgium 36.5	Germany 25.6	Italy 6.7	Netherlands 33.6	Portugal 21.9	Portugal 10.1
12.	France 35.8	Belgium 24.6	Belgium 6.6	Norway 33.4	Sweden 19.1	Iceland † 8.6
13.	Spain 35.7	Luxembourg* 23.6	Germany 6.6	Germany 32.2	Japan 18.6	France 8.2
14.	Canada 33.0	Turkey 22.1	Turkey 5.1	Belgium 31.2	U.S.A. 18.6	Luxembourg* 8.1
15.	Australia 32.4	Japan 21.9	France 5.0	Turkey 27.2	Switzerland 15.0	Italy 7.7
16.	Germany 30.5	Austria 20.6	Sweden 4.7	Portugal 26.3	Turkey 14.8	Denmark 6.8
17.	Sweden 29.9	Ireland* 18.4	Austria 4.6	Ireland 25.9	U.K. 13.8	Norway 6.1
18.	U.K. 29.8	Italy 11.2	Norway 3.6	Austria 25.2	Finland 13.2	Spain 6.1
19.	Switzerland 27.2	France 11.0	Switzerland 3.5	Iceland† 24.7	Ireland 8.1	Germany 5.6
20.	Netherlands 26.5	Spain 11.0	Denmark 2.6	Spain 19.8	Denmark 7.9	Netherlands 4.1
21.	Luxembourg* 24.6	Greece n.a.	Greece n.a.	Italy 17.9	Canada 7.0	Belgium 3.4
22.	Japan 24.0	Portugal n.a.	Portugal n.a.	France 16.0	Iceland† 6.6	Finland 2.4
23.	U.S.A. 19.0	Iceland n.a.	Iceland n.a.	Greece* 11.7	Australia —	Sweden 2.2

SOURCE: Organization for Economic Cooperation and Development, *Revenue Statistics of OECD Member Countries 1968-1970, 1972.*

* 1968 and 1969 only.

† 1969 only.

TABLE 19
ADJUSTED GROSS INCOME, TAXABLE INCOME, AND
EFFECTIVE TAX RATES ON FEDERAL INCOME TAX RETURNS, 1972

Adjusted Gross Income Class	Adjusted Gross Income (in billions)	Taxable Income (in billions)	Untaxed Income*	Effective Tax Rate on	
				AGI	TI
Total	$746.6	$444.8	40.4%	13.0%	21.0%
No AGI	−2.7	—	—	—	—
Under $5,000	64.4	13.9	78.4	5.2	15.1
$5,000 to under $7,000	53.7	24.5	35.8	7.9	16.2
$7,000 to under $10,000	103.3	55.6	46.2	9.3	16.9
$10,000 to under $15,000	189.0	113.1	40.2	10.6	17.7
$15,000 to under $25,000	201.9	136.0	32.6	13.2	19.5
$25,000 to under $50,000	83.9	61.4	26.8	17.8	24.3
$50,000 to under $100,000	31.9	24.4	23.5	26.8	34.9
$100,000 to under $200,000	11.9	9.2	22.7	34.6	44.8
$200,000 to under $500,000	5.4	4.0	25.9	40.9	54.9
$500,000 to under $1,000,000	1.8	1.3	27.8	45.6	63.0
$1,000,000 and more	2.1	1.4	33.3	47.2	69.0

SOURCE: U.S. Internal Revenue Service, *Statistics of Income, 1972, Individual Income Tax Returns* (Preliminary), 1974.

* Difference between AGI and TI as percentage of adjusted gross income.

TABLE 20
CURRENT GOVERNMENT EXPENDITURES IN OECD MEMBER COUNTRIES, 1972
(As a Percentage of Gross Domestic Product)
Average (Mean) 29.7%

		Percentage of GDP
1.	Sweden	40.8
2.	Norway	40.3
3.	Netherlands	39.0†
4.	Italy	37.4
5.	Denmark	36.8*
6.	Belgium	35.5
7.	Germany	34.3
8.	Canada	34.2
9.	France	33.6
10.	United Kingdom	32.9*
11.	Ireland	32.9*
12.	United States**	30.9*
13.	Austria	30.3*
14.	Finland	29.0
15.	Luxembourg	28.7†
16.	Iceland	24.9§
17.	Greece	23.7†
18.	Australia	23.5
19.	Switzerland	22.2‡
20.	Portugal	20.2*
21.	Spain	20.1
22.	Turkey	17.4*
23.	Japan	14.9*

SOURCE: *The OECD Observer*, February 1974.

* 1971.

† 1970.

‡ 1969.

§ 1968.

** According to national income accounts governmental expenditures in calendar year 1971 totaled $340.2 billion, which equals 32.2 percent of GNP. The corresponding figure for 1972 is 32.1 percent *(Survey of Current Business* (July 1973)). This still leaves the United States in the relative position shown above: twelfth among twenty-three countries, which is exactly in the middle.

TABLE 21
FEDERAL EXPENDITURES, 1952 AND 1972

	Expenditures (in millions)		Percent Increase 1952–1972	Expenditures as a Percentage of GNP		Percentage of Total Expenditures	
	1952	1972		1952	1972	1952	1972
Total expenditures	$ 71,045	$244,576*	244%	20.6%	21.1%	100.0%	100.0%
National security and cost of past wars	54,122	98,314	82	15.7	8.5	76.2	40.2
National defense	46,745	78,722	68	13.5	6.8	65.8	32.1
International affairs	2,380	3,608	52	0.7	0.3	3.4	1.5
Space research and technology	—	3,353	—	—	0.3	—	1.4
Veterans benefits and services	4,997	12,631	153	1.5	1.1	7.0	5.2
Interest on debt	4,599	15,309	233	1.3	1.3	6.5	6.3
Domestic services	12,324	130,920	962	3.6	11.3	17.3	53.5
Education, welfare and health	5,915	89,703	1416	1.7	7.8	8.3	36.7
All other	6,409	41,217	543	1.9	3.5	9.0	16.8
Exhibit: Education	323	6,551	1928	0.1	0.6	0.5	2.7
Social security and welfare	5,161	77,731	1406	1.5	6.7	7.2	31.8
Health, hospitals, medical insurance, and sanitation	431	14,492	3262	0.1	1.3	0.6	5.9
Population of the U.S. (in thousands)	157,553	208,842	33				
GNP (in billions)	345.5	1,155.2	234				
Consumer price index (1967=100)	79.5	125.3	58				
Implicit price deflator (GNP) (1958=100)	87.5	146.1	67				

SOURCES: 1952: U.S. Department of Commerce, Bureau of Economic Analysis, *The National Income and Product Accounts of the United States*, a Supplement to the *Survey of Current Business*, 1966.

1972: U.S. Department of Commerce, Bureau of Economic Analysis, *Survey of Current Business, National Income Issue*, July 1973.

* Includes wage accruals less disbursements not included in the functional distribution of expenditures or in national income accounts expenditure categories: $33 million in 1972.

TABLE 22

STATE AND LOCAL EXPENDITURES, 1952–1972

	Expenditures in (in millions)		Percent Increase	Expenditures as a Percentage of GNP		Percentage of Total Expenditures	
	1952	1972	1952–1972	1952	1972	1952	1972
Total expenditures	$ 25,253	$164,023*	550%	7.3%	14.2%	100.0%	100.0%
Domestic services	24,680	163,623	563	7.1	14.2	97.8	99.8
Social welfare†	14,869	107,273	621	4.3	9.3	58.9	65.4
General government	2,190	18,453	742	0.6	1.6	8.7	11.3
All other	7,621	37,897	397	2.2	3.3	30.2	23.1
Net interest paid	287	– 448	–256	0.08	–0.04	1.1	–0.2
All other	286	699	144	0.08	0.06	1.1	0.4
Exhibit:							
Education	8,263	65,606	694	2.4	5.7	32.7	40.0
Social security and welfare	2,841	22,586	695	0.8	2.0	11.3	13.8
Health, hospitals and sanitation	3,098	16,932	447	0.9	1.5	12.3	10.3
Population of the U.S. (July 1) (in thousands)	157,553	208,842	33				
Consumer price index (1967=100)	79.5	125.3	58				
GNP (in billions)	345.5	1,155.2	234				
National income (in billions)	291.4	941.8	223				
Personal consumption (in billions)	216.7	726.5	235				
Implicit price deflator (GNP) (1958=100)	87.5	146.1	67				

SOURCES: 1952: U.S. Department of Commerce, Bureau of Economic Analysis, *The National Income and Product Accounts of the United States, 1929-65*, a Supplement to the *Survey of Current Business*, 1966.
1972: U.S. Department of Commerce, Bureau of Economic Analysis, *Survey of Current Business, National Income Issue*, July 1973.

* Includes wage accruals less disbursements not included in the functional distribution of expenditures: $149 million in 1972.
† Includes education; health, hospitals and sanitation; social security and public welfare; labor; housing and community development. Includes expenditures from federal grants. Therefore table 22 (state and local expenditures) and table 21 (federal expenditures) together total more than table 23 (governmental expenditures). Federal grants to state and local governments would have to be netted out to equal total governmental expenditures.

224

TABLE 23

GOVERNMENTAL EXPENDITURES IN THE UNITED STATES, 1952 AND 1972

	Expenditures (in millions)		Percent Increase	Expenditures as a Percentage of GNP		Percentage of Total Expenditures	
	1952	1972		1952	1972	1952	1972
Total expenditures (federal, state, local)	$ 93,652	$370,922*	296%	27.1%	32.1%	100.0%	100.0%
National security and cost of past wars	54,218	98,392	82	15.7	8.5	57.9	26.6
National defense	46,795	78,806	68	13.5	6.8	50.0	21.3
International affairs	2,380	3,603	51	.7	.3	2.5	1.0
Space research and technology	—	3,288	—	—	—	—	.9
Veterans benefits and services	5,043	12,695	152	1.5	1.1	5.4	3.4
Net interest paid	4,886	14,861	204	1.4	1.3	5.2	4.0
Domestic services	34,548	257,487	645	10.0	22.3	36.9	69.4
Social welfare†	19,101	178,052	832	5.5	15.4	20.4	48.0
All other	15,447	79,435	414	4.5	6.9	16.5	21.4
Exhibit: Education	8,387	67,500	705	2.4	5.8	9.0	18.2
Social security and public welfare	6,664	84,578	1169	1.9	7.3	7.1	22.8
Health, hospitals, and sanitation	3,414	20,264	494	1.0	1.8	3.6	5.5
Population of the U.S. (July 1) (in thousands)	157,553	208,842	33				
Consumer price index (1967=100)	79.5	125.3	58				
GNP (in billions)	345.5	1,155.2	234				
National income (in billions)	291.4	941.8	223				
Personal consumption (in billions)	216.7	726.5	235				
Implicit price deflator (GNP) (1958=100)	87.5	146.1	67				

SOURCES: 1952: U.S. Department of Commerce, Bureau of Economic Analysis, *The National Income and Product Accounts of the United States, 1929-65,* a Supplement to the *Survey of Current Business,* 1966.

1972: U.S. Department of Commerce, Bureau of Economic Analysis, *Survey of Current Business, National Income Issue,* July 1973.

* Includes wage accruals less disbursements not included in the functional distribution of expenditures or in the national income accounts expenditures categories: federal, + $33 million in 1972; state and local, + $149 million in 1972.

† Includes education; health, hospitals and sanitation; social security and public welfare; labor; housing and community development.

225

TABLE 24
FEDERAL EXPENDITURES, 1952–1972

	Total Expenditures (in millions)	National Defense (in millions)	Domestic Services (in millions)	All Other (in millions)				
				Total	Space Research and Technology	International Affairs and Finance	Veterans Benefits and Services	Interest on Debt
1952	$ 71,045	$46,745	$ 12,324	$11,976	$ —	$2,380	$ 4,997	$ 4,599
1953	76,989	49,428	15,911	11,650	—	2,216	4,742	4,692
1954	69,728	41,974	16,180	11,574	—	1,989	4,789	4,796
1955	68,094	39,362	16,693	12,039	—	2,264	5,027	4,748
1956	71,866	41,113	18,220	12,533	—	2,147	5,153	5,233
1957	79,568	45,015	21,452	13,101	—	2,076	5,343	5,682
1958	88,870	46,725	28,923	13,222	30	2,153	5,615	5,424
1959	90,988	46,904	29,605	14,479	263	2,228	5,639	6,349
1960	93,016	45,885	31,813	15,318	574	2,233	5,668	6,843
1961	102,086	48,896	37,258	15,932	893	2,530	6,143	6,366
1962	110,256	52,787	40,275	17,194	1,796	2,585	5,954	6,859
1963	113,857	52,130	42,161	19,566	3,370	2,611	6,210	7,375
1964	118,079	51,566	44,782	21,731	4,629	2,648	6,141	8,313
1965	123,497	51,868	48,318	23,311	5,591	2,674	6,370	8,676
1966	142,750	62,628	55,486	24,636	5,947	2,858	6,397	9,434
1967	163,594	74,509	63,958	25,127	4,857	2,690	7,124	10,456
1968	181,509	80,776	74,288	26,445	4,548	2,553	7,666	11,678
1969	189,207	81,234	79,785	28,188	3,898	2,655	8,524	13,111
1970	203,927	77,878	94,982	31,067	3,641	2,873	9,782	14,771
1971	221,039*	75,366	113,110	32,602	3,465	3,317	11,245	14,575
1972	244,576*	78,722	130,920	34,901	3,353	3,608	12,631	15,309
Percent increase 1952–1972: 244.3%		68.4%	962.3%	191.4%	—	51.6%	152.8%	232.9%

SOURCES: U.S., Department of Commerce, Bureau of Economic Analysis, *National Income and Product Accounts of the United States, 1929–1965, Supplement to the Survey of Current Business,* August 1966; idem, *Survey of Current Business, National Income Issue,* July 1967–1973.

* Includes wage accruals less disbursements not included in the national income accounts expenditure categories: − $39 million in 1971 and + $33 million in 1972.

226

TABLE 25

GOVERNMENTAL EXPENDITURES IN THE UNITED STATES, 1952–1972
(FEDERAL, STATE, LOCAL)

	Total Expenditures (in millions)	National Defense (in millions)	Domestic Services (in millions)	All Other (in millions)				
				Total	Space Research and Technology	International Affairs and Finance	Veterans Benefits and Services	Interest on Debt
1952	$ 93,652	$46,795	$ 34,548	$12,309	$ —	$2,380	$ 5,043	$ 4,886
1953	101,183	49,472	39,689	12,022	—	2,216	4,789	5,017
1954	96,711	42,021	42,715	11,975	—	1,989	4,789	5,197
1955	97,637	39,411	45,634	12,592	—	2,264	5,111	5,217
1956	104,102	41,167	49,869	13,066	—	2,147	5,179	5,740
1957	114,867	45,051	56,097	13,719	—	2,076	5,422	6,221
1958	127,206	46,748	66,553	13,905	30	2,153	5,694	6,028
1959	130,989	46,921	68,838	15,230	262	2,228	5,700	7,040
1960	136,131	45,907	74,133	16,091	572	2,232	5,745	7,542
1961	148,968	48,909	83,255	16,804	890	2,526	6,256	7,132
1962	159,901	52,777	89,091	18,033	1,785	2,578	5,990	7,680
1963	166,918	52,116	94,465	20,337	3,351	2,605	6,232	8,149
1964	175,433	51,564	101,456	22,413	4,606	2,643	6,163	9,001
1965	186,864	51,896	111,175	23,793	5,550	2,669	6,391	9,183
1966	212,281	62,648	124,703	24,930	5,907	2,851	6,407	9,765
1967	242,857	74,534	142,991	25,332	4,816	2,684	7,152	10,680
1968	270,300	80,859	162,990	26,451	4,488	2,547	7,699	11,717
1969	287,888	81,329	178,602	27,957	3,836	2,650	8,599	12,872
1970	312,692	77,958	204,102	30,632	3,574	2,868	9,857	14,333
1971	340,169*	75,446	232,557	32,375	3,398	3,312	11,310	14,355
1972	370,922*	78,806	257,487	34,447	3,288	3,603	12,695	14,861
Percent increase 1952–1972	296.1%	68.4%	645.3%	179.9%	—	51.4%	151.7%	204.2%

SOURCES: U.S. Department of Commerce, Bureau of Economic Analysis, *National Income and Product Accounts of the United States, 1929–1965*, Supplement to the *Survey of Current Business*, August 1966; idem, *Survey of Current Business, National Income Issue*, July 1967–1973.

* Includes wage accruals less disbursements not included in the national income accounts expenditure categories: federal, –$39 million in 1971, +$33 million in 1972; state and local, –$170 million in 1971, +$149 million in 1972.

TABLE 26
Public and Private Consumption, 1952 and 1972

	1952 (in millions)	1972 (in millions)	Percent Increase
Personal Consumption Expenditures	$216,679	$726,506	235%
Food	68,357	157,892	131
Clothing and personal care	29,198	83,795	187
Housing and household operation	58,149	210,347	262
Medical care	10,225	57,431	462
Transportation (includes automobiles)	25,097	100,159	299
Recreation	12,102	47,826	295
Private education and research	1,870	12,008	542
All other	11,681	57,048	388
Government Expenditures for Domestic Services	34,548	257,487	645
Education	8,387	67,500	705
Social services and public welfare	6,664	84,578	1169
Health, hospitals and sanitation	3,414	20,264	494
All other	16,083	85,145	429

SOURCES: U.S., Department of Commerce, Bureau of Economic Analysis, *National Income and Product Accounts of the United States, 1929-1965,* Supplement to the *Survey of Current Business,* August 1966; idem, *Survey of Current Business, National Income Issue,* July 1973.